Dead Secrets

Yale University Press

New Haven & London

Tamar Heller

Dead Secrets

Wilkie Collins and the Female Gothic

Published with the assistance of the Frederick W. Hilles Publication Fund of Yale University.

Designed by Nancy Ovedovitz and set in Century Expanded type by Marathon Typography Service, Inc. Printed in the United States of America by Vail-Ballou Press, Binghamton, New York.

Library of Congress Cataloging-in-Publication Data
Heller, Tamar, 1959–
Dead secrets : Wilkie Collins and the female gothic / Tamar Heller
p. cm.
Includes bibliographical references and index.
ISBN 0-300-04574-3
1. Collins, Wilkie, 1824–1889 — Criticism and interpretation. 2. Gothic revival (Literature) 3. English fiction — 19th century — History and criticism. 4. Feminism and literature. I. Title.
PR4497.H4 1992 91-27533
823′.8 — dc20 CIP

The paper in this book meets the guidelines for permanence and durability of the Committee on Production Guidelines for Book Longevity of the Council on Library Resources.

10 9 8 7 6 5 4 3 2 1

to Chuck

Contents

Acknowledgments ix

Introduction: Dead Secrets 1

1. Reigns of Terror: The Politics of the Female Gothic 13

2. Becoming an Author in 1848: History and the Gothic in the Early Works of Wilkie Collins 38

3. *Basil*: Femininity, Ressentiment, and the Male Artist 58

4. Writing after Dark: Collins and Victorian Literary Culture 82

5. *The Woman in White*: Portrait of the Artist as a Professional Man 110

6. Blank Spaces: Ideological Tensions and the Detective Work of *The Moonstone* 142

Epilogue: The Haunted Narrative 164

Notes 169

Index 197

ACKNOWLEDGMENTS

I would like to thank J. Hillis Miller and Margaret Homans for their advice and kind encouragement in the earliest stages of this project. Williams College granted me the leave and financial support that allowed me to complete this book. I have benefited from the helpful comments of Suzanne Graver, Clement Hawes, Donna Heiland, Susan Meyer, Stewart Moulthrop, Linda Peterson, and Jennifer Wicke. Sue Lonoff not only read my manuscript and made valuable suggestions but also generously shared with me her knowledge of Collins.

I am grateful to the people I have had the pleasure of working with at Yale University Press. I would especially like to thank my editor, Ellen Graham, for her encouragement of my work; Eliza Childs; and Cynthia Carter Ayres, who gave me invaluable help with my manuscript.

Many thanks, and much gratitude, are owed to my family—Anita, Stanley, and Jackie Heller—for their love and support through the years. Barry and Mary Hatten made my task much easier by giving me their set of the Collier edition of Collins' novels. Kerry Batchelder and Susan Bianconi came to my aid at crucial moments. And, finally, my most incalculable debt is to my husband, Charles Hatten, who never tired of talking with me about my work, giving me superb advice, and urging me on: he has been my best reader and best friend.

Dead Secrets

Introduction: Dead Secrets

In a paradigmatic instance of an image that is central to his work, acts of writing and reading by women structure Wilkie Collins' fourth novel, *The Dead Secret* (1857).[1] At the beginning of the novel Sarah Leeson, housemaid to a wealthy Cornish family, writes down with trembling reluctance her mistress' deathbed confession, which she hides in the crumbling and disused part of the family manor; in the second part of the novel the heiress to the estate, hearing rumors of this buried secret, becomes a detective who tracks down the paper's hiding place, only to find that it reveals she is not really a Treverton of Porthgenna Hall but instead Sarah Leeson's illegitimate daughter, whom the barren Mrs. Treverton had passed off as her own child through an intricate fraud.

The plot of *The Dead Secret*, with its focus on buried writing, typifies many characteristic themes in Collins' writing. Transgressive secrets —often, as in *The Woman in White* and *No Name*, concerning a character's illegitimacy—abound in Collins' novels; as in *The Dead Secret*, such secrets can be concealed, and later revealed, by writing that is hidden or buried. Through the recurrent image of buried writing Collins represents social and textual marginality, as well as a subversiveness lurking beneath the surface of convention. *The Moonstone* (1868), one of Collins' most famous novels and an important predecessor for modern detective fiction, contains two striking and disturbing images of buried writing that recall the hidden paper in *The Dead Secret*. Ezra Jennings, an outlandish-looking doctor and social outcast, requests that all his papers, including his original new book on psychology, be buried with him in an unmarked grave; Rosanna Spearman, like Sarah Leeson a servant, records her transgressive love for an upper-class man in a letter that is sunk beneath the surface of the quicksand into which she later throws herself. The authors of these buried texts are typically either feminine, like Rosanna, or, like the outcast Ezra Jennings (who claims that he has a "female" constitution),[2] in a powerless and hence stereotypically feminine position.

In *The Dead Secret,* Sarah Leeson, a nerve-racked and obsessed loner, figures both women and the working class as the Other in Victorian gender and class hierarchies. When Rosamund Treverton discovers that she is Sarah's daughter, she too is dispossessed in class terms by losing her inheritance; in addition, literally and symbolically cast out of the will of the father, she embodies Victorian women's legal and economic identitylessness, a position in which she, like a later illegitimate heroine of Collins', Magdalen Vanstone, has "no name."

Women's dead secret in Collins' novels, however, is not just that of their powerlessness but also that of their transgression. We see such a transgression in the conspiracy between Sarah and her mistress, Mrs. Treverton, which attacks both patriarchal privilege and class hierarchies by fraudulently installing an illegitimate and working-class child as heir to the father's estate. Moreover, Mrs. Treverton and Sarah's plot involves their traveling together and switching places when Sarah is pregnant, so that Sarah acts the lady and her mistress—a former actress—the maid, further confusing "proper" class distinctions.

If the image of buried writing in Collins' novels is affiliated with a thematics of secrecy, transgression, and illegitimacy, *The Dead Secret* is an especially clear instance of how his work embodies these thematics generically. The genre *The Dead Secret* recalls is the Gothic, which has long been concerned with such themes, and particularly in this case the tradition of Gothic writing by women known as the female Gothic. As developed by such figures as Ann Radcliffe, who popularized the genre in the 1790s, the female Gothic maps a plot of domestic victimization. In the Radcliffean Gothic, the castles in which the heroines are imprisoned are nightmarish images of the home, and the coercive villains versions of male authority figures. In spite of its absence of villainous males, *The Dead Secret* is one of Collins' purest examples of the classic Radcliffean plot found in such novels as *The Mysteries of Udolpho.* Feminist critics have read the female Gothic as a narrative about mothers and daughters, in which a daughter who has lost her mother either discovers that she is not dead or finds mother substitutes in her place.[3] These maternal figures are regarded with ambivalence by the daughter because they represent the grim fate of women in a male-dominated society. In *The Dead Secret* the daughter, like the

Radcliffean heroine, is a female detective who traces clues that lead her—appropriately, in the most Gothic section of the house—to her lost mother; this discovery, however, is also the symbolic revelation of both her mother's and her own alienation and powerlessness.

Collins, however, uses the Gothic not only to tell a story about female victimization, but also to encode a plot of feminine subversion that resembles a narrative pattern feminist critics have identified in nineteenth-century women's writing. Thus Sandra Gilbert and Susan Gubar, in reading *Jane Eyre*, see the Gothic figure of the raging and incendiary madwoman, Bertha Mason Rochester, as expressing a subversive subtext of Brontë's novel; such a covert subtext, they suggest, is paradigmatic of nineteenth-century women's writing.[4] Collins' Sarah Leeson, always "fearing and failing" (209), as she puts it, may not be so robust an image of female rage as Bertha. Nonetheless, like Brontë's confined madwoman, she embodies all the novel's repressed female subversion, not just through her participation in the plot to pass off Rosamund as a Treverton, but also through her representation, as a fallen woman, of a disruptive feminine sexuality.

Collins' use of a female-centered plot in *The Dead Secret*—a plot which is structured by its Gothic perspective on feminine experience, and in which the Gothic encodes feminine subversion—typifies an aspect of his art that has long attracted note. Of the relatively few critics who approached Collins' work earlier in this century, several—Dorothy Sayers, Maurice Richardson, and Robert Ashley[5]—have noticed that his portrayal of women is particularly sympathetic and unconventional for a Victorian male novelist. More recent reevaluations of Collins, contesting the long critical neglect of his novels, have found in him an important and able commentator on nineteenth-century gender politics. In their study of male novelists and the Victorian sexual system, for instance, Richard Barickman, Susan MacDonald, and Myra Stark claim that Collins is "the most directly concerned with issues of women's rights and the most openly irreverent toward Victorian sexual conventions" of the writers they examine.[6] Barickman, MacDonald, and Stark argue that Collins' "bizarre" plots—by which they presumably mean his Gothic plots—can be read as a critique of Victorian gender ideology, "parodies of conventional sexual alignments."[7]

Indeed, the plots of several of Collins' novels, in addition to containing the Gothic elements already discussed, target specific inegalitarian aspects of Victorian marriage laws by exemplifying the female Gothic plot that Joanna Russ has aptly characterized as "Somebody's Trying to Kill Me and I Think It's My Husband."[8] In *The Woman in White*, the diabolic husband Percival Glyde tries to seize his wife's fortune by incarcerating her in a lunatic asylum and claiming that she is not herself, but a dead mental patient she closely resembles; this plot expresses a critique of a legal and economic system that robbed women of their social identity by transferring them and their wealth to their husbands' control. Similarly, *Man and Wife* (1870) attacks abuses in Scottish marriage laws by displaying a Gothic gallery of abused wives: Anne Delamayn, whose husband does indeed try to kill her, and the mute cook Hester Dethridge, who, in another image of buried writing, carries concealed on her body an autobiographical narrative of how her husband abused her and how—in a subversive twist of the Radcliffean Gothic—she murdered him.

Like other critics who use a feminist perspective to assess Collins' work,[9] I am concerned in this book with the gender politics of Collins' novels. But I place my analysis of Collins' representations of gender in a more fully historicized context. In examining Collins' representation of gender through the female Gothic plot, I link the relation of Collins' generic choices to his position as a male writer in the Victorian literary marketplace. This should then help explain why, for Collins, the image of buried writing is a compelling one, not just as a figure for a feminine subversiveness, but as a self-reflexive commentary about the influence on his work of one of the major nineteenth-century genres associated with women writers, the Gothic.

The image of buried writing could well stand for Collins' own literary reputation, since critics—like Rosamund finding the hidden paper in a forgotten part of the manor—have been discovering his previously marginalized works. Besides the renewed interest in Collins on the part of feminist critics, there have also been other important studies, such as Sue Lonoff's careful examination of Collins' "rhetoric of authorship" and his relationship to his audience.[10] Three articles on *The*

Moonstone illustrate the variety of methods critics now use to read Collins. John Reed argues that the novel about a lost Indian jewel constitutes a cogent critique of British imperialism; Albert Hutter, in a psychoanalytic approach, sees Collins as a detective or diagnostician of his society's repressed and buried desires; D. A. Miller, in a Foucauldian essay, reads detection in *The Moonstone* as part of a thematics of social regulation and surveillance.[11] Like feminist readings of Collins, such critical reevaluations are influenced by new types of literary criticism that seek to evaluate the political and social dimensions of literature. Whereas Collins' concern with, and thematics of, such social issues as gender relations have made him an attractive candidate for these types of reevaluation, the renewed interest in his work has also benefited from the expansion of critical attention beyond the boundaries of the traditional literary canon. Collins' career can be illuminated by an interrogation of the politics of the formation and maintenance of literary canons, and also, since he has long been pigeonholed as a mystery writer, from recent studies of popular genres hitherto deemed subliterary. Certainly, in the early years of the twentieth century, a period of aggressive canonization, Collins' association with "subliterary" genres caused him to be considered a minor author not worthy of serious critical study.

One purpose of this book is to explore these issues—the renewed critical interest in the social and political dimensions of literature and that of canonization—in the context of Collins' critical reputation during his lifetime. If Collins' literary reputation was particularly low during the first half of the twentieth century, it had already begun to decline during his career, which spanned forty years, from 1848 until his death in 1889. Although often admiringly compared in the 1850s and 1860s to such figures as Dickens and Thackeray, at the same time he was frequently disparaged as an ingenious constructor of melodramatic plots: "Mr. Wilkie Collins is an admirable story-teller," declared one reviewer of *The Woman in White*, "though he is not a great novelist,"[12] and a reviewer of *The Moonstone* sneered that the word "novel" is "an absurd misnomer" when applied to stories that are "simply conundrums."[13]

That the novels referred to are the two works of Collins since admitted to "classic" status is ample proof of the shifting beliefs in what constitutes literary value. Such aesthetic values, however, also reveal social values. What offended contemporary critics of Collins was not just the form of what he wrote, but what he wrote about. Throughout his career critics who described his art as aesthetically marginal often responded negatively to his depiction of socially marginal groups: criminals, fallen women, the underworld of Victorian culture. One reviewer of Collins' *No Name* (1862), in which an illegitimate heroine marries for money in a vengeful campaign to regain her lost inheritance, regretted her "pollution."[14] Another criticized Collins for portraying the "'sinks and sewers'" of society in *Armadale* (1866), a novel that prominently features the murderess and adventuress Miss Gwilt: "What artist would choose vermin as his subjects?"[15]

The criticisms of his contemporaries, then, reveal the ineradicable link between literary judgments and the political and social contexts from which they spring. The most negative criticisms of Collins from his contemporaries employ a traditional spatial map for class relations to determine aesthetic value: if the lower classes are visualized as lower, the artist who depicts the "sinks and sewers" of this social detritus is aligned with genres that were aesthetically "low" or degraded within Victorian literary hierarchies, like the sensation novel, with whose development Collins was credited. If class is an important term in this mapping of aesthetic value, however, so is gender: Collins' literary "fallenness" is associated with fallen women as well as with lowness in class terms.

Collins, however, was associated with women not only in a thematic sense—through his depiction of fallen and "polluted" femininity—but also in a literal sense, because of his generic choices and the changing face of the Victorian literary marketplace during his career. As a writer of popular melodrama, Collins had a wide female readership. Moreover, although other Victorian male novelists, such as Charles Reade and, early in his career, Charles Dickens, were classified as sensation novelists, the genre was insistently linked with women writers, such as Mary Elizabeth Braddon and Mrs. Henry Wood. This sensation fiction by women writers is, in turn, heavily influenced by the female Gothic.

Collins' association with Gothic or sensation fiction that was both literally and symbolically feminized suggests his ambiguous place in Victorian literary culture. In her recent study of gender and the Victorian literary marketplace, Gaye Tuchman has shown how the novel's status during the nineteenth century was elevated by making writing, like so many of the more prestigious Victorian occupations, a profession rather than simply a trade. Since the professions were the province of men, this professionalization of literature was in fact its masculinization, eventually "edging out" of prominence within the market the women writers with whom the novel, hitherto an unprestigious form, had been associated.[16] Although women writers remained numerous and popular during the mid-nineteenth century, the "period of invasion" of male writers into the novel-writing field,[17] women's status was generally lower than that of their more prominent male colleagues. Collins' position in this changing Victorian literary marketplace was in many ways a double one, both feminine and masculine. Collins was associated with the "low" and heavily feminine genres of the Gothic and sensation fiction, yet he was an active participant in the process of professionalization. Although he was an immensely popular writer well versed in the techniques of selling his wares in the marketplace —"Make 'em cry, make 'em laugh, make 'em wait" was one of his mottoes—he saw himself, and was seen by many contemporaries, as a serious artist who was indubitably professional in his industry and perseverance at his writing. Such a view was particularly pronounced during the first two decades of his career, when he was establishing and defining his position in the literary world. Just as *The Dead Secret* was finishing its serial run in Dickens' journal *Household Words*, Edmund Yates, in a laudatory appreciation of Collins' writing, compared him to other types of male professionals: "No barrister or physician ever worked harder at his profession, devoted more time, or thought, or trouble to it, was prouder of it, or pursued it with more zeal or earnestness than Mr. Collins has done with regard to literature."[18] This encomium makes literature a kind of science and serious business for men; such a status, in which literature was seen, like other professions, as protecting and promoting the social values and institutions that undergirded Victorian life, diverged from the questionable and dubious status of sensation fiction, which was seen by its critics as socially subversive and blurring (rather than underscoring) class and gender hierarchies.

This context of the professionalization of literature explains why, for Collins, the female Gothic plots in his novels are at once the source of inspiration and ambivalence. The Gothic, as I have suggested, gave him a way of being a social critic, and of writing about his often liberal views on social issues, including gender, while also offering him an avenue for portraying types of alienation and subversion. But Collins' professional aspirations drew him in a more conservative direction. His tendency to evade the full implications of a feminist critique could be seen as determined by the ideological climate of his era, and by his desire not to offend readers shaped by conservative values. But that many of his works, even the most "feminist" ones, end with the containment of female power and subversion, must also be seen as a function of his aspiration for professional status, and of his investment in the ideology of professionalism, which, as historians have argued, strongly reinforces the division between male labor and female domesticity.[19]

Collins' novels, in fact, are often paradoxically Gothic plots that end with the containment of the Gothic as the site of subversion and literary marginality. *The Dead Secret*, which makes the connection between the female Gothic and feminine alienation and transgression, is a good example of this type of narrative containment. Jenny Bourne Taylor calls both *The Dead Secret* and the earlier *Hide and Seek* (1854) "much less risqué domestic melodramas" than *Basil*, Collins' flamboyant first Gothic melodrama, which had shocked critics with its frank portrayal of sex and crime.[20] Unlike Taylor, I would not dismiss *The Dead Secret* as a bland novel, but see it as one haunted by the ghosts of feminine sexuality and subversion. Still, this haunting is precisely the point: just as Porthgenna Hall is supposedly visited by the specter of a beautiful but wicked woman, so versions of feminine transgression, the dead secrets of the text, are finally rendered ghosts or traces, subsumed within a domestic plot suitable for publication in Dickens' respectable *Household Words*. By its conclusion the novel notably tones down and tames the subversive possibilities that it has used the Gothic to suggest: Sarah Leeson becomes such a nervous wreck that she is subjected on several occasions to the diagnostic gaze of male doctors, and "cured" only when she is, just before her death, restored to her proper position as mother to Rosamund, who has also become a mother. This channeling of Rosamund's energies into maternity and marriage is the more significant because she had also briefly appeared as a figure for the writer: trying to gather courage to tell her snobbish husband about her real class origins, she pretends she is telling him a story: "Why not? More women write novels now than men. What is to prevent me from trying?" (279).

This representation of a major woman character as a writer suggests at once Collins' association, and rivalry, with women writers. Viewing Collins as a writer in both a masculine and a feminine position in the marketplace will undergird my reading of the significance of female Gothic in this study. As I shall define it, female Gothic is important source material from which Collins derives inspiration for his representation of gender and also (drawing particularly on Shelley's *Frankenstein*) class. This is not to say that Collins was not influenced by male forms of Gothic or by other male writers (such as Balzac, Dickens, or Scott), but to underscore the special importance of female Gothic in shaping his stories about gender. Although I address the continuity between the female Gothic tradition and Collins' novels,[21] I do not simply dwell on a comparison between the two so much as suggest how Collins uses the female Gothic to write narratives about forms of power and authority—literary, familial, political—in Victorian culture. As my discussion of Collins' position in the literary marketplace indicates, the term *female Gothic* has a meaning in this study beyond that of a genre written by female writers; in light of the politics of the marketplace, the Gothic becomes for Collins a feminized discursive category, associated with what is "other," subversive, and marginal, and thus the site of ambivalence for him as a Victorian professional writer.

By reading the Gothic in this way, I hope to suggest some new ways of discussing literary transmission. Clearly, to examine a male writer's influence by a feminine tradition revises the model of literary transmission proposed by Harold Bloom, in which a male artist is inspired by major masculine predecessors, and also the model articulated by such feminist critics as Gilbert and Gubar, which characterizes the feminine tradition as that of "Milton's daughters," exiled from the linguistic authority accorded to men.[22] Neither model fully accounts for Collins' position in literary history. Certainly a male writer's indebtedness to a feminine tradition associated with the lack of authority must be particularly complex and troubled. Collins' problematic relation to a maternal (rather than a Bloomian paternal) tradition can be seen, for example, in *The Dead Secret*. Through Rosamund's discovery of her maternal origins, Collins self-reflexively thematizes his own return to the matrilineal tradition of the female Gothic; this maternal literary tradition, though, is linked to marginality and buried writing. Such an association with marginality cannot be reduced to Collins' "anxiety of influence" about his Gothic predecessors. Rather, I ground my discussion of Collins' relation to them, not in the abstract and ahistorical terms of many models of literary transmission, but, through the context of the Victorian literary marketplace, in the politics of a specific historical and economic moment.

Emphasizing the maternal and the matrilineal, my first chapter examines the politics of the female Gothic as a feminine tradition with a strong focus on mother-daughter narratives. Focusing on works of Ann Radcliffe, Mary Wollstonecraft, and Mary Shelley, I explore the treatment of gender issues in the female Gothic by linking the genre to the period of its development, the French Revolutionary era and its aftermath. I argue that the ideological tensions surrounding gender (and, in the works of Wollstonecraft and Shelley, of class also) reflect and engage responses to types of debates about gender and power during this revolutionary period. Collins, who claimed he became an author in 1848, the beginning of another period of revolutionary uprising throughout Europe, similarly makes revolution an important theme in many of his works, including his most famous novels, *The Woman in White* and *The Moonstone*, both set during the 1848 period. For Collins, revolution becomes not only a sign for the outbreak of types of gender and class rebellion, but also the backdrop for a drama about the male intellectual's often conflicted relation to this rebellion, which is coded through and associated with the Gothic.

To address these issues, the second chapter discusses Collins' two earliest full-length works, the memoirs he wrote of his father, the landscape painter and Royal Academician William Collins, and his first novel, *Antonina*, a seemingly uncharacteristic historical fiction set during the fall of Rome. This chapter examines the development of Collins' early career by considering what it meant to become an author in 1848, the year in which he published the biography of his father. Both these early works chart the decline of a world of fathers and patriarchs, and the rise of the Gothic amid the disruptions of history, characterized by the rebellion of women and the lower classes.

The third, fourth, and fifth chapters treat, respectively, *Basil* (1852), the short-story collection *After Dark* (1856), and *The Woman in White* (1860) as meditations on the marketplace that share a narrative pattern. These works all contain figures for the male artist who, although outcasts themselves, are still ambivalent about their association with women characters connected to or embodying the female Gothic. These narratives, I argue, represent a strong ambivalence toward the female Gothic heightened by Collins' position in the literary marketplace. One of the most emblematic is the frame narrative of the story collection *After Dark*, which splits the artist into two figures, a temporarily blinded portrait painter and his wife, who conceives the idea of making money by collecting her husband's Gothic stories, gathered from his sitters' histories, into a book. The confusion over how much power the wife actually has in this partnership figures the tensions about female Gothic and women's power in the marketplace that I discuss elsewhere in the chapter. *The Woman in White*, one of Collins' most brilliant revisions of the Radcliffean Gothic, expresses these anxieties about women's power and masculine professionalism even more dramatically by making its central figure a professional man who, by the novel's end, reasserts the division between male professionalism and domesticity.

The final chapter reads *The Moonstone* as Collins' subtlest exploration of ideological and generic tensions in his work. The novel seems to be the clearest instance in Collins' canon in which the female Gothic is revised to become the traditionally "masculine" genre of detective fiction. Yet *The Moonstone*, I argue, is a novel that tells two stories, a masculine one about the triumph of male reason, and a feminine one about buried writing, associated with the subversive discourses of the Gothic and radical Romanticism that cannot be wholly effaced. In *The Moonstone,* as in the other works I examine, the female Gothic is thus, like Sarah Leeson's hidden paper, the dead secret that is alternately repressed and resurrected. One of Collins' most compelling images of buried writing is that of Rosanna Spearman burying her letter in the quicksand into which she despairingly throws herself. But the writing is not buried so completely as is her body in its nameless grave. Her letter is locked in a box that can be retrieved by means of a chain that pulls it to the surface, like Sarah Leeson's Gothic secret coming to light in the crumbling mansion. Like these buried texts, the female Gothic may be contained by the conservative narratives of professionalization and domesticity in Collins' fiction, yet always resurfaces to tell its story of subversion.

One

Reigns of Terror: The Politics of the Female Gothic

As the revolutionary Reign of Terror raged in France, another reign of terror invaded the realm of English letters. In England in the 1790s, while voices were raised both for and against the French Revolution and the reforms it represented, Gothic novels—or "horrid" novels, as they are called in Jane Austen's *Northanger Abbey*—became the most popular fictions of the day. The relation between the rise of the Gothic during the last decades of the eighteenth century and the period's tumultuous political and intellectual climate has long been the subject of critical inquiry. In 1928, Michael Sadleir declared that Gothic novels were "as much an expression of a deep subversive impulse as the French Revolution."[1] Although the extent to which the Gothic is subversive has remained controversial, critics have seen the genre as linked to and reflecting the rise of the bourgeoisie and the decline of a feudal aristocracy during the late eighteenth century. The Gothic castle, a site of exoticism and mystery but also of imprisonment and terror, evokes a feudal system that is archaic and outmoded, a symbolism that mirrors the political debate about tradition and change during the French Revolutionary period. Writing from the conservative viewpoint, Edmund Burke, in his *Reflections on the Revolution in France*, likens the French constitution before the revolution to a castle that, though it has suffered "waste and dilapidation," is yet a "noble and venerable" castle on whose traditions, or "foundations," the French might have built rather than destroying them.[2] In *A Vindication of the Rights of Men*, however, Mary Wollstonecraft voices the opposing radical view when she asks, "Why was it a duty to repair an ancient castle, built in barbarous ages, of Gothic materials?"[3] Though the typical Gothic is not a work of Jacobin propaganda, it nonetheless records a similar reaction against a crumbling ancien régime figuratively rendered by the Bastille-like convents and castles from which enterprising Gothic heroes and heroines free themselves.

For the feminist critic, however, the subversive nature of the Gothic extends beyond its reflections on the French Revolution to its exploration of the troubled politics of domestic ideology. Underscoring the genre's focus on family stories, such feminist critics as Ellen Moers, Margaret Anne Doody, Claire Kahane, and Kate Ellis have shown how Gothics are particularly compelling fictions for the many women who read and write them because of their nightmarish figuration of feminine experience within the home.[4] Moers coined the term "female Gothic" to describe how a tradition of women writers, beginning with Ann Radcliffe, use the genre's paraphernalia of claustrophobic castles, villainous dominating men, and beleaguered heroines to thematize women's sense of isolation and imprisonment within a domestic ideology fast becoming hegemonic by the end of the eighteenth century.

But whereas feminist critics have stressed the radical critique of the family in the genre, the female Gothic of the 1790s more generally tells a double story about women and domesticity inflected by the different and conflicting discourses about gender during the French Revolutionary period. The position of women was crucial to the ideological systems of both English Jacobins—supporters of the French Revolution—and anti-Jacobins. Including women with other oppressed groups, such as the working classes and slaves, radical intellectuals expanded their campaign, as Mary Wollstonecraft did, from championing the "rights of men" to defending "the rights of woman." Conservatives like Burke, meanwhile, expatiated on the "horrible consequences of taking one half of the species wholly out of the guardianship and protection of the other,"[5] seeing the liberation of women as the deathblow to a paternalistic order in which state and family are both ruled by benevolent father figures.

Influenced by different views of gender and class, Jacobin and anti-Jacobin political rhetoric constructed their own versions of Gothic. The radical Gothic of English Jacobin writing is a carceral world in which walls—of Bastilles, feudal manors, despotic families—unjustly imprison the individual. The conservative Gothic of Burke's political treatises, however, is animated by a fear of the dissolution of boundaries that delimit the proper places of various stations of society, causing a concomitant explosion of repressed and anarchic rebellion. In Burke's most horrifically Gothic visions in his political writing on the revolution, women, no longer dependent beings to be protected, are the instigators of revolt who image the monstrous disruptions of the social order signified by the revolution. "La Révolution" and "La Terreur" are feminine terms, and for Burke, as for many later writers, the figures who symbolize the revolution are the market women who marched on Versailles, called in his *Reflections on the Revolution in France* the "furies of hell . . . in the abused shape of the vilest of women."[6] The market women resemble the Gothic and specifically feminine specter who rises from the grave of the father-king whom she has slaughtered in her parricidal revolt: "Out of the tomb of the murdered monarchy in France has arisen a vast, tremendous, unformed spectre, in a far more terrific guise than any which ever yet have overpowered the imagination, and subdued the fortitude of man . . . despising all common maxims . . . that hideous phantom overpowered those who could not believe it was possible she could at all exist."[7]

Unlike the Burkean Gothic with its nightmarish images of rightful authority overturned, the female Gothic is animated to a large extent by an antiauthoritarian spirit. An offspring of the novel of sensibility, which placed a new emphasis on feminine consciousness and yet did so to reflect and shape the centrality of women within bourgeois domestic ideology, the Radcliffean Gothic does not in any simple way reject conventional gender roles.[8] Still, the emphasis on female subjectivity in the Radcliffean Gothic has radical tendencies, pitting the Gothic heroine against father figures who are coercive rather than (as Burke would have them) benevolent. The hyperbolically virtuous Gothic heroine—seemingly, the perfect domestic woman—thus can use language that is reminiscent of Paine and Wollstonecraft in asserting her rights. "I can endure with fortitude, when it is in resistance of oppression," declares Emily to the villainous Montoni in *The Mysteries of Udolpho*,[9] and in *The Italian* Ellena proclaims, "My own voice never shall sanction the evils to which I may be subjected" and "the immortal love of justice . . . will sustain my courage."[10] In this context, it is not surprising that in some cases the female Gothic has, as Margaret

Anne Doody notes, developed into the novel of "feminine radical protest,"[11] attracting Jacobin sympathizers and such feminists as Charlotte Smith and Mary Wollstonecraft who, in novels like *Desmond* (1792) and *Maria* (1797), exploit the parallel between the degraded status of the French people under the ancien régime and that of women.

Influenced by the double message about women in both radical and conservative political ideologies of the period, however, the Radcliffean Gothic, as distinguished from its more radical offshoots, resonates with an ambivalence about the extent of women's rebellion against a male-dominated society. Female Gothic, indeed, is animated by the paradigm that such feminist critics as Sandra Gilbert and Susan Gubar have identified as characteristic of women's writing: a double voice of both rebellion and acquiescence to convention.[12] The female Gothic, however, in many ways inverts the narrative pattern that Elaine Showalter has described, in which the subversive plot is coded within the conventional one: "The orthodox plot recedes, and another plot, hitherto submerged in the anonymity of the background, stands out in bold relief like a thumbprint."[13] In female Gothic, the subversive nature of the text appears uppermost, in its dark and prisonlike images of feminine experience within domesticity, and in its representation of terror caused by women's imprisonment by despotic male authority figures like Montoni. Yet in the Radcliffean Gothic, terror can play an ambiguous role. A narrative mechanism that simultaneously expresses and contains the genre's more radical tendencies, terror as a theme and a narrative device suggests the influence of conservative ideologies of gender and domesticity on the female Gothic.

Even in its most ideologically conflicted guises, however, the female Gothic continues to be a political text that not only reflects but also actively engages debates about the meaning of women's role. It is the female Gothic's ability to engage the political dimensions of gender —even when the text appears to avoid the public, male realm of politics to focus instead on the private world of women—that will be of greatest significance to such Victorian Gothicists as Wilkie Collins. In his own version of Gothic, Collins will rediscover and develop the potential of the genre to tell a narrative about both gender and class.

This chapter prepares for this reading of Collins by examining several versions of the politics of gender in the female Gothic. First, I look at Radcliffean Gothic—not the first example of female Gothic but the most formative and influential in defining a narrative of the incarceration of women within domesticity that will influence Collins in novels like *Basil* and *The Woman in White*. Yet I also trace the ambivalence about feminine rebelliousness in the female Gothic that will similarly prove important as a narrative paradigm for representing ideological tensions about gender in the Victorian Gothic text. This discussion of the Radcliffean Gothic is followed by one of Wollstonecraft's *Maria*, which, as an explicitly feminist version of the genre, anticipates the most radical ways in which Collins uses the Gothic as a vehicle for social protest. Finally, I conclude with a reading of Mary Shelley's *Frankenstein* (1818, 1831), a work that, written and revised in a transitional period spanning the era between the French Revolution and the Victorian age, will be a particularly influential text for Collins because of his interest in representing both class and gender. *Frankenstein* is the most significant example of a Gothic novel that develops a discourse of class—a subject of especial concern for Victorians—that is analogous to and intersects with its discourse of gender.

Radcliffean Gothic: Terror and the Daughter

In its most characteristic form, Radcliffean Gothic tells a story of mothers and daughters. In a paradigmatic scene from one of her earliest works, *A Sicilian Romance* (1790), the heroine, Julia, discovers a woman imprisoned in the depths of her father's castle:

> The door opened, and she beheld in a small room, which received its feeble light from a window above, the pale and emaciated figure of a woman, seated, with half-closed eyes, in a kind of elbow chair. . . . Her features, which were worn by sorrow, still retained the traces of beauty, and in her air was a mild dignity that excited in Julia an involuntary veneration.
>
> She seemed as if about to speak, when fixing her eyes earnestly and steadily upon Julia, she stood for a moment in eager gaze, and suddenly exclaiming, "My daughter!" fainted away.[14]

In this scene the walls of the father's dungeon are transformed into a version of the body of the mother, a womb-like space that surrounds the meeting of mother and daughter. Such a narrative becomes a Utopian one where the daughter has the chance to save the mother from her imprisonment; soon after their meeting, Julia exclaims, "Surely Heaven can bless me with no greater good than by making me the deliverer of my mother" (II, 177).

The desire of the daughter to save the mother is evidence of the continuity of an oppressive feminine experience in the Radcliffean Gothic. Even as Radcliffe imagines the possibility of the daughter's saving the mother, she describes a world in which the daughter's fate is perpetually on the verge of reproducing the mother's in oppressiveness. Julia discovers her mother's dungeon as she herself is fleeing from a marriage arranged by her despotic father, who of course is also her mother's jailer. Not knowing of the imprisonment of Julia's mother, people think that she was killed by her husband's harshness: "the arrogant and impetuous character of the marquis operated powerfully upon the mild and susceptible nature of his lady; and it was by many persons believed, that his unkindness and neglect put a period to her life" (I, 5–6). The man whom Julia's father wishes her to marry, the Duke de Luovo, shares with this harsh patriarch the "love of power" as his "ruling passion; . . . He had been twice married, and the unfortunate women subjected to his power, had fallen victims to the slow but corroding hand of sorrow" (I, 129). Radcliffe's pun on "Luovo" locates both romantic love and the "love of power" as the weapon of male tyrants.

Thus the plot that Claire Kahane has identified as central to the female Gothic—the daughter's search for the lost mother[15]—is based on a reading of women's position that resembles Wollstonecraft's prophecy in *A Vindication of the Rights of Woman*, "The weakness of the mother will be visited on the children!"[16] Wollstonecraft characterizes women's unequal role in the family as an inheritance from the disempowered mother to the daughter she socializes: "Women are told from their infancy, and taught by the example of their mothers, that a little knowledge of human weakness, justly termed cunning, softness of temper, *outward* obedience, and a scrupulous attention to a puerile kind of propriety, will obtain for them the protection of man" (*VRW* 19). Though Radcliffe is not so radical in her critique of gender roles as Wollstonecraft, she shares a recognition that women's disadvantaged position is caused by an economic dependence on men rewritten as and reinforced by sexual domination. Julia's father and her would-be husband the Duke de Luovo are examples of Wollstonecraft's claim that "tyrants and sensualists . . . endeavour to keep women in the dark, because the former only want slaves, and the latter a play-thing" (*VRW* 24).

Although Julia's reunion with her mother in *A Sicilian Romance* embeds in the Gothic text an ecstatic vision of women rescuing each other from oppression—a vision that, as we shall see, is at the heart of Wollstonecraft's own feminist Gothic, *Maria*—Radcliffe's novels emphasize the mother's powerlessness more frequently than they do the daughter's salvific power. In Radcliffe's most famous Gothic, *The Mysteries of Udolpho* (1794), the daughter's discovery, after her own mother's death, of the powerlessness of a series of mother substitutes encodes the plot that feminist critics have identified as "matrophobia," or the daughter's fear of becoming as powerless and oppressed as the mother. Emily St. Aubert, a virtuous orphan, is imprisoned in the castle of Udolpho along with her aunt, who has married Montoni, Emily's coercive guardian. In a darker version of the scene from *A Sicilian Romance* where Julia finds her lost mother, Emily discovers that her aunt, whom Montoni had forcibly separated from her, is dying as a result of the ill treatment she has received:

> She rushed towards a bed . . . and drew aside the curtains. Within, appeared a pale and emaciated face. She started back, then again advanced, shuddered as she took up the skeleton hand, that lay stretched upon the quilt; then let it drop, and then viewed the face with a long, unsettled gaze. It was that of Madame Montoni, though so changed by illness, that the resemblance of what it had been, could scarcely be traced in what it now appeared. She was still alive, and, raising her heavy eyes, she turned them on her niece. (364)

Madame Montoni's death figures her economic inferiority as a wife: her husband starves her to death in an attempt to force her to sign away the money from her marriage settlements. ("You may understand," he had warned her earlier, "the danger of offending a man, who has an unlimited power over you" [305]). Emily has reason to be particularly terrified by Madame Montoni's fate because there is every sign that it will shortly be her own, as Montoni tries to gain control over her inheritance by marrying her to Count Morano, a man she does not love.

Emily's "unsettled gaze" as she looks at her dying aunt uncovers the contradiction between the domestic ideal, according to which husbands protect and provide for their wives, and the real world, an increasingly mercantile and materialistic society where husbands are sole owners of their wives' property. By confronting such ideological tensions, the image of the female gaze in Radcliffe's novels recalls a passage in Wollstonecraft's *Vindication of the Rights of Woman* in which she likens the origin of both familial and political power to a "dark abyss" which "no eye must dare to explore, lest the baseless fabric should totter under investigation" (*VRW* 225). In this feminist revision of the Pandora myth, the regulation of women's conduct prevents them from seeing, and changing, the origins of their oppression. Similarly, the gaze of the female "eye" in *Udolpho*—an image for the developing subjectivity of the female "I"—suggests the power of the heroine to identify and hence to escape her fate as her mother's daughter.

Emily makes repeated attempts to negotiate the "dark abyss" of her lack of knowledge of her mother's fate. Prior to the scene where she draws aside the bed curtains to see her dying aunt, in a clandestine trip at night through the halls of Udolpho, Emily attempts to uncover a veiled picture; her brief glimpse of this mysterious object causes her to drop senseless to the floor (249). Because we find out only later that the object was a wax statue, we have no way of knowing at this point that it isn't, as Emily herself seems to think, the body of the "late lady of the castle" (248), Signora Laurentini, whom Montoni was suspected of murdering. Radcliffe had earlier raised a doubt about the identity of Emily's real mother by showing her father kissing the miniature of an unknown woman; thus Signora Laurentini, the ghostly feminine presence in the backdrop of *Udolpho* who was rumored to have had a hopeless love affair, becomes yet another of the novel's series of mother substitutes. Later in the novel, Emily discovers the fate of the Marchioness de Villeroi, who turns out to be the woman in the miniature her father kissed, and actually his sister rather than Emily's mother. Compelled to marry one man while in love with another, the Marchioness died young; after hearing her aunt's dismal story, Emily, in another image of unveiling the fate of mother substitutes, lifts the black veil the Marchioness laid down in her bedroom before her death (533).

The multiplicity of mother figures in *Udolpho*—dead mothers, aunts, mysterious mistresses of castles—suggests the inevitability of women's nightmarish fate. This same multiplicity, however, allows a distinction to be made between these otherwise similar figures as they are divided into good and bad women. Such a distinction dilutes the critique of the family in the Gothic by blaming women's woes not on a male-dominated familial system, but on those women who have imperfectly assumed their domestic functions. As Tania Modleski has argued, by killing off Emily's own impossibly good mother early in *Udolpho* and replacing her with Madame Montoni, who before her disastrous marriage disliked and dominated her ward, Radcliffe displaces ambivalence about the role of mothers in socializing their daughters onto this fairy-tale image of the vicious stepmother.[17] This pattern of segregating good from bad women is repeated more spectacularly with the contrast between Signora Laurentini, the "late lady" of *Udolpho*, and the Marchioness de Villeroi, Emily's aunt. Whereas Emily had feared that Signora Laurentini was another victim of domestic violence, she turns out to be a murderer, having poisoned the Marchioness, with whose husband she was having an affair. This adultery plot shifts the blame for sexual impulses from the Marchioness, who before her loveless marriage wished to marry another man. To underscore this moral, Signora Laurentini ends up a demented nun in a convent and warns Emily not to indulge the "evil passions" (646) that caused her downfall; in this way, the incipient plot about the Marchioness as a victim of sexual repression is obscured by a cautionary tale about a woman who is a victim of her own unruly sexual desire.

Of course, Radcliffe's figures of dominating men—the Duke de Luovo in *A Sicilian Romance*, Montoni in *Udolpho*—suggest that a fear of male sexuality is one root of this distrust of feminine passion. In the *Vindication of the Rights of Woman* Wollstonecraft claims that women who marry because of their desire for men become their husbands' sexual and economic slaves; she prefers relationships in which sexual attraction is subservient to intellectual and emotional companionship. Similarly, Radcliffe marries Emily not to a dark, sexually aggressive figure like Montoni, but to the bland and domesticated Valancourt. Nevertheless, the adultery plot in *Udolpho* suggests an anxiety not just about male, but also about female, sexuality as a socially disruptive force. Signora Laurentini's participation in an adulterous liaison signifies adulteration, a Burkean allegory of the dissolution of social and gender boundaries caused by a woman who rebels against her properly passionless and affective role within domestic ideology.

Like designating female characters as good or bad women, the use of terror as a narrative device in the Radcliffean Gothic—to stimulate the heroine's and the reader's fear—emphasizes the contiguity of the heroine to the taint of potential transgression while also removing her from it. On the most obvious level, the experience of terror in Radcliffean Gothic records women's fear of male domination, as in a scene where Emily's unwanted suitor, Count Morano, tries to persuade her to elope with him by bursting into her room and "springing towards the bed" with "a sheathed sword" (261). This scene recalls the famous one that Burke describes in his *Reflections*, where armed revolutionaries startle the terrified and half-naked Marie Antoinette in her bed. But encoded within this scene's Burkean image of threatened domesticity is a more complex response to women's subjectivity and sexuality. As a spurned lover who threatens, when words will not persuade Emily to elope with him, to use "force" (265), Count Morano epitomizes the male tyrant of the Gothic. Yet by "springing towards the bed" he also externalizes the "passions" that similarly threaten Emily, who is often, as Mary Poovey argues, the victim of the excessive fears generated by her "undisciplined imagination."[18] The novel's anxiety about feminine subjectivity is typical of the ideology of sensibility, in which women's feelings are central to but also potentially threaten their affective role within domestic ideology by placing emphasis upon the self rather than on social duties. The wariness about feminine subjectivity in the ideology of sensibility was only heightened in this period, as Marilyn Butler points out, by anti-Jacobin propaganda that associated a subjective viewpoint with the "sentiments of extreme individualism" voiced in the works of radicals.[19] Radcliffean Gothic expresses this pervasive fear of extreme subjectivity, figuring it through and connecting it with a feminine sexuality that is similarly viewed with apprehension.

This anxiety about feminine sexuality is encoded through the linking of terror to the typical sexual plot of the Gothic.[20] Terror becomes a way of coding the sexual feelings of the Radcliffean heroine separated from her lover—as is *Udolpho*'s Emily, Adeline in *The Romance of the Forest*, or Ellena in *The Italian*—by insistently referring to her body; Gothic heroines are always sighing or fainting or shivering. Female Gothic functions like prescriptive, medical, and other literary discourses about sexuality that, as Foucault argues, simultaneously express and channel it.[21] For while the experience of terror embodies the Gothic heroine by expressing her sensations—and thus, frequently, her desire—such experiences usually end in a moment of silence and vacuity where she loses power over her body, either by fainting or by becoming mute and inarticulate.

When Emily is surprised by the armed Count Morano we can see how the containment of feminine sexuality and autonomy in Gothic terror functions. Although Emily is "almost fainting with terror," she

> had yet sufficient command over herself, to check the shriek, that was escaping from her lips, and, letting the curtain drop from her hand, continued to observe in silence the motions of the mysterious form she saw. It seemed to glide along the remote obscurity of the apartment, then paused. . . . Certain remembrances now struck upon her heart, and almost subdued the feeble remains of her spirits; she continued, however, to watch the figure, which . . . advancing slowly towards the bed, stood silently at the feet, where the curtains, being a little open, allowed her still to see it; terror, however, had now deprived her of the power of discrimination, as well as of that of utterance. (261)

This scene elaborately codes its references to feminine sexuality. Watching from her bed, Emily is both the object of voyeurism for the as-yet-unseen male intruder and a voyeur herself. The insistence on her need to control her body underscores the significance of her bodily responsiveness to this scene set in her bedchamber. Nevertheless, terror causes her to control not only her body but also, significantly, her voice. The movement of the passage is from this control ("sufficient command") to the silencing of that voice through excessive terror. Emily first checks a shriek and observes in silence—reasonable precautions under the circumstances—but then "certain remembrances" (of the earlier scene where she lifted the veil before the picture?) "subdued" the feeble remains of her spirits. Finally, terror deprives Emily of control and of utterance; in imposing a power over her that will not let her speak terror re-creates the control that Montoni wishes to wield over her. Several pages later, when Emily learns that Montoni would have "sold" her in marriage to Morano (262)—a terminology that recalls the Wollstonecraftian equation between women and slaves—she cannot save herself from either man, and again cannot speak: "terror had so entirely disordered her thoughts, that she knew not how to plead to Morano, but sat, mute and trembling, in her chair" (265).

This fall of the Gothic heroine into silence and terror allows the Radcliffean Gothic, finally, to evade the implications of its most radical messages about women's position.[22] In the scene discussed earlier where Emily lifts the veil before what she thinks is Signora Laurentini's body, she drops "senseless on the floor" (249): "When she recovered her recollection, the remembrance of what she had seen had nearly deprived her of it a second time. She had scarcely strength to remove from the room, and regain her own . . . Horror occupied her mind, and excluded, for a time, all sense of past, and dread of future misfortune" (249). This moment where the female gaze would penetrate the "dark abyss" of male power dissolves into a scene of feminine panic: Emily is not sure what she has seen and, as we find later, has been an unreliable detective. Her withdrawal from the room to her private chamber—something she has scarcely strength to do—is a significant shift back to domestic space. At the moment of uncovering a revelation of women's history, Emily loses all sense of history in an attack of near amnesia: "Horror . . . excluded, for a time, all sense of past, and dread of future misfortune." The end of Radcliffe's novel similarly returns to an idealized domesticity isolated from all sense of history as Emily marries Valancourt and returns to the paternal estate.

In Balzac's *Les paysans*, a villainous male character makes the sinister but pragmatic claim that terror controls the common people, women, and children,[23] and the female Gothic consistently critiques such blatant authoritarianism. (Montoni, after all, treats Emily like a dependent child.) The terror in the genre, however, controls female characters by diffusing their power, voice, and sexuality. Feminist critics have characterized the Gothic as a "paranoid" genre that records women's fear and resentment of male domination.[24] Yet whereas women's paranoia may be generated by their oppression, paranoia itself can be oppressive in its ability to stifle the female voice. We can understand how terror functions in the Gothic novel when considered in the context of the redefinition of discipline and authority in the late eighteenth century. Douglas Hay argues that the more blatant forms of judicial terror that safeguarded bourgeois property were replaced as the eighteenth century progressed by a subtler (but no less efficient) use of terror as a means of discipline. This argument is akin to Michel Foucault's analysis of how during the same period in France harsh punishments were replaced by systems of internalization and normalization that reinforced rather than relaxed the mechanisms of social control.[25] The "system of terror"[26] within the Radcliffean Gothic novel represents a form of resistance to a society that treats women as the property of men. Yet the Gothic, like the changing legal and judicial discourses of the period, provides through terror a form of internalization for women—heroines and readers—that diffuses the most radical implications of the revolt of mothers and daughters that it evokes.

Maria*: Feminist Gothic*

Whereas the carceral landscape of Radcliffe's Gothic, when it achieves its most radical critique of the family, exemplifies Wollstonecraft's critique of women's position in *A Vindication of the Rights of Woman*, Wollstonecraft's own Gothic novel written after the *Vindication* is distinctively Radcliffean. Wollstonecraft's last novel, *Maria* (1797), left unfinished at her death, borrows Radcliffean conventions to signify the "wrongs of woman" while also acknowledging that they are insufficiently horrific to depict the nightmare of women's lives: "Abodes of horror have frequently been described, and castles, filled with spectres and chimeras, conjured up by the magic spell of genius to harrow the soul, and absorb the wondering mind. But, formed of such stuff as dreams are made of, what were they to the mansion of despair, in one corner of which Maria sat, endeavouring to recall her scattered thoughts!"[27]

Even as Wollstonecraft claims that fiction cannot adequately convey women's oppressive reality, this passage that begins *Maria* suggests her anxiety that her fiction resembles Radcliffe's as much as it does. Wollstonecraft will not name her most important female predecessor, the phrase "magic spell of genius" evoking rather than specifying Radcliffe's reputation as the Great Enchantress. Yet Wollstonecraft's disclaimer that she is not Radcliffe emphasizes how her heroine's fate is, if anything, more Gothic than those of Radcliffe's protagonists. Maria's imprisonment within social conventions will not end, as does Emily's, with her escape from the paradigmatically Gothic prison—here, a madhouse—in which her husband has immured her.

Just as the beginning of *Maria* emphasizes the continuity between feminine versions of the Gothic crafted by Wollstonecraft and Radcliffe, so the story is concerned with the Radcliffean theme of the link between the fate of mothers and daughters. In *Maria*, however, the emphasis is on the mother rather than on the daughter. Whereas in Radcliffe's Gothics the daughter searches for evidence of the mother's fate, here it is the mother who self-reflexively becomes a figure for the woman writer of Gothic, recording an account of her life for the daughter from whom imprisonment has separated her. As Maria's narrative shows how she has become as disempowered as her own mother, the servant Jemima, who is assigned to tend Maria in the madhouse, also recounts how her life has mimicked that of her mother, who suffered seduction, poverty, and starvation. These interlocking cycles of mother and daughter stories figure the daughter's inability to achieve difference from the mother; in her prison Maria "mourned for her child, lamented she was a daughter, and anticipated the aggravated ills of life that her sex rendered almost inevitable" (24). Although Maria's written account of her childhood illustrates Wollstonecraft's claim that women are taught to assume an unequal place in society by the example of their mothers, it also represents at the same time an attempt to reverse this negative example by instructing one daughter to avoid her mother's errors.

The written text bequeathed from mother to daughter thus represents a more positive version of inheritance from the mother than is usually found in the female Gothic's matrophobic narrative. Reminiscent of the Utopian vision in *A Sicilian Romance* where the daughter rescues the mother, *Maria* invokes the power of feminine solidarity to transform oppressive domestic histories. Such solidarity unites mothers and daughters of different classes; the character of Jemima, who from being Maria's jailer becomes her friend and ally, inserts a narrative about class foreign to the Radcliffean Gothic, where the heroines are elite women and their servants usually only a form of comic relief. That Jemima's story echoes Maria's, however, demonstrates Wollstonecraft's point in her preface that "different classes of women" (22) share the same wrongs. Jemima is Wollstonecraft's revision of Burke's rebellious revolutionary viragos; unlike Burke's ideology, which would pit lower-class women against threatened and passive queens, Wollstonecraft promises a potential friendship and alliance between women of radically different backgrounds.[28]

This implicitly political vision of women's solidarity contrasts with the pessimism that elsewhere shadows *Maria*. Unlike Radcliffe's novels, set in a distant past, Wollstonecraft's Gothic is set amid the actual history its author experienced, the political repression in the wake of the French Revolution and England's entry into war with France. Although Maria's defiance of women's traditional fate and her decision to leave her husband for her lover once she escapes from the madhouse enact a "REVOLUTION in female manners" more radical even than Wollstonecraft calls for in her *Vindication* (*VRW* 192), this rebellion is met with a reaction similar to that which met other English Jacobins in the 1790s. Dismissing Maria's eloquent written plea, which she asks to be read when she is brought into divorce court, the judge decries the influence of "French principles" (149) that would "legalize adultery" and violate the "sanctity of marriage" (150).

This representation of political repression, coupled with a projected outline for the end of the novel in which her apparently liberal and sensitive lover soon abandons Maria, reflects and prophesies the way both radical and conservative social agendas in the late 1790s avoided the possibility of redressing the "wrongs of woman." Living in France during the Terror, Wollstonecraft witnessed the suppression of women's clubs and feminist discourse by the French Jacobins, including the execution of such prominent women activists as Olympe de Gouges and Madame Roland. In England, meanwhile, anti-Jacobin reaction reinforced the increasingly conservative definition within domestic ideology of woman's role as wife and mother that would become hegemonic by the nineteenth century.[29]

In *Maria*, this thematics of political repression is figured as textual marginalization. The force of Maria's writing is overwhelmed by the repressive voice of the judge following her vindication of her conduct, which he reads as an example of "the fallacy of letting women plead their feelings" (149). This judicial voice-over imposes a single repressive interpretation on a text composed of multiple voices—the narrator's, Maria's, Jemima's, Maria's lover Darnford's—and ending with Wollstonecraft's notes for the projected conclusion. It would be mistaken, however, to ascribe the textual disorder of *Maria* solely to its unfinished state at Wollstonecraft's death (ironically, in childbirth). The fragmentation of the narrative is in many ways deliberate and ideologically motivated: the novel's multiple narrative voices, recorded through dialogue, monologue, letters, and other writing, draw on the epistolary tradition in a radical attempt to give speech to those—women and the lower classes—who would otherwise be silenced. Even the theme of madness in the novel, although it suggests utter unintelligibility, exposes a culture that systematically exiles and dispossesses women and other outcasts. The women's narratives, which mimic the manic rhythm of Maria's "scattered thoughts" at the beginning of the novel, pose the voice of feminine rebellion, stigmatized by the dominant culture as madness, against the oppressive "sanity" of ideological hegemony.[30]

Given Wollstonecraft's aesthetics of multiplicity in *Maria*, it is perhaps appropriate that even the novel's closure is doubled. In the posthumous edition of the work, William Godwin published the two endings that Wollstonecraft left in draft, which posit two radically different fates that might befall her rebellious heroine. One of these traces a dismal new domestic history: "Divorced by her husband—Her lover unfaithful—Pregnancy—Miscarriage—Suicide" (152). The other, however, sketches the restoration by Jemima of Maria's lost daughter, presumed dead, a revelation that causes her to renounce her plan of suicide and to claim "I will live for my child!" (153). Whereas the first ending writes a narrative of political pessimism, the second breaks the Gothic chain of the dismal repetition of the mother's fate, promising, moreover, through Jemima's help in finding the lost child, a future for daughters in a community of women.

Frankenstein: *Gender and Class in the Nineteenth-Century Gothic Novel*

Mary Shelley drew on her mother's feminist narrative to create her own version of postrevolutionary Gothic. Influenced in *Frankenstein* by Wollstonecraft's analysis of women and the lower classes as social outcasts, Shelley was also indebted to the radical Gothic of her father's *Caleb Williams* for a tale of men of differing class backgrounds engaged in a paranoid cycle of quest and evasion. Closely allied with radical Romanticism, and yet written in a period of increased political repression, Shelley's Gothic novel is shaped by the same ideological tensions surrounding the question of the woman writer's relation to rebellion that shaped the Radcliffean Gothic. In *Frankenstein*, Shelley makes her monster embody *ressentiment*, or lower-class envy of and rebellion against class privilege. The nineteenth-century ideologeme of ressentiment, however, often suggests (if with great anxiety) the participation of the author in this rebellion.[31] Although in her characterization of the monster Shelley develops the discourse about class in the Gothic to a new degree of explicitness, her ambivalence about being implicated in this subversion causes the novel to shift between feminist and Burkean registers. The story of *Frankenstein* embeds the analogy between gender and class, employed from radically opposed political perspectives in *Maria* and Burke, but also finally obscures this parallel. *Frankenstein* is thus a particularly double-voiced and conflicted narrative. Shelley creates a Gothic story whose familial plot more insistently refers to politics and history than does the typical female Gothic; yet in her resolution of this plot she anticipates a strategy of depoliticization in nineteenth-century fiction that distinguishes the public story of class from the private one of gender in order to emphasize the power of domestic ideology to heal and prevent class disruption.

The extent to which class and gender are linked in *Frankenstein* remains a question in most recent studies of ideology in the novel. Unsurprisingly, feminist critics have tended to focus on gender ideology in the narrative, situating their interpretations in the context of both familial and literary history. In her famous discussion of female Gothic, Ellen Moers reads the novel not as a story about fathers and sons in which the mother—central to the Radcliffean Gothic—is absent, but as a classic mythicization of birth trauma, in which a woman writer records her ambivalent feelings about maternity and childbirth.[32] Other feminist critics, such as Sandra Gilbert, Susan Gubar, and Margaret Homans, have gone on to show how Shelley underscores the parallel between nineteenth-century familial and literary history, figuring the way that women's works are, in a male-dominated tradition that denies them authority, dispossessed and monstrous, "hideous progeny," as Shelley called her novel in the 1831 preface.[33] In apparent contrast to the internal history that feminist critics tell about gender and the novel—internal because it focuses on women's history within the family, within literary history, within their own minds where the conflict between convention and subversion is waged—is the history of politics and class foregrounded by those critics who situate their reading of the text outside the family, and literary genealogy, in a turbulent society. Ronald Paulson characterizes *Frankenstein* as a "retrospect" on revolutionary history, and Lee Sterrenburg argues that the monster's ragged ugliness and Otherness evokes the specter of working-class rebellion that continued to be the source of bourgeois panic after the French Revolutionary period.[34] Sterrenburg underscores the apparent distinction between these internal and external histories that causes Shelley to evade the connection between gender and class concentrated in figures like Burke's market women and Wollstonecraft's Jemima; by turning her monster into a "lone male," Sterrenburg claims, Shelley "denies herself many of the sexual and political implications already inherent in the image of the female, parricidal monster."[35]

In spite of its apparent avoidance of a clear connection between femininity and the lower classes, however, *Frankenstein* suggests a signifying system in which gender and class evoke each other. Although he is not a feminine outcast like Jemima, the monster suggests both her, and Wollstonecraft's radical text itself, through allusion. The monster's description of himself as an "abortion" (222) recalls Jemima's account of having an abortion and her sense of herself as monstrous. As Gilbert and Gubar note, the monster's eloquent autobiographical narrative has its origins in Jemima's speech to Maria in which she calls herself an "object of abhorrence" (55).[36] Similarly, the monster's query "Was I then a monster, a blot upon the earth, from which all men fled, and whom all men disowned?" (120) echoes Jemima's "Who ever acknowledged me to be a fellow creature?" (69).

Whereas *Frankenstein* thus makes by allusion the analogy between the monster as class Other and outcast women, Shelley implies through these references to her mother's text that women's writing, too, is alien and exiled, both in its subversiveness and in its exclusion from male authority. In her preface to *Maria*, echoing the graphic images of Jemima's abortion, Wollstonecraft hopes that her political tale will not be dismissed as the "abortion of a distempered fancy" (21); her daughter's description of her own novel as "hideous progeny," however, suggests that women's texts are such literary abortions. Sewn together from fragments, Shelley's monster recalls Wollstonecraft's fragmented and unfinished radical Gothic. Yet although this imagery of monstrous fragmentation hints at a negative reading of the literary value of her mother's work, Shelley borrows and develops one of the original aspects of Wollstonecraft's narrative experimentation in *Maria* that further suggests the relation between the monster and women. Structurally, the first-person narratives of Shelley's novel mimic the accounts of Jemima and Maria in her mother's novel; like the narrative given to Jemima, the monster's story, which follows his demonic characterization by his creator, has the subversive function of allowing a dispossessed and alien character a sympathetic voice.

Like his monster, who thus embodies Shelley's link between women and social outcasts and alludes to a maternal tradition of Gothic, the figure of Frankenstein also provides a way of connecting gender and class issues in the novel. At first, this connection seems to be made in the most conservative manner, as the novel indicates that the instigators of class revolt are arrogant male rebels against female-centered domesticity. If the monster symbolizes the specter of class rebellion, Frankenstein is the radical reformer or "metaphysician" who, as Burke claimed, resembles in his cold-blooded attempts to reorder society the "cold malignity of a wicked spirit" rather than "the frailty and passion of a man."[37] The image of the Jacobin as hubristic intellectual, Frankenstein is the rebellious son who in his rejection of the family spawns rebellious offspring. Shelley's portrait of the male intellectual who strays outside the affective bonds of domesticity echoes anti-Jacobin propaganda; it also records her hostility to radical theories —including, as Mary Poovey has argued, Romanticism itself[38]—that exclude women. Just as the promise of equality held out by the French Revolution gave way to the imperialism of Napoleon, so Frankenstein is finally not so much a radical as a Papa-Emperor, musing to Walton that "A new species would bless me as its creator and source . . . No father could claim the gratitude of his child so completely as I should deserve theirs" (54). This representation of the tyrannical father echoes Wollstonecraft's radical writings, specifically her depiction of exacting parents in the *Vindication of the Rights of Woman*: "Parents often love their children in the most brutal manner . . . to promote . . . the future welfare of the very beings whose present existence they embitter" (*VRW* 225).

Shelley's image of the Jacobin as imperialist represents his domination of a feminine Nature. In characteristically "phallic language," as Andrew Griffin calls it,[39] Frankenstein desires to "penetrate . . . [the] misty veil" of Nature (96); he urges Walton's mutinous sailors to conquer the North Pole, which Marc Rubenstein sees as a symbol for the maternal principle exiled from the male world where the father has usurped the role of mother.[40] This gendered allegory of imperialism is continued as the monster, hiding in the woods near the De Lacey home, weeps over the fate of North American natives when he hears Felix and Safie read from the Jacobin historian Constantin Volney's *Ruins of Empire.* Himself the class alien, the monster identifies with a woman's grief over imperialism: "I heard of the discovery of the American hemisphere, and wept with Safie over the hapless fate of its original inhabitants" (119). At this moment a feminist narrative—feminist because Safie is a woman oppressed by a tyrannical father—intertwines with a critique of class inequality. The monster hears Felix instruct Safie about class relations from the Volney text: "the strange system of human society was explained to me. I heard of the division of property, of immense wealth and squalid poverty; of rank, descent, and noble blood" (120).

This critique of imperialism, one of the novel's most feminist elements, shows the category of the feminine, which includes women and Nature, dominated by men. Such symbolism apparently renders the major female characters in *Frankenstein*—Caroline Beaufort, Elizabeth Lavenza, and Justine Moritz—merely passive victims. Distinguishing them from the novel's rebellious males, indeed, Barbara Johnson dismisses these women as "selfless, boring nurturers . . . who never experience inner conflict or true desire."[41] But viewed more subtly, the women in *Frankenstein* are linked with rebellion and hence, indirectly, with the embodiment of rebellion, the monster.

Like the monster, all three women are associated in some way with the lower classes. A servant, Justine Moritz becomes a part of the Frankenstein family in a way that parallels the adoption of Frankenstein's childhood companion and fiancée, Elizabeth Lavenza. Although Elizabeth is described in the most sanctified of domestic terms—"the saintly soul of Elizabeth shone like a shrine-dedicated lamp in our peaceful home" (38)—she is the daughter of an Italian nationalist who is described as one of the "*schiavi ognor frementi*" (slaves always fretting) for freedom. Such a lineage links Elizabeth both to rebellion and to slavery, and she is appropriately enough discovered by Frankenstein's mother, Caroline, in a peasant household. Caroline herself had been adopted by her fatherly husband, who saved her from the poverty in which she had been compelled to perform wage labor. The monster's murder of William, the second male heir of the Frankensteins, draws Justine and Elizabeth into a plot of rebellion. Although Justine is innocent, she is seen as a kind of class monster by those who believe her guilty; Frankenstein's father, a syndic of Geneva, murmurs sadly that he grieves to discover "so much depravity and ingratitude in one I valued so highly" (80). The injustice of Justine's condemnation drives the gentle Elizabeth to a quiet but significant dissent from her adoptive father's opinion. "Violently agitated" as she defends Justine in court, Elizabeth is radically disillusioned with men's justice when her plea fails: "Before, I looked upon the accounts of vice and injustice . . . as tales of ancient days . . . but now . . . men appear to me as monsters thirsting for each other's blood" (92). Elizabeth's speech locates monstrosity not in the class outcasts—Justine, the monster—but in the establishment and legal system with which her father, one of the city's chief magistrates, is associated.

Shelley's novel, however, employs a strategy for dealing with the problem of feminine subversion similar to that in the Radcliffean Gothic, in which the heroine's rebellion is contained and displaced onto the Other Woman. It is revealing, indeed, that the most horrible monster in the novel is a feminine one that is never created, the mate that Frankenstein refuses to provide for the monster because it would endlessly reproduce rebellious offspring. It is a tribute to how Shelley writes female revolt out of the text that the monster, the class Other, takes the place of the Radcliffean Other Woman, implicating the female characters only unwittingly and unwillingly in his plot of rebellion. Although Elizabeth labels herself a monstrous mother at William's death ("I have murdered my darling child" [72]), neither she nor Justine is actually responsible. Yet it is significant that Elizabeth links the crime to a miniature of Caroline Beaufort, which she gave William to wear, because she thinks its value attracted a robber. Even as the miniature does attract the monster with its evocation of the feminine domesticity from which he—who has no mother—has been barred, the sanctified image of domesticity represented by the mother's face is transformed from a beneficent influence into what Marc Rubenstein calls a "malignantly destructive" force.[42] That the miniature is a mother's legacy to her adoptive daughter recalls the theme of maternal inheritance in the Radcliffean Gothic; it also suggests the radical heritage represented by Shelley's own mother, Wollstonecraft. By making the maternal image a domestic, not a political, one, and by absolving the women from more than unconscious complicity in the monster's crime, Shelley bleaches her narrative of all but a trace of feminine rebellion. Finally, it is the monster's class ressentiment that slays William, who had taunted him with a reminder of his own privileged position: "my papa is a Syndic . . . he will punish you" (142).

This displacement of female rebellion onto a demonized image of class ressentiment undoes the narrative connection between class and gender inequality, and thus diffuses the most radical aspects of Shelley's novel. The parallel between gender and class oppression is rewritten as opposition when the monster's attacks on his unequal status lead to assaults on women; he not only causes Justine's death, but he also strangles Elizabeth Lavenza on her wedding night. That Elizabeth's body is thrown across her marriage bed implicitly makes the male monster an icon for men's domination of women within marriage.[43] Yet given the Burkean resonance of the scene, which echoes the account in the *Reflections* of Marie Antoinette's near-violation by revolutionaries, the criticism of Frankenstein as a figure for bourgeois male dominance is deflected onto his monster, the bestial lower-class male. Thus Shelley's critique of male domination is subsumed within a kind of domestic feminism (male monsters kill wives and mothers) that is hard to distinguish from Burke's horror at the dissolution of the family. The Gothic image of the murdered wife recalls the slaughter of "mothers and daughters" by the monster of Jacobinism that Burke imagines in *Letters on a Regicide Peace*: "Let us suppose, then . . . [the] exemplary queen, at the head of the matronage of this land, murdered . . . with hundreds of others, mothers and daughters."[44]

Even when most clearly alluding to Wollstonecraft in the story of Safie, Shelley rejects the legacy of her mother's radicalism. Safie, with whom the monster weeps over the fate of native Americans, is the novel's most overt tribute to Wollstonecraft; although she embodies the seraglio trope that figures male domination in *A Vindication of the Rights of Woman*, she might also be read as a figure for Mary

Shelley herself, since she is said to inherit a love of women's liberty from her mother (123–24). Safie rejects the monster, rushing away when she first sees him (135), once again fracturing an alliance between women and the working classes; symbolically turned away by a figure for feminism, the monster asserts his class ressentiment by burning down the De Lacey home. Not only is the monster repulsed as a figure for the working classes, but also Wollstonecraft's *Vindication* is itself symbolically expelled from her daughter's text as Safie rushes out of the narrative. This expulsion of the mother's text is rendered more significant because, as Rubenstein notes, Safie's story lies at the center of the concentric series of narratives in the novel;[45] in a microcosm of the rejection of radicalism, when Safie runs away the centrality of the mother's text vanishes and gives way to a more conservative and Burkean version of Gothic.

Safie's rejection of the monster, although it transcribes Shelley's ambivalence about male and female radicalism, finally reflects the historical split between bourgeois feminism and movements for working-class suffrage in the postrevolutionary period. In this sense, *Frankenstein* mirrors the post-Romantic historical vision that sees social change as either self-destructively violent or simply impossible; by the end of the narrative, the violence of the struggle between the monster and his creator has precipitated a kind of stasis, killing both radical creator and his monster. *Frankenstein* ends with a vision in which history outside the family—science, and figuratively, revolution—is reduced to a disruption of the family and censored with the hubristic son's death and his monster's imminent self-immolation. This conservative plot anticipates and provides a model for the narrative paradigm that Nancy Armstrong has traced, in which the distinction between a domestic plot and a political one becomes a standard strategy for eliding divisive class politics and underscoring the hegemony of domestic ideology in nineteenth-century versions of the domestic novel.[46]

In his revision of *Frankenstein* and other Gothic fictions, Wilkie Collins would in many ways reverse the tendency to depoliticization exemplified by Shelley's novel. From *Frankenstein*, Collins borrowed the plot of class ressentiment and the figure of a monstrous and disfigured social outcast to make, as Shelley does, a parallel between the situation of women and that of the lower classes. The recurrent outcast figures in Collins' works—Robert Mannion, Sarah Leeson, Anne Catherick, Ezra Jennings—are either women or in stereotypically "feminine" and disempowered positions. These characters, vehicles for Collins' plots of social protest, are usually even more sympathetically portrayed than Shelley's monster, and to do so Collins borrowed from Shelley the structure of the multiply voiced narrative used both in *Frankenstein* and in Wollstonecraft's feminist Gothic, *Maria*. The many narrative voices in Collins' most famous novels (*The Woman in White* and *The Moonstone*) not only give a voice to women and other outcasts, but also, like *Maria*, imply an aesthetics of multiplicity over an aesthetic unity that signifies the hegemony of a male-dominated and bourgeois culture.

At the same time that Collins uses Gothic conventions (the vision of domesticity as "feminine carceral,"[47] the figure of the class and gender outcast) to encode a critique of domesticity and the Victorian class system, however, his works also record an ambivalence to rebellion and revolution similar to that in the Radcliffean and Shelleyan Gothic. In the case of Radcliffe and Shelley, this ambivalence can be traced to the conflict experienced by the woman writer between subversion and acquiescence to conventional gender roles. For Collins, however, this ambivalence stemmed from his position as a male writer who defined his authority through the distinction between male professionalism and the domestic world of women. For Collins, then, as for Radcliffe and Shelley, the Gothic was the site of ideological conflict, a vehicle through which at once to criticize domesticity and to pose its values as a barrier against rebellion and social change.

Two

Becoming an Author in 1848: History and the Gothic in the Early Works of Wilkie Collins

Wilkie Collins' first work, published in 1848 when he was twenty-four, was a biography of his father, the respected painter and Royal Academician William Collins. In contrast to the matrilineal tradition of the female Gothic, *Memoirs of the Life of William Collins* is a monument to the male artist that celebrates the bond between father and son. Chronicling William's Franklinesque rise from poverty to prosperity through unrelenting industry, Collins eulogizes his father as an exemplary family man and, above all, an empowering predecessor. The *Memoirs* were, however, an anomaly in the career their publication launched. Not only was Collins to turn from writing biography to writing fiction, but the filial piety of the *Memoirs* was to be replaced by a melodramatic Gothicism that would have shocked the father who reportedly avoided in his painting all that was "coarse, violent, revolting, fearful"[1]—everything, in other words, that came to be associated with his son's art.

The *Memoirs*, then, can be seen as a generic dead end for Collins, as can his first novel, *Antonina* (1850), a bustling historical epic in the style of Scott and Bulwer-Lytton. Yet these often neglected early works have an important place in Collins' oeuvre as fictions of origins in which he interrogates the sources of his art and experiments with representational strategies. Most significant, the *Memoirs* and *Antonina* draft the kind of plot that was to become characteristic of Collins' later and more mature work from *Basil* onward, in which a narrative about literary authority is cast as a story about gender and, in particular, as a family romance in which the father is invested with the social and artistic power from which the mother is excluded.

In *Basil*, the son who is the figure for the emergent bourgeois artist defies the authority of his father and is subsequently disinherited.

The plot concerning rebellion against the father is already embedded in the early works that are the focus of this chapter, but it is complicated by a nostalgia for the patriarchal power beginning to decline in the *Memoirs* and dramatically waning in the novel about the Fall of Rome, home of the paterfamilias. As I suggested above, the figure of William Collins looms large in the *Memoirs* as an image for masculine authority and as the Romantic predecessor, since he not only was a friend of Wordsworth and Coleridge, but also practiced in his landscapes a Romantic fidelity to Nature. Yet the father's Romanticism (like that of Wordsworth and Coleridge in their later years) was of a conservative variety that eschewed political radicalism in favor of "Toryism" (II, 55). If the *Memoirs* were a dead end for Collins, it was because the work suggested the end of the (paternal) line for this Romanticism as a form of art worthy of the son's emulation, not only because he was more liberal than his father but also because William's conservative philosophy no longer had validity in the politically stormy world of the 1830s and 1840s. Collins declared in a brief autobiographical sketch written in the early 1860s, "An author I became in the year 1848,"[2] and his early works are about what it meant to launch an artistic career in the period culminating in the European revolutions of that year, but beginning in England with the movement for Chartist reform that Collins refers to in the *Memoirs* and represents in his historical narrative in *Antonina*.

Becoming an author in 1848 suggests an oedipal narrative in which the son can produce only once he has acknowledged, through the publication of the *Memoirs*, the death of his Tory father. Yet even as the *Memoirs*, and particularly *Antonina*, which is more explicitly about defying the father's rules, show how Collins departs from William's example, they are also pervaded by a sense of the newfound absence of paternal authority—a loss figured in his first novel as a crisis of male power that will become pronounced rather than diminished in the later fictions. This narrative about a crisis of male power is really about a crisis of definition, in which the post-Romantic and bourgeois male writer attempts to define his own authority in the absence of the father's. The fall of the father's authority is connected in turn with the rise of a hitherto repressed maternal or feminine power that, in a way similar to the fictions discussed in the previous chapter, is associated both with revolution and with the Gothic. It is in fact Collins' uneasy relation to the Gothic, which comes to inspire his art, that forms the major generic and ideological tension of *Antonina,* a novel in which patriarchal Rome is besieged by the Gothic army that is embodied in a monstrous female figure of ressentiment. In this narrative, as would become more evident in such later novels as *Basil* and *The Woman in White,* Collins is simultaneously attracted to the rebellion associated with the feminine and repulsed by it, as he seeks to constitute an aesthetic authority structured by the ideology of bourgeois manliness.

Mapping the Fatherland: Memoirs of the Life of William Collins

In the *Memoirs,* William Collins' art becomes a synecdoche for his life, which is elided by an account of his professional existence. Although Collins includes excerpts from letters and journals, the two-volume biography is organized around word pictures that describe William's paintings in excruciating detail—a tally of productivity that almost parodies his work ethic in its scrupulous particularity. Whereas this emphasis on William's career correspondingly deemphasizes his relationship with his family, Collins further suppresses this private history in his treatment of the correspondence he does include. As Verlyn Klinkenborg has shown in his comparison of William's original letters with the versions in the *Memoirs,* Collins "altered, rearranged, and recombined" his sources to edit out, among other things, hints of conflict with his father over his own choice of a profession.[3]

Although William was not the melodramatically stern patriarch that Nuel Pharr Davis has made him out to be,[4] there was some friction over his eldest son's career; Collins did not pursue ordination in the Anglican Church as his father had originally wished, but he tried several other professions—a stint as apprentice to a tea merchant and study for the bar—before announcing his desire to become a writer. William did not contest this decision, and even commissioned his son to write the *Memoirs.* Yet that Collins took so long to articulate his choice of profession might explain why he refers, in an 1860s autobiographical sketch, to the sources of his art as clandestine and even illicit, claiming that he first began to write "in secret."[5]

In the *Memoirs* the erasure of this history of generational conflict erases in turn the character of the son who, as Kenneth Robinson claims, "so seldom intrudes upon his father's story."[6] Yet although such self-suppression makes the son who began to write in secret even more of a hidden presence, it also reinforces his authority by linking it more securely to that of his father. Klinkenborg argues that by censoring both William's nicknames for his son and his teasing references to his early writing, Collins protects his own seriousness as author.[7] It is also true, though, that Collins' intervention in his father's correspondence—which, by cutting his jokes, makes William more priggish and aloof than ever—underscores the predecessor's monumental seriousness as a source of inspiration for his son's art.

Although it is a gesture of self-authorization, this emphasis on the father as precursor also suggests the extent to which he really was an influence on his son. Even as the biography displays the qualities that distinguished William from his more bohemian son—his "Toryism" (II, 55), his orthodox Anglican piety—it reveals the devotion to art and to professionalism that Collins was to emulate in his own career. The *Memoirs* in fact define the son's art as literally a translation of the father's; Collins' word pictures transform his father's painting into his own medium and anticipate, as one critic has noted, the landscape descriptions in his novels.[8] Although Collins was to transform William's idealized pastoral landscapes into eerie Gothic ones, he returned to his father's Romantic ideals of fidelity to Nature even while apparently rejecting them, claiming, for instance, in the preface to his famously melodramatic *Basil* that the artist should portray the "poetry of everyday truth."[9]

What is most striking about the *Memoirs*, indeed, is the way they reflect Collins' desire to construct a masculine artistic identity empowered by the father's example. The *Memoirs* certainly associate artistry with masculinity, especially forms of male power. The world of the text is like a stag club: not only is there an implicit bond between father and son, but also the biography maps a narrative of what Eve Kosofsky Sedgwick calls "male homosocial desire" in the close personal and professional friendship between William Collins and the Scots painter Sir David Wilkie.[10] Named after both these men (Collins' baptismal name was William Wilkie), the son presumably inherits the social and artistic power vested in male networks.

Whereas the *Memoirs* trace these bonds between men, the mother is absent. Even given the biographical focus on William, the degree to which Collins edited his mother out of his account of family life is the more striking because she was, in Kenneth Robinson's words, "the dominant influence in the forming of Wilkie's character," and a staunch supporter of his early artistic career.[11] In an interview in the 1880s, Collins even claimed that he inherited from his mother "whatever of poetry and imagination may be in my composition."[12] That Collins so completely suppresses his mother's role in shaping his art to emphasize instead a paternal predecessor is symptomatic of the ambivalence toward the influence of female precursors displayed throughout his future work. Far more than the emphasis on his father in the *Memoirs* would call for, Collins limits the mention of his mother, a woman of considerable intelligence and cultivation, to brief notes on her birth and her marriage to his father; she is the addressee of William's letters, yet not one letter from her to him is included. Sir David Wilkie gets far more attention than Harriet Collins, and indeed the fusion of the names of the two male friends in the son's implies that, like Shelley's monster, he is the offspring of male bonding rather than of the heterosexual union between father and mother.[13]

If the mother is excised as a literal presence, however, the category of the feminine enters the text figuratively through a description of Nature. One critic of William's landscapes, in fact, declared that Nature was his bride: "Mr. Collins was wedded to Nature, and the match has turned out a happy one" (II, 296). The marriage metaphor that this critic uses echoes Romantic images of Nature as a feminine or maternal presence, such as Wordsworth's "spousal verse" in the Prospectus to *The Excursion,* which, as Margaret Homans argues, assumes a union between a masculine "Mind of Man" and a traditionally feminine Nature.[14] A Wordsworthian vision of Nature as beneficent spouse and mother is the backdrop for the male artist's self-expression, a relationship that mirrors that between women and men in nineteenth-century marital ideology and in which the silencing of forthright Harriet Collins is overdetermined.

Still, just as feminine Nature in *Frankenstein* embodies the revolutionary content of Romanticism, Nature in the *Memoirs* is not so placid as it might seem from Collins' many descriptions of his father's idyllic landscapes. This stormy vision of feminine Nature is particularly apparent in Collins' lengthy description of a painting his father completed in the late 1820s, "Morning after a Storm." The description of this painting is important because it reinserts the mother's voice into the narrative, if only in the most covert form. In a letter to R. H. Dana written after the publication of the *Memoirs*, Collins explains that he had just seen for the first time the canvas of this painting and another called "A Frost Scene," both of which he described in the *Memoirs*, because they had been in the private collection of Sir Robert Peel. Though he conceals this fact in the *Memoirs*, Collins' description of these paintings is thus derived not from the father's originals but from, as he puts it, "my Mother's recollections."[15]

Since both the paintings that his mother described are called by Collins in his letter to Dana "classics of the English School of Painting,"[16] his version of how he became familiar with them does not empower the mother's voice so much as it makes her a conduit for the father's power: she is only a copyist, or amanuensis, of William's art, a version of which is transmitted to the son. If the mother is associated with the repression of the feminine, however, the painting whose subject is the passing of a storm depicts a feminine Nature that has just burst out of bounds. This version of natural conflict apparently contradicts the father's professed desire to paint only what is "beautiful in Nature" (II, 313) and not "violent" or "fearful" (II, 311); in the painting a fisherman's wife anxiously awaits, with her children, her husband's return on the morning after a storm that may have killed him. The narrative suggested by this scene is a Gothic fiction, stressing feminine vulnerability caused by the possible dissolution of the family, a threat underscored by the "wild broken clouds" and "vexed waters" still "in process of subsiding from their recent agitation" (I, 315).

Yet although William's painting focuses on the quelling of the "agitation"—the morning *after* the storm—his son's description lingers on what is threatening about the landscape, the "powerful and beautiful" contrast between the "brilliant action of the elements" and the Gothic "fear" of the waiting woman (I, 315). This emphasis on the contrasts of Nature as "powerful" yet "beautiful"—an echo of the Romantic sublime—reinserts the feminine into the masculine landscape of the *Memoirs*, albeit as an unruly and disruptive, possibly even man-killing, force. This narrative of an "agitation" that threatens the family—which recalls the ideological contours of the Burkean, or conservative, Gothic—is significant given the figuration of political "agitation" elsewhere in the *Memoirs*, as Collins records his father's reactions to the stormy decade of the 1830s.

William's reaction to the rise of the Chartist movement in the 1830s was typically conservative; professing his distaste for the English "mob" (II, 2), he declared in a letter that "Of the two scourges now afflicting us [a cholera epidemic and Reform Bill riots], I know not which is the worst" (II, 3). In one passage Collins himself catches up his father's imagery in both the letter and the painting "Morning after a Storm":

> Those momentous public occurrences, the outbreak of the cholera, and the Reform Bill agitation, of which England was the scene during this year [1835], produced that long and serious depression in the patronage and appreciation of Art which social and political convulsions must necessarily exercise on the intellectual luxuries of the age. The noble and the wealthy, finding their lives endangered by a mysterious pestilence, and believing that their possessions were threatened by a popular revolution, which was to sink the rights of station and property in a general deluge of republican equality, had little time . . . to attend to the remoter importance of the progress of national Art. (I, 344–45)

The reference to "mysterious pestilence" in this passage, like the father's reference to cholera, implies a likeness between the fever epidemic and the threat of revolution. Similarly, the word "agitation" echoes Collins' description of natural agitation in "Morning after a Storm."

The above passage, however, does not simply reproduce the father's discourse. Collins does not explicitly endorse the Reform Bill himself, echoing bourgeois paranoia about lower-class revolt by repeating his father's imagery of disease and stormy agitation. Yet the passage displays a curious form of indirect discourse; the description of a popular revolution "which was to sink the rights of station and property in a general deluge of republican equality" reproduces the language of the "noble and the wealthy," rather than of Collins himself. (We might assume, however, that the hyperbole of the flood metaphor ["general deluge"] is self-consciously, if covertly, witty.) Collins also suggests that a relation between art and politics is unavoidable: "that long and serious depression in the patronage and appreciation of Art which social and political convulsions *must necessarily exercise* on the intellectual luxuries of the age" (my emphasis). Collins' association of art (including the father's) with aristocratic luxuries subtly contrasts with his championship of the "progress of national Art" that politics has impeded.

Collins' claim that politics affects the patronage of art seems an obvious point rather than a radical opinion. Yet a subtle tension between the father's view of art and the son's sense that history intrudes upon art is evident when a passage like this one is compared with a description of William's aesthetic philosophy. Despite his Wordsworthian depiction of Nature and the lower classes, William Collins scrupulously avoided the critique of society in radical Romanticism. Collins claims his father never portrayed class struggle or extreme poverty: "no representations of the fierce miseries, or the coarse contentions which form the darker tragedy of humble life, occur among them" (II, 311). The happy villagers in William's paintings provide their audience (which presumably was largely bourgeois or upper class) with a preindustrial fantasy stressing the contentment of the rural lower classes rather than the discontent of the urban and industrial working class. This avoidance of "coarse contentions" dovetails with William Collins' aesthetic ideal, which "led him intuitively to the contemplation of all in Nature that was pure, tranquil, tender, harmonious; and to the rejection of all that was coarse, violent, revolting, fearful" (II, 311).

In contrast to his father's philosophy of separation and exclusion,

Collins dwells on images of fluidity and indeterminacy in William's paintings. His description of "Morning after a Storm" blurs the terms he had used to express his father's art: what is "violent" and "fearful" (stormy Nature) is juxtaposed with what is "pure" and "tender" (the waiting woman) to form, rather than to undermine, a "harmonious" composition. Immediately following the description of "Morning after a Storm," Collins discusses a painting entitled "Summer Moonlight," which also focuses on a moment of natural transition. Evoking "the dreamy, mysterious softness of the atmosphere, neither twilight nor moonlight, but partaking of both" (I, 316), Collins again underscores an image of miscegenation rather than separation, and of flux rather than stasis. As if to associate his father with what is balanced and moderate, Collins claims that his father's chiaroscuro combines equal portions of light and shade (II, 323) and that William had a horror of "blackness" (I, 284). Yet "Summer Moonlight" is an image not only of night and blackness, but also of a "mysterious" indeterminacy that contrasts with the movement toward morning and clarity in "Morning after a Storm."

By emphasizing images of instability in William's art, Collins destabilizes the terms of his father's aesthetic philosophy, but also attempts to transform the limitations of that philosophy into virtues worthy of his own emulation. That he describes what his father left out of his paintings, however, underscores the extent to which William remains a problematic as well as an empowering predecessor. References to the conservative cast of William's vision suggest that he might be not just an unsatisfying model for his more liberal son, but also an inadequate one in a period of rapid historical change.

On the last page of the *Memoirs*, Collins is clearly worried that the paternal ideal may have lost its validity in 1848:

> Whether . . . it can be hoped, that in these times of fierce political contention, and absorbing political anxiety, they [the *Memoirs*] should be important enough to awaken the attention, or even to amuse the leisure of others, are doubts which cannot now be resolved; and which, could they be penetrated, I should at this stage of my undertaking be little willing to approach. (II, 337)

Collins here expresses anxiety that his father's biography not only might be meaningless in 1848, but might not even prove one of the "intellectual luxuries" he described earlier ("even to amuse the leisure of others"). This anxiety is surely the more prominent because the life of an artist who did not believe in representing class conflict or political strife would seem outdated in a world where the disruptions of history could no longer be avoided. The language of the passage conveys the instability of the patriarchal ideal after the father's death. History raises doubts that cannot be "penetrated," an image that underscores the male writer's apparent lack of power. The subjunctive "whether" draws attention to the way these doubts "cannot now be resolved," and Collins claims he would be reluctant to deal with them even if they were demystified. Amid these impenetrable doubts, the "fierce" agitation of history escapes, with the repetition of the word "political," from the son's efforts to control it and render it subordinate to the record of the father's life.

Despite Collins' attempts in the *Memoirs*, then, to establish William as a monumental predecessor, the authority that his son inherits is a diminished one. Collins attempts to cloak himself in his father's definition of character by claiming that his principal goal is to "trace character in a painter. . . . To emulate, in the composition of the following Memoirs, the candour and moral courage which formed conspicuous ingredients in the character that they are to delineate . . . is all that I can further promise to the reader" (I, 2–4). Presumably Collins absorbs his father's character by writing the *Memoirs*, but in a curious diminution of this achievement, imitating William is "all" he can do. The son can thus have a character only by writing about his father, yet the patriarchal character is history, the dead who perhaps can no longer be resurrected. The nostalgia for the father's character is the more marked because that character is associated with aesthetic form and artistic success. "I generally want a form in my pictures," William complains in an early journal entry reproduced in the *Memoirs*, after declaring that he desires to "become a master. . . . I propose to aim more at method and order" (I, 72).

The elegiac note in Collins' description of his father is particularly marked in passages where, while he celebrates William's power over feminine Nature, he associates this vision of the masterful male artist with the past. Like the Romantic poet, or Shelley's Frankenstein, William Collins is a detective of Nature, which he regulates by seeing or viewing it. Collins says of his father that "his power of observation . . . thus regulated, it was seldom that the smallest object worthy of remark escaped its vigilance" (II, 310). This detection gives his paintings their "inflexible adherence to Nature and truth" (II, 310). In several memorable scenes, Collins portrays his father as a solitary figure observing Nature but not troubled by its agitations, in one case imperturbably sketching under stormy skies: "Mr. Collins, with one knee on the ground, steadying himself against the wind" (II, 223). In another case a description of his father walking on the beach inserts a miniature narrative into the text:

> Had Hastings in 1816, been what Hastings is in 1848, the fashionable loiterers who now throng that once unassuming little "watering-place," would have felt no small astonishment . . . in beholding, at all hours, from earliest morning to latest evening, and in all places, from the deck of the fishing boat, to the base of the cliff, the same solitary figure, laden, day after day, with the same sketching materials, and drawing object after object, through all difficulties and disappointments, with the same deep abstraction and the same unwearied industry. (I, 91–92)

In the modern period associated with change ("that once unassuming little 'watering-place'"), the changeless aspect of the paternal figure ("day after day, with the same sketching materials") would provoke astonishment, if not, one assumes, laughter. Collins conjures up the ghost of the dead father to haunt the present age, but William's power belongs to the past.

Antonina*: The Invasion of the Gothic*

After he had finished eulogizing his father as patriarch and predecessor, Collins returned to the "classical romance"[17] he had interrupted to write the *Memoirs*. In doing so, he turned from a narrative in praise of the father to one about rebellion against fathers. In *Antonina; or,*

The Fall of Rome, published in 1850, the Roman paterfamilias Numerian, an ascetic bent on reforming the corruptions of the early Church, discovers his daughter Antonina hiding a lute, which she has been playing despite his commands that she avoid sensual pleasures. Smashing the instrument to pieces, he orders her to her room, where she is visited that night by Vetranio, the dissolute young aristocrat who gave her the lute and who forces this clandestine entrance in order to seduce her. In the midst of this scene, Antonina is again discovered by her puritanical father, who incorrectly assumes that she has been succumbing to temptation rather than virtuously resisting it. Dramatically disinheriting her, he exiles her from his house, thus thrusting her into the events surrounding the Fall of Rome and, figuratively, into the tumultuous history that lurks behind the stately facade of the *Memoirs*.

Collins himself drew the parallel between the events of antiquity in *Antonina* and the type of contemporary "fierce political contention" he alludes to at the end of the *Memoirs*. In a letter to Richard Bentley, the editor who accepted *Antonina*, he referred to the revolutionary events of 1848, and especially to the siege of Rome that followed: "I have thought it probable that such a work might not inappropriately be offered for your inspection, while recent occurrences continue to direct public attention particularly on Roman affairs."[18] In making such analogies between his own world and that of the past, Collins had many antecedents. The nineteenth-century historical novel, developed most influentially by Scott, was often a vehicle for encoding responses to contemporary events. Moreover, the subgenre of historical fiction to which *Antonina* belongs—the novel about the decline of empire—was a particularly popular way of representing, as Lee Sterrenburg argues, "anatomies of failed revolutions" in the aftermath of the French Revolution and the Napoleonic Wars.[19]

The details of the siege of Rome in *Antonina* could have been influenced by accounts of the events of 1848–49, but the novel is more generally inspired by the idea of revolution itself, since Collins had started it prior to 1848. In particular, the portrait of Roman society in *Antonina* recalls how the class-stratified British society of the 1830s was startled by the emergence of the Chartist movement, which suggested the possibility of a new English revolution. The setting of the novel, indeed, illustrates the scene Collins described in the *Memoirs* where, during the "social and political convulsions" accompanying Reform Bill agitation in the 1830s, the "noble and wealthy," threatened by the "popular revolution" symbolically mirrored by the "mysterious pestilence" of cholera, had "little time . . . to attend to the remoter importance of the progress of national Art" (I, 344–45). *Antonina* begins with the Roman aristocracy, an Epicurean and "effeminate" lot,[20] reluctantly but rapidly engulfed by the famine and plague overwhelming the city during the blockade of Rome by the Goths. The artist-figure Vetranio, the brilliant but debauched poet who gives Antonina her lute, is an image for the artistic and social decadence precipitating the Fall of Rome. Collins' diagnosis of the excesses of the Roman elite is reminiscent of the portraits in such other Victorian narratives of the corrupt ancien régime before the French Revolution as Carlyle's *The French Revolution* (1837) and Dickens' *A Tale of Two Cities* (1859). The Goths at the gate in *Antonina* externalize the forces within Roman society that resist the venal tyranny of rulers called "the oppressors of the world" (375). Upper-class luxury and cruelty are juxtaposed with hints of covert lower-class mutiny and ressentiment, and the narrator claims that the "dangerous and artificial" position of the "poorer classes" was "one of the most important of the internal causes of the downfall of Rome" (76).

In the context of this political allegory, Collins' portrayal of the Fall of Rome tells a different story from the *Memoirs* of what it means to become an author in 1848. The biography clings to the image of the father as predecessor, even as it suggests that his art is no longer viable in 1848. *Antonina*, however, is a novel about how, amid a "worldwide revolution" (341), the power of fathers has come to lack meaning for the emergent artist, who is now aligned with the forces of rebellion against established hierarchies. The expulsion of Antonina from her father's house for insubordination (her presumed sexual fall figures her fall into art) is the darker narrative of familial conflict that the filial piety of the *Memoirs* papers over. With Numerian recalling, as Nuel Pharr Davis points out, the harsher and more intolerant qualities of William Collins,[21] *Antonina* spells out the oedipal narrative, hinted at in the father's biography, in which the transgressive child becomes an artist by being thrust out of the father's house into an atmosphere of turbulent historical change. Such a narrative associates the father with the outmoded aristocracy the revolution replaces, not inappropriately since, although William Collins is portrayed as the heroic bourgeois in the *Memoirs*, his patrons were largely aristocratic.

This oedipal narrative, however, is complicated by the sex change that transforms the portrait of the artist as a young man into the portrait of the artist as a young girl. Making the artist into a daughter revises the patrilineal plot of the *Memoirs*, in which the son inherits the father's artistic power. To feminize the figure for the son, in fact, hyperbolically underscores his alienation from the father's art; when Antonina is expelled from her father's house, she is cast out from the entire patriarchal tradition represented by the Fathers of the early Church who are Numerian's inspiration. In the absence of a masculine tradition, the artist is aligned with a feminine one that resurrects the figure of the mother repressed in the *Memoirs*, even if only to associate her with illegitimacy and exclusion from authority. By playing the lute, Antonina becomes connected in her father's eyes with her dead mother (a Spaniard, a foreigner), whom she dimly remembers singing to her "hour after hour, in her cradle" (122). Since Antonina's mother was unfaithful to her father, this feminine tradition is linked not only to art but also to adultery; as Numerian says when he discovers Vetranio in his daughter's room, "her mother was a harlot before her!" (195).

This association of feminine art with actual or presumed sexual fall implies that the feminine tradition is a renegade one that represents rebellion against the father's law. Such feminine rebellion, although it switches the sex of the child protagonist in the oedipal plot, retains that plot's emphasis on a struggle with the father. Still, Antonina's rebellion, unlike her mother's, is of the most mild-mannered kind, since she is neither a harlot nor defiant after her brutal treatment by her father; her greatest desire, in fact, is to be reconciled with him. In this case, then, femininity represents not so much an alternative form of artistic power to the father's as it does powerlessness and vulnerability. Not only does Antonina become an icon of terrified passivity (she spends vast portions of the novel either frightened or asleep), but she soon ceases to be a figure for the artist, preserving a fragment of her smashed lute but never again playing it.

In this sense, transforming the artist into a daughter minimizes the extent of the rebellion against the father, since she leaves his house only to be immediately transferred to the protection of another male figure. Wandering accidentally into the Gothic camp, Antonina is shielded by Hermanric, a young warrior, who swiftly falls in love with her. Antonina and "Her Man" are then exemplars of an embryonic domesticity that provides a private haven in a heartless world: "While a world-wide revolution was concentrating its hurricane forces around them . . . they could . . . completely forget the stormy outward world, in themselves" (341). This domestic ideal represents the new bourgeois ideology that rises, phoenix-like, from the fall of the aristocracy.[22]

Hermanric in particular emerges as a figure for the bourgeois manhood who, by controlling women within domesticity, is an alternative to the other classes, which are either too emasculated (the effeminate aristocracy) or too emasculating (the lower classes who revolt against those above them). Early in the novel, Collins ecstatically prophesies the rise of the middle classes following a vignette in which a stalwart Roman farmer vehemently denounces the aristocratic "tyrants" whose "rank had triumphed over my industry" (83):

> By this time he had lashed himself into fury. His eyes glared, his cheeks flushed, his voice rose. Could he then have seen the faintest vision of the destiny that future ages had in store for the posterity of the race that now suffered throughout civilized Europe, like him —could he have imagined how, in after years, the "middle class," despised in his day, was to rise to privilege and power; to hold in its just hands the balance of the prosperity of nations; to crush oppression and regulate rule; to soar in its mighty flight above thrones, and principalities, and ranks and riches, apparently obedient, but really commanding—could he but have foreboded this, what a light must have burst upon his gloom, what a hope must have soothed him in his despair! (83–84)

This paean to the messianic middle class accumulates clauses with a rhetorical feverishness that echoes the farmer's outburst. The bourgeois man thus seems to be allowed the rebellion against the ancien régime ("apparently obedient, but really commanding") denied to both the daughter Antonina and the insolent lower classes. Yet Hermanric, the novel's principal figure for this emergent bourgeois manhood, is rendered singularly powerless. Although in the passage following the farmer's speech Collins synecdochically compares the bourgeoisie to "just hands," Hermanric's hands become immobilized. To punish him for his transgression in protecting his Roman enemy Antonina rather than killing her, Hermanric's angry sister Goisvintha severs the tendons in his hand with a knife. That he is shortly afterward slain as a deserter by a posse of vengeful Huns adds an appropriate finale to this symbolic castration.

The eruption of the sister into the scene of proto-domesticity between Antonina and Hermanric points both to Goisvintha's importance in the novel and to the energy with which she disrupts its conventions. Literally female Gothic, she also figuratively signals the invasion of the Gothic genre into Collins' art. In the most obvious sense, her crazed desire to revenge her family, massacred by the Romans, recalls the obsessed melodramatic figures in the Gothic tradition. Goisvintha evokes Gothic conventions in a general way, but through her the genre also is associated more specifically with images of feminine power and violence. To explain her "mysterious and powerful influence" over her brother (217), Collins emphasizes how Gothic culture is structured around women's position as priests and seers, a "remarkable ascendency of the woman over the man" (215). In her first scene with Hermanric in the novel, indeed, it appears as if she had "changed sexes" (20) with her brother; the phallic woman, she seizes the knives and swords he will not wield against Antonina in an attempt to use them herself. Throughout the novel, the narrative voice disapprovingly comments on Goisvintha's usurpation of the male role: she is "harsh and unwomanly" (213), the "unappeasable and unwomanly Goisvintha" (381), who speaks in a "broken, hoarse, and unfeminine" voice (23).

This emphasis on Goisvintha's rebellion against gender roles links her to her Roman enemy Antonina (whom at one point she stabs with her ever-ready knife) as an embodiment of the daughter's covert rebellion against her father. In this position as doppelgänger, Goisvintha recalls the prominence of such doubles in the Gothic tradition, while also, more importantly, evoking the genre's representation of revolution. In *Antonina*, the Gothic gives Collins a language for figuring revolution, even as it aligns that language with the feminine. Goisvintha is the novel's figure for revolution; an early version of Dickens' Madame Defarge (for whom she may have been a model),[23] she seethes with ressentiment against Roman tyrants. Her iconic embodiment of the monstrous mother (it is the death of her children that fuels her outrage) recalls Carlyle's image of the "insurrection of women" during the French Revolution as an uprising of mothers, "Judiths" and "Menads" defined by their power to mutilate and disempower men, as Goisvintha does to Hermanric.[24]

Goisvintha's feminine "insurrection" again ties her to Antonina, for if the female Goth is a rebellious mother, Antonina is connected through her mother with a tradition of feminine revolt against the father's law. Whereas the rise of the feminine rebellious energy that Goisvintha represents precipitates the waning of patriarchal power —during the course of the novel the rigidly ascetic Numerian becomes weak and senile—it poses an even more significant threat to the new bourgeois order signified by the domesticity of Hermanric and Antonina. In this bourgeois ideology, woman is not a rebellious but a submissive partner, a solace amid the storms of history (surely it is appropriate that Goisvintha stabs Antonina in the throat, as if to emblematize this type of silencing). Goisvintha, however, is sacrificed—quite literally—to restore domesticity. Captured by the demented Ulpius, who is obsessed with reviving the cult of the pagan gods, she is offered to them, as if in parody of her own phallic energy, by being impaled on a large sword. Yet Goisvintha's violent chastisement, which excises both feminine power and the Gothic energy that figures it, ultimately excludes history itself from the novel. After the deaths of both the female Goth and her crazed assailant, the energy of the historical narrative dissipates, allowing for the reconciliation of Antonina with her repentant father and the reestablishment of domesticity, albeit (since Hermanric is dead) in an impotent and desexualized form.

This exclusion of history has the paradoxical effect of making the novel subtitled "The Fall of Rome" elide that event. Concluding the story after the first blockade of Rome by the Goths, the narrator turns from the image of Antonina and her father mourning over Hermanric's grave to ask:

> Shall we longer delay in the farmhouse garden? No! For us, as for Vetranio, it is now time to depart! While peace still watches round the walls of Rome; while the hearts of the father and daughter still repose together in security after the trials that have wrung them, let us quit the scene! Here, at last, the narrative that we have followed over a dark and stormy tract, reposes on a tranquil field; and here let us cease to pursue it!
>
> So the traveler who traces the course of a river, wanders through the day among the rocks and precipices that lead onward from its troubled source; and, when the evening is at hand, pauses and rests where the banks are grassy and the stream is smooth. (656)

The transitory nature of this final scene ("while peace still watches round the walls of Rome") reminds the reader that this domestic sunniness is soon to be interrupted, and perhaps destroyed, by the "dark and stormy" history it holds only imperfectly at bay.

In terms of *Antonina*'s representation of 1848, such an ending is in one sense appropriate. By concluding the novel after the Goths' first blockade, the "world-wide revolution" of Rome's fall is still in the process of happening, just as, presumably, social conditions were ripe for revolutionary movements, even though the 1848 revolution did not travel to England. Still, the narrator's "No!" after he asks if he should linger in Rome recalls what Georg Lukács referred to as the "denial of history" in bourgeois literature following 1848. Surveying the historical novel after Scott, Lukács examines how the bourgeoisie, who had portrayed themselves prior to 1848 as revolutionary heroes in a drama of historical "progress," react to the threat of proletarian uprisings that contest their power as much as that of the upper classes. The form that this bourgeois reaction takes after 1848, Lukács argues, is to elide the representation of history as a type of rebellion of one class against another, dwelling instead on narratives that suggest the inevitability of bourgeois hegemony.[25]

Some recent critics have adopted and elaborated on Lukács' theory to trace how literature uses domestic ideology as a particularly powerful means of naturalizing bourgeois authority in the 1848 period. In his study of the English historical novel, Nicholas Rance locates 1848 as the moment of a shift from the historical fiction of Scott and Bulwer-Lytton to domestic fiction that normalizes bourgeois ideology.[26] A more detailed history of this shift is provided by Nancy Armstrong, who underscores the separation between political themes and domestic ones that became pronounced in English fiction by the 1840s. As Armstrong argues, novels of the 1840s imply that the world of politics should be isolated from domesticity, even as they suggest that struggles between classes can be regulated in the same way as rebellions within families.[27]

By moving, at the end of *Antonina*, beyond history to take refuge in a patently fragile domesticity, Collins both participates in this narrative economy and points to its inherent weakness. Although *Antonina* embodies the energy of revolution and rebellion in female characters and then silences them, this maneuver does not restore male authority over the family, history, or the narrative itself: Numerian is senescent and powerless, and Hermanric is dead. Moreover, the conclusion of *Antonina* does not solve the problem of Collins' own literary authority, of his becoming an author in 1848. The novel that rejects the law of the father imagines art and rebellion as the provenance of female figures, who are in turn contained and circumscribed. In this novel about the invasion of the Gothic, the power concentrated in the figure of Goisvintha represents the narrative energy of the Gothic that invades Collins' art even as, in this revolutionary moment, he turns farther away from the father's example. The attempt to exorcise the Gothic or to hold it at bay anticipates the narrative pattern that would become more pronounced in the novels that follow *Antonina*, in which a crisis of power for the male artist is linked with the rise of a female power associated with or figured by the Gothic. The male artist's efforts to ally himself with or to contain the power of these female and Gothic figures form the major narrative tension of Collins' later fictions. In *Antonina*, however, these tensions are resolved only by an evasion of closure that suggests an inability to tell the narrative of 1848. Although the novel figures the waning of the patriarchal power eulogized in the *Memoirs*, at this early moment in his career Collins could not imagine an alternative image of either male or female authority.

Three

Basil: Femininity, Ressentiment, and the Male Artist

The publication of *Basil* in November 1852 precipitated a marked change in the critical reception of Collins' novels. Reviewers from such journals as the *Spectator*, the *Athenaeum*, and *Bentley's Miscellany*, publications that reflected the increased emphasis on the aesthetic and moral value of fiction in the Victorian literary establishment, had hailed Collins' earliest efforts; of *Antonina*, a reviewer in *Bentley's* claimed that "the author, in his first work, has stepped into the first rank of romance writers."[1] With *Basil*, however, began the mixed and often dismissive criticism that was to become characteristic of reviews of Collins' fiction. The novel had its admirers, including Charles Dickens, who included it among his favorite books and wrote a complimentary letter to Collins in December 1852. Yet the response of the *Athenaeum* is emblematic of the swift decline in Collins' literary reputation. Its redoubtable reviewer H. F. Chorley, who had praised *Antonina* as a "richly-coloured impassioned story, busy with life, importunately strong in its appeals to our sympathy," had nonetheless advised Collins to shun "the vices of the French School";[2] evidently D. O. Maddyn, who reviewed *Basil* for the journal, felt that the warning had not been heeded. Scolding Collins for not imitating his father's art—"the son of an eminent painter . . . should know that the proper office of Art is to elevate and purify in pleasing"—he exclaimed in horror over the plot of the novel: "the vicious atmosphere in which the drama of the tale is enveloped, weighs on us like a nightmare. The jail, the gibbet, and the madhouse are the accessories of the story:—the adultery of a wife, the jealous torture of the ignored husband, the ferocious thirst for revenge of the detected paramour, are its themes!"[3]

Maddyn's comments all too obviously reveal the reasons for critical outrage over *Basil*. The "vices of the French School" were surely muted by the historical distance between the world of *Antonina* and the world in which it was written. *Basil,* however, subtitled "A Story of Modern Life," was the first of Collins' novels to place a Gothic plot in a contemporary setting. Moreover, *Basil* was a descendant not only of Radcliffean Gothic, but also of the tale of criminality known as the Newgate novel. (Maddyn inveighed against Collins' "aesthetics of the Old Bailey.") By the 1860s, critics would find a name for works like *Basil*: the sensation novel.

The label sensation novel is part of a Victorian discursive framework that seeks to segregate the "high" (moral, elevating novels) from the "low," fiction that depicts sexuality, the criminal underworld and the lower classes, and fallen, rather than domestic, women (hence Maddyn's horror at the "adultery of a wife"). The next chapter will explore at greater length the ideological implications of the term *sensation fiction* and consider how attacks on the literary value of Collins' fiction were linked both to his association with this genre and to its figuration of gender and class issues. In reading *Basil,* however, I trace a conservative impulse in Collins' fiction that would become as characteristic of his novels as their transgressively "sensational" elements.

Critics of *Basil* who objected to Collins' depiction of adultery obviously believed that he wanted to write sensational, and hence not morally elevating, fiction. One reviewer, who claimed that Collins had not lived up to the ideal of the Victorian novelist as a writer with a "high and holy mission," was particularly outraged that he "makes a woman given up to evil the heroine of his piece."[4] By ignoring the centrality of Basil, the cuckolded husband, the reviewer fails to notice that the "evil" woman—Margaret, his adulterous wife—is not the heroine but the villainess leagued against Basil with her lover Mannion, a clerk who is a figure for the rebellious class subordinate. *Basil* is thus not so much about the desire to transgress as it is about the desire to escape the taint of the transgressors, a plot rendered the more significant by Basil's being a figure for the writer. Even more explicitly than *Antonina, Basil* represents the fate of the male writer after 1848, while demonstrating, like that earlier work, a deep ambivalence about the writer's relation to both feminine rebelliousness and class ressentiment. This ambivalence is reflexively expressed by an ambivalence about the genre that shapes it, since, as in *Antonina*, the female Gothic is associated both with revolution and with a threatening female influence over men. The ideological tensions that surround the role of the male writer and his indebtedness to the female Gothic make it appropriate that the Gothic text *Basil* most obviously revises is Mary Shelley's *Frankenstein*, a novel that also figures the artist's relation to revolution in a postrevolutionary world.

Family and Revolution in Basil

Unlike *Antonina*, with its figure of the covertly rebellious daughter, *Basil* elaborates on the oedipal plot elided in the *Memoirs* of the son who defies his father's beliefs. That Collins continued to be interested in the political implications of the oedipal plot is evinced by his publishing, several months prior to *Basil*, "Nine O'Clock!" a ghost story about fathers and sons set during the period of the French Revolution.[5] The way Collins uses the family romance in *Basil* as a signifier for revolution makes the novel, for all its contemporaneity, a development of historical fiction rather than a departure from that genre. *Basil* is an earlier version of the kind of narrative that Albert Hutter has identified in Dickens' historical novel *A Tale of Two Cities*, in which, structured as it is by "two revolutions, one generational and the other political," the "iconography of father-son conflict carries a particularly powerful social resonance."[6] Like the story of Charles Darnay's decision to reject his aristocratic heritage, *Basil* traces a historical allegory about the rise of the bourgeoisie. Son of a gentleman who, as a member of a family that is "one of the most ancient" in England,[7] has inflexible notions about birth and breeding, Basil is disinherited because of his "descent into the middle class" (as the back of the Dover edition melodramatically puts it)[8] when he secretly marries Margaret Sherwin, a linen draper's daughter.

This miscegenation of classes begets an adulterous triangle that is as shocking to Basil as the idea of an improper marriage is to his father. To avoid losing the monetary and social advantages of his daughter's marriage should Basil's father immediately disinherit his son, Margaret's unbearably slimy father stipulates that the marriage must remain not only secret but also unconsummated for a year while Basil tries, presumably, to prepare his father for the blow. As if this symbolic deferral of Basil's manhood were not humiliating enough, Margaret is seduced by Mannion, her father's clerk, who thus revenges his father's execution years before as a forger based on evidence given by Basil's father. The night on which he is to consummate his marriage Basil tracks Margaret and Mannion to a hotel and, hiding in a nearby room, overhears "my wrongs in all their nameless horror" (160). He subsequently hideously disfigures and half-blinds Mannion by throwing him facedown on a newly macadamized road (ah, the perils of modern progress!). Although Mannion's disfigurement only literalizes his monstrous ressentiment, he is understandably less than appreciative and malevolently haunts Basil's steps until he, rather than his prey, is killed. Meanwhile, Margaret dies of typhus, allowing Basil's reconciliation with his father, who had predictably cast him out when he heard about the marriage. Although his father had ripped the page devoted to his son out of the book of family lineage, Basil is finally reunited, much as Antonina is with Numerian, with the once tyrannical but now repentant patriarch. As in *Antonina*, too, the class allegory of this plot is written as an allegory of gender, with the erotic bond between Margaret and Mannion figuring revolution as the inversion of both class and gender hierarchies that Basil's rebellion produces.

The uncomfortable ménage-à-trois that results from these multiple transgressions is a demonic version of the Shelleyan notion of the romantic triangle. Indeed, the reflexively literary character of the text, which represents "modern life" as a series of fictional formulas run amok, underscores its meditation on the role of the writer. For Basil is a figure for the Victorian writer who, in a representation of the ambiguous status of Victorian fiction, begins (like the young Collins himself) to write in secret. Yet he is terrified of the transgressive characters born of his plot of defiance, a fear encoded in his language of hysterical sexual revulsion. Dreaming of Margaret and Mannion after he has discovered their betrayal, Basil imagines them as "two monsters . . . leaving on their track a green decay, oozing and shining with a sickly light. . . . fiend-souls made visible in fiend-shapes" (173–74).

"Indescribable Influence": Domesticity, Female Gothic, and the Literary Marketplace

Although in *Basil's* revision of *Frankenstein*, the intellectual, Basil, creates monsters he is not able to control—a reading I shall return to later—Margaret and Mannion are not the only threat to his perilously feeble bourgeois manhood. Maddyn's disgruntled comment that the novel was "almost revolting in its domestic horrors"[9] is an unwitting pun on how its Gothicism locates domesticity as the site of a potential revolt against the male authority that presumably controls it. In *Basil* the home is the place not only where women are oppressed, but also where they threaten male virility, either by rendering men as powerless as themselves or by subverting their authority.

Unlike *Antonina*, where Goisvintha is a feminized version of the Gothic rather than a signifier for the female Gothic itself, *Basil* alludes more specifically to the devices and themes of the Radcliffean narrative of "domestic horrors" and its covert critique of domestic ideology. Since the Gothic exemplifies feminine duplicity, an indirect rather than openly rebellious form of feminine writing,[10] it is appropriate that the women in *Basil* should be doubles of each other, with the demonic woman externalizing the rebellion of the domestic one. Just as Goisvintha and Antonina had been Gothic mirrors of each other, Basil's wife, Margaret, and his seemingly pure and submissive sister, Clara, are another version of this feminine doubling. Collins pointedly underscores the dichotomy between the two women through the conventionally Victorian division between dark and fair women: Clara is blue eyed and pale, whereas Margaret is voluptuous and dark, "darker than usual in English women" (30). Making Margaret into a version of the racial Other (a fitting complement to Mannion's class Other) does not, however, blur the similarity between her and Clara. Both women are associated with the female Gothic as a literary influence on the male writer, and as an image for a feminine rebelliousness that threatens to contaminate his work.

Indeed, the repeated use of the word "influence" in the novel suggests a comparison between Clara's and Margaret's influence on Basil and the influence of the female Gothic on his writing. We hear that

Clara has "some indescribable influence" mingled with her "untiring good-nature" (22). "Influence" here is a code word for the role of moral guide that women are supposed to play within domesticity. But Clara's influence, benign as it is, is also proleptic of "the fatal influence of the dark beauty" (41), Margaret. When Basil first meets Margaret (on an omnibus, no less), he describes her effect on him in terms that echo those he used to evoke Clara's "indescribable" influence: "I felt her influence on me directly—an influence that I cannot describe—an influence which I had never experienced in my life before, which I shall never experience again. . . . Had I the same influence over her? Or was it I that received, and she that conferred, only? I was yet destined to discover; but not then—not for a long, long time" (29). In this scene, Margaret is a walking embodiment of female Gothic, wearing the veil that is one of the most ubiquitous of Gothic symbols and which signifies here the veiled power of women. Basil is both attracted to and terrified by this power; the questions he asks about Margaret's influence suggest his fear that he is unable to control this mysterious femininity and the literary influence it embodies. "Had I the same influence over her? Or was it I that received, and she that conferred, only?"

Basil's anxiety about whether he can control or supersede his female precursors is underscored by his being surrounded by echoes of female Gothic texts. Not only is Margaret a quotation from the female Gothic, but so is Clara, who as sister and intellectual companion plays Elizabeth Lavenza to Basil's Frankenstein. Whereas Frankenstein says that "the saintly soul of Elizabeth shone like a shrine-dedicated lamp in our peaceful home" (*F* 38), Basil refers to Clara as his "brightest" domestic "influence" (21). In sublimated sexual terms, he describes the "sweet days . . . of uninterrupted intercourse" (24) with Clara, with whom he is accustomed to converse in the family's "old gothic library" (140).

This punning reference to the "old gothic library" implies that Clara has sprung from a Gothic text, and as such a Gothic presence she literally shapes Basil's work. She strings together the loose pages of Basil's first novel (39), which is, not surprisingly given the autobiographical mirroring of Collins in Basil, a "historical romance" (25).

She is also the first reader and critic of this work; Basil claims that "my first pages of manuscript . . . were read by my sister, and never penetrated into my father's study" (9). The rejection of the father's elitism would seem to signal the birth of bourgeois manliness, but this is not the case; the phrase "never penetrated" implies that, as son and father grow apart, Basil is threatened by the loss of his manhood. Although the aristocratic father recalls William Collins' dependence on the aristocracy and gentry for patronage, the figure for Collins, the son who enters the marketplace, is associated not with manly self-reliance but with womanliness, specifically with writing for a female audience represented by Clara.

This association of the male writer with feminine writing brings with it a symbolic threat to male identity, figured as sexual potency. The hint of sexual anxiety in "never penetrated" deepens in Basil's later description of Clara's management of his study:

> Clara . . . augurs wonderful success for my fiction when it is published. She is determined to arrange my study with her own hands . . . and sort my papers herself. She knows that I am already as fretful and precise about my literary goods and chattels . . . as if I were a veteran author of twenty years' standing; and she is resolved to spare me every apprehension on this score, by taking all the arrangements of my study on herself, and keeping the key of the door when I am not in need of it. (25)

The sister domesticates the male writer's study, now associated with the marketplace ("literary goods and chattels"), by keeping the key and thus symbolically usurping command of the phallus. The sexual imagery implicit in this arrangement is underscored by Basil's tribute to Clara's "first inestimable sympathies with my first fugitive vanities of embryo authorship" (24). Clara at once holds the key and guards the "embryo," that is, the offspring of the son's "fugitive" rebellion against his father's values, which he had already begun to criticize while in college (3).

Indeed, Basil's embryonic work figures what Mary Shelley had called the "hideous progeny" of the Gothic. Clara's incubation of Basil's novel anticipates the entrance of Gothic into the text in the form of Clara's mirror image, Margaret, for whom Basil records his love in the imagery of monster birth: "this giant-sensation of a day's growth, was first love" (42). Basil meets Margaret in the omnibus during the time he is writing his historical romance, so that her influence on him figures the influence of the Gothic on the historical romance, and thus recalls the invasion of Gothic in Collins' own first novel, *Antonina*. The site of their meeting, the omnibus, suggests how the Gothic genre is linked with a disturbingly commonplace and public version of the literary marketplace.

In this sense, *Basil* establishes an opposition between paternal law, signified by the father's conservative belief in primogeniture, and the maternal word associated with the Gothic tradition. This theme of a female literary genealogy illuminates the novel's figuration of the family romance: the theme of feminine influence in the novel may be traced beyond Margaret and Clara back to Basil's dead mother. Basil tells us that although Clara strikingly resembles his father, "her expression . . . must be very like what my mother's was" (18). It is particularly in his sister's "silent and thoughtful" moments that she "has always appeared to freshen, and even to increase, my vague, childish recollections of our lost mother" (18). This lost mother, who suffered the Wollstonecraftian fate of dying shortly after giving birth to her daughter (2), figures the Gothic as a feminine influence that, once discovered by the male writer, overpowers his obedience to the father's law.

This literary allegory explains why Basil's lost mother is recalled not only through her daughter, whom the father calls a "representative" of the mother (10), but also through representation itself. The portrait of the mother that hangs above the fireplace in the father's study, which recalls the two images of the dead mother in *Frankenstein* (the miniature and the "historical subject" that hangs above the Frankenstein fireplace), is associated, as were those images, with both feminine domesticity and incipient revolution. Basil stops before his dead mother's portrait before going to his clandestine wedding:

> The picture had an influence that quieted me; but what influence I hardly knew. Perhaps it led my spirit up to the spirit that had gone from us—perhaps those secret voices from the unknown world,

> which only the soul can listen to, were loosed at that moment, and spoke within me. While I sat looking up at the portrait, I grew strangely and suddenly calm before it. (94)

Evoking "secret voices," the mother is subtly associated with the type of doubleness and duplicity that Basil himself practices in resisting the father's law. Although the portrait reminds Basil that his mother is now among "the angels of God" (94), it gives him the strength to persist in his marriage to Margaret, whom he later likens to a fiend (174). This wedding day, which comes after Basil's first serious rift with his father—when his father suspects, but does not yet know, the full extent of his son's disgrace—is dark and stormy: "black clouds . . . overspread the whole firmament. . . . For the last ten days the sun had shone almost uninterruptedly—with my marriage-day came the cloud, the mist and the rain" (92). This darkness obscures the "sun" of paternal favor that has hitherto governed the son's life: up to this time, "For me, the morning sunshine of life was life without a cloud" (4–5).

Basil's marriage to Margaret, then, raises from the dead both his mother's indescribable influence ("what influence I hardly knew") and revolution, imaged by a dark and stormy feminine Nature as it was in both the *Memoirs* and *Frankenstein*. As in the *Memoirs*, this stormy maternal Nature tropes the disruptions of history: the clock strikes while Basil looks at his mother's portrait, recalling him to the time of the marriage ceremony and drawing him from the isolation of domesticity to the demands of the "outer world" (95). When Basil meets the Sherwins before the ceremony, he notices that the occasion has spread its "agitating influence" (95) over them as well as himself. Although we later hear that the Sherwins' agitation is caused by the encroaching influence of Mannion over Margaret, it symbolically mirrors the agitation connected with the seemingly calm and domestic influence of the mother.

Given the legacy of depictions of female oppression in the Gothic, it is unsurprising that women's influence is linked to oppression and secrecy, an implication hinted at in Basil's reference to "secret voices" in describing his mother's portrait. Clara's expression best resembles her mother's in "silent and thoughtful moments," and in the original edition the mother's silence was caused by some mysterious "great sorrow" (I, 33 [1852]). By inheriting the mother's sorrowful silence, Clara recalls Radcliffe's theme of the ambiguous legacy of mothers to daughters, as well as her description in *The Mysteries of Udolpho* of Emily's "silence and solitude." Basil in fact revises Radcliffe's phrase at the end of a description of his sister:

> The strong and deep feelings of my sister's nature lay far below the surface—for a woman, too far below it. Suffering was, for her, silent, secret, long enduring; often almost entirely void of outward vent or development . . . there was no sighing, no weeping, no speaking even. . . . The very strength of her emotions was in their silence and their secresy. (23)

This emphasis on the repression of women (recalling the veiled figure of Margaret) represents their situation through the Gothic plot of the feminine carceral. Thus it is ironic that Basil claims that Clara's feelings are too hidden "for a woman," since, despite her role as a mediator of sentiment, she and the other women in *Basil* are consistently associated with what is hidden and imprisoned. When Basil follows Margaret home, he sees her playing with a caged bird (37), recalling Wollstonecraft's metaphor for women as "confined then in cages like the feathered race" (*VRW* 98). As if to literalize this metaphor, Margaret's mother, Mrs. Sherwin, is a wretched invalid imprisoned within a horrifying marriage.

In sharp contrast to this vein of feminist imagery in the novel is the Burkean juxtaposition between revolutionary women and beleaguered matrons, here demonstrated by Margaret's scorn for her mother. This imagery allows Collins at once more openly to depict female resistance to subordination and to punish it. Revising his depiction of the revolutionary woman in *Antonina,* in a "fury of passion" (134) Margaret grabs a poker to kill her mother's cat, which has killed her pet bird, a version on a smaller scale of the moment where Goisvintha seizes her brother's knife to threaten Antonina. Quickly disarmed of her weapon, Margaret launches into a "fit of hysterics" (135), sobbing with "frightful violence, and pouring forth a perfect torrent of ejaculations of vengeance against the cat" (134). This hysterical and far from silent feminine violence is contrasted with the silence of the suffering mother, who speaks only to warn Basil of Mannion's influence and, on her deathbed, to reproach her daughter for her promiscuity.

Yet by emblematizing the Gothic, even the more conventional and less violent women in the novel, the silent Clara and Mrs. Sherwin, appear as "frightful" images. In the scene where Basil's father disinherits him, Clara defends her brother, dramatically interrupting the scene between father and son: "the look of terror which changed to unnatural vacancy the wonted softness and gentleness of her eyes, her pale face, her white dress, and slow, noiseless step, made her first appearance in the room seem almost supernatural; it was as if an apparition had been walking towards us, and not Clara herself!" (206). Basil's father identifies this Gothic appearance as a form of rebellion: "Clara! are you so changed, that you can disobey me to my face?" (207). This rebellious daughter silences the father's voice: "as she approached my father, he pronounced her name in astonishment; but his voice sank to a whisper, while he spoke it" (206). Although Gothic terror paralyzes Clara, changing her expression to "unnatural vacancy" and making her almost a somnambulist, she thus embodies the very "void" of silence and secrecy with which she had previously been associated. In her white dress, in fact, Clara is the first version of Collins' woman in white, who, in the later novel by that name, would also figure the silent and secret rebellion of women under male authority. Whereas Clara's "supernatural" appearance recalls the "unknown world of spirits" that the mother's portrait evokes, another Gothic mother follows fast upon her footsteps. The zombie-like Mrs. Sherwin, who "never told . . . her sufferings or her sorrows" (105), comes to life with preternatural strength in a scene soon after Clara's resistance of her father. Interrupting the startled Basil and Mr. Sherwin, the dying woman refutes her husband's story of what happened between Margaret and Mannion, moving Basil to ask: "Had the grave given up its dead? I stood awe-struck, neither speaking nor moving while she walked towards me. She was clothed in the white garments of the sick-room—they looked on *her* like the raiment of the tomb" (215).

Like his father, whose voice was silenced by Clara's spectral presence only several pages earlier, Basil is paralyzed by Mrs. Sherwin ("I stood . . . neither speaking nor moving"). Recalling Freud's figure of Medusa's Head, these silent women paralyze, silence, and symbolically castrate men,[11] not least because, as images of the Gothic, they are frightening mirrors of what the male artist fears to become. In fact, Basil's silence and secrecy during the year he hides his marriage from his father makes him resemble the women, a likeness strengthened after his disinheritance, when his name is torn from the father's book of family lineage and he loses access to the father's name and its concomitant public identity. In his own narrative, he says, "a blank occurs wherever my father's name should appear" (3), a terrifying erasure that suggests how the Gothic "whiteness" of the women figures for the male artist a blank page.

The whiting out of the father's name, and of the masculine authority it represents, is linked to Basil's entrance into the literary marketplace. Before he leaves his father's house, Basil does not yet have to write for money; "the struggle for fame could never be identical —terribly, though gloriously identical—with the struggle for bread" (4). Although the language of this passage assumes that earning money is intertwined with the quest for literary fame ("terribly, though gloriously identical"), once Basil leaves his father's house this description of authorship as a kind of male heroism gives way to an association of writing with drudgery and wage slavery. Although Basil never claims he is writing for money, he speaks as if he must. He calls his narrative his "labours," here catching up the association of the term with the lower class; elsewhere he refers to his writing as "employment" (1) and even "toil," the "penance of this poor taskwork" (148).

Although Basil becomes a figure for the writer as wage-slave after he is disinherited, this degradation of his class status is intimately linked to his romance with Margaret, that figure for the female Gothic, recalling Gaye Tuchman's argument that male writers anxious to elevate their status in the literary marketplace fear an association with degraded and "feminine" genres. Whereas in the days before he had to "struggle for bread" Basil claimed that he could devote himself "wholly and unreservedly to literature" (4), after he meets Margaret he writes her love letters in which "composition was an instinct now, an art no longer" (56).

Basil's inability to write literature ("an art no longer") is coupled with a new consciousness of his financial situation; his meeting with Margaret occurs after he has deposited his "quarter's allowance of pocket-money" at the bank (27). Thus the marketplace is the site not of male self-definition, but of the erasure of masculine identity through an economic neediness that makes men like women. Women are associated with lack of economic independence either through their feminine reliance on men within the Victorian family or, alternatively, through their unfeminine dependence on the marketplace when they are writing for money. Although both the market for and authorship of Victorian fiction, including Gothic, or sensation novels, were composed of men and women, Collins, like so many of his contemporaries, figures an anxiety about the drudgery of the marketplace through images of women writers and of voracious feminine audiences. Clara embodies both the female reader and the female writers Hawthorne disgustedly referred to as a "d——d mob of scribbling women":[12] even as she reads Basil's writing she claims, in a passage cut from the 1862 edition, that she wants to "go down to posterity" with him as the "amanuensis" who copies the extracts he needs for sources (I, 92 [1852]).

Although being merely a copyist of Basil's writing does not make Clara a threat to her brother's literary authority, the phrase "go down to posterity" inserts a significant hint of rivalry in her relationship to Basil's writing. Being an amanuensis is a covert means for Clara to insinuate her voice into her brother's narrative (as, in the *Memoirs*, it had been the mother's voice that described the father's picture). And Clara's presence as a Gothic source for Basil's work makes her copying sources for him more significant, since it implies her priority over his writing rather than a secondariness to it.

Thus Clara, like Margaret, symbolizes the double-edged threat of the female Gothic and of femininity itself to the male writer who, despite his rebellion against the father, wishes to share his masculine authority. Because Basil's story echoes the women's, the narrative of his quest for masculine literary potency unwittingly becomes a female

Gothic plot about exclusion from the social order. Moreover, Basil's entrance into the marketplace symbolically emasculates him, rendering him like the women who are symbolized by absence and blankness but also subjecting him to the threat of their veiled power.

The imagery of emasculation is particularly pronounced when Basil implores Clara to be the primary reader of his text: "May *your* kind eyes, love, be the first that fall on these pages, when the writer has parted from them for ever! May *your* tender hand be the first that touches these leaves, when mine is cold! Backward in my narrative, Clara, wherever I have but casually mentioned my sister, the pen has trembled and stood still" (18). This paralysis of the phallic pen, which "has trembled and stood still," signifies emasculation as a loss of control over language. After he addresses Clara, Basil claims that his hand, like his pen, "trembles" and that he must stop writing: "my courage and my calmness fail me" (18). That thoughts of Clara cause this trembling suggests that, once Basil writes for women, he shares their lack of social and linguistic authority. Yet the power of women seems as threatening as their powerlessness, since Basil implies that the female reader of his work will become his rival. At the beginning of his narrative, Basil claims that he is writing a "plain and true record" (1) of his story, although he admits that "Others will be found, when I am no more, to carve, and smooth, and polish to the popular taste of the day this rugged material of Truth which I shall leave behind me" (311). But since Basil bequeathes his narrative to his sister ("may *your* tender hand be the first that touches these leaves, when mine is cold"), he implies that she, who had earlier been his female editor, will be one of those to smooth and polish the male writer's ruggedly truthful text to fit the "popular taste."

Fiction and Indeterminacy

Although Basil claims that this dilution of masculine rugged Truth by feminine popular fiction will take place only after his death, it happens even as he writes. As Basil enters the marketplace, he writes a feminine language, which Collins defines, in the image of the pen trembling in Basil's hand, as a lack of linguistic authority. Yet it is implied that, to write fiction, the writer must, at least symbolically, be a woman. Both femininity and fiction (what is smoothed and polished for the popular taste) are seemingly antithetical to the "plain and true record" of facts with which Basil seeks to reestablish the masculine identity he has lost. Basil's claim that he writes only a "plain and true record" recalls Collins' assertion that the *Memoirs* represent only "unvarnished Truth," the "faithful record of a life" (I, v). In *Basil*, the son's name is ripped out of the book that is, like the *Memoirs*, a "biographical history" of the father's family (201). In both the *Memoirs* and the novel, the world of the father is associated with a stable social and linguistic order in which signification is clear and in which fiction that blurs fact has little place. And, in both works, fiction making is a transgressive activity for the son. In the *Memoirs*, for instance, the son's art is evinced through the figurative subtext of the work that subtly undoes the father's aesthetic economy, as in Collins' description of the painting "Morning after a Storm," in which beauty and terror are mingled, and that of "Summer Twilight," which by blurring darkness and light confuses the seemingly crisply defined terms of the father's art.

In *Basil*, too, confusion invades the male writer's narrative once he can speak of his father only "in the past tense" (5)—an indeterminacy linked to fiction, if not least because of the profusion of figurative patterns—darkness, paralysis, loss of vision—that trope it. This indeterminacy exposes a paradox at the heart of Collins' meditation on fiction and the marketplace. Collins' vision of writing for the "popular taste" draws on the traditional association of fiction with lying, or blurring truth in order to entertain. Yet it becomes increasingly clear in Basil's narrative that fiction is also a means of telling unpleasant truths, and of questioning the social order symbolized by the father's law. Hence the female Gothic can be at once a trope for writing popular fiction in the marketplace, and for writing subversively. Since this subversion is associated, in Clara's and Mrs. Sherwin's case, with a kind of indirect or ironic feminine writing—with the feminist subtext of Radcliffe's and Shelley's Gothic fiction—it can lead to aesthetic complexity rather than to the devaluation of art that Basil associates with popular fiction ("an instinct now, an art no longer").

Throughout his narrative, however, Basil persists in a negative association of indeterminacy with the femininity and class degradation he fears. Once he enters the marketplace, he characterizes his writing as a failure because it can no longer reproduce the coherence and clarity that mark his father's ideology. Not only does he open his narrative with a question—"What am I now about to write?" (1)—but he confesses that he does not know exactly why he is writing. Although he claims that writing his private "history" (1) will explain the "error" of his marriage and make the descendants of the family from which he has been disinherited remember him kindly, he also admits to other motives "which I feel, but cannot analyse" (1). This inability to read may actually be a refusal to read, since "cannot" could mean "must not": Basil may not wish to record his resentment against his father for rejecting him, although this anger surely motivates his text. In the absence of a discourse about rebellion, however, Basil falls back on a language of confusion and impotence. He claims that he cannot judge the characters of either himself or the other people in his story: "We can neither know nor judge ourselves; others may judge, but cannot know us" (5). The son's inability to judge differs from the father's ability to judge him for transgressing class boundaries (and, indeed, the scene of Basil's disinheritance is a melodramatic revision of the Last Judgment or of the expulsion from Paradise). Although he describes the members of his family, he warns the reader that "I make no attempt to judge their characters: I only describe them—whether rightly or wrongly, I know not—as they appeared to *me*" (5).

The substitution of subjective for objective knowledge occurs after Basil first sees Margaret, whom he surreptitiously follows home as the "fair summer evening was tending towards twilight" (37). This mysterious twilight, which recalls Collins' image of indeterminacy in his description of his father's painting "Summer Twilight," suggests that Basil's vision becomes blurred not only literally but figuratively as he responds to the imaginative energy that Margaret figures. As he strays into a new type of imaginative world at the sight of the veiled Margaret, he can no longer see as he once did: "Her features and her expression were but indistinctly visible to me. I could just vaguely perceive that she was young and beautiful; but, beyond this, though I might imagine much, I could see little" (29–30). The ability to imagine, when evoked by Margaret's veiled female influence, is purchased by blindness. Imagination is couched in the subjunctive ("I might imagine much"), but the emphasis is on loss of sight ("but indistinctly visible"; "just vaguely perceive"; "I could see little"). As Basil sums it up: "My powers of observation, hitherto active enough, had now wholly deserted me" (30).

Observation, and sight itself, are associated in the novel with Basil's father, who is always alert to the signs of class difference. The father's social vision, which perceives sharp distinctions between classes, recalls the minute observation of Nature that Collins ascribes to his father in the *Memoirs*; in both cases the father's sight symbolizes his power over what he sees (the classes "beneath" him, feminine Nature). After his attack on Mannion, Basil likens himself to a blind man whose sight is only partially restored—an ironic simile given his own half-blinding of the clerk (168). Yet Basil's action was presumably intended to reestablish social distinctions, by punishing the clerk for committing adultery with his wife and aspiring to revenge himself on those responsible for his outcast status. Blinding Mannion, however, cannot efface the likeness between him and his assailant. Not only does Basil's assault on the clerk make him an outcast like Mannion, but Mannion, as an image for class ressentiment, becomes his double.

Redefining Monstrosity: Mannion and the Crisis of Male Authority

Thus Mannion, like the women in the novel, is a Gothic mirror of what Basil fears to become. Collins' depiction of the relationship between Mannion and Basil is mediated by a revision of *Frankenstein*, in which the clerk is both the monster that Basil has created and what is monstrous within himself.[13] Collins' rewriting of Shelley's novel in many ways preserves the more conservative aspects of her social vision, particularly on issues of class. Yet Collins also redefines monstrosity, by developing through Mannion's story the allegory of the writer in the marketplace that the novel has already delineated, and by using

Basil's relationship to the clerk to represent the Victorian writer's relation to revolution.

Echoes of *Frankenstein* cluster around the description of Mannion, who, like Frankenstein's monster, is with his creator on his wedding night. Recalling the monster's cry to Frankenstein—"Remember, that I am thy creature. . . the work of your hands" (*F* 100–101)—Mannion taunts Basil at Margaret's grave: "'Do you know me for Robert Mannion?' he repeated. 'Do you know the work of your own hands, now you see it?'" (303). Yet if Basil's disfigurement of Mannion inscribes upon the clerk's body the hostility to class privilege that motivates him, Basil is not the only creator of Mannion's monstrosity. Mannion reveals his history to Basil in a letter that, since it is a first-person narrative like the monster's relation of his origins, presents him in a sympathetic light. This letter, however, makes it clear that Basil is not responsible for Mannion's "creation" so much as Basil's father is, whose implication in a system of class privilege kills Mannion's father and dooms his son to a life of poverty and social namelessness.

Mannion's father was hanged as a forger because he resorted to a fiction—writing the name of Basil's father on a bond to evade his creditors. Although Mannion claims that his father was a "great respecter of the wide gaps which lay between social stations in his time" (227), the forgery represents a kind of class resentment, because Basil's father, a member of Parliament, had failed to procure him a government sinecure as he had promised. Most significant, however, the charge of forgery conflates literary authority with criminality, implying that the artist in the marketplace has lost the authentic presence of the paternal word and can attempt only to copy it; driven by economic necessity, Mannion's father, a "gentleman" by birth, pretends to possess Basil's "ancient" family name. The disgrace the son inherits from his father makes him, like that father, unable to take up a profession, "as distinguished from a trade" (227), finally causing him to become a "hack-author" (231) who, by translating other works, lives off the "offal of literature" (232), "plagiarising from dead authors, to supply the raw material for bookmongering" (232).

With this history, Mannion embodies the figure, so popular in the nineteenth century, of the ressentiment-ridden intellectual. The class degradation he suffers implicates the Victorian writer in the "proletarianization" of the working class. Although the class status of the Victorian writer is nominally (like Mannion's or Basil's) that of gentleman, the writer's dependency on the marketplace is linked to an experience of wage slavery and drudgery, and even a kind of mechanization; like Melville's "Bartleby, the Scrivener" and Dickens' figure of Nemo, the legal copyist, in *Bleak House* (both texts published in 1853, the year after *Basil*), Mannion rewrites what others have written rather than creating his own original art.[14]

This proletarianization of the writer, figured in Mannion and Basil, is also a kind of feminization; Mannion's copying other works into English resembles Clara's role as Basil's amanuensis, who transcribes his sources. Like the women, too, Mannion practices a veiled and secretive revolt against authority; in one scene where Basil visits him before he recognizes his villainy, Mannion acts as the deferential subordinate until, as a flash of lightning illuminates his face, "he absolutely seemed to be glaring and grinning on me like a fiend, in the one instant of its duration" (130). This suppressed hostility, however, echoes Basil's own secret anger against his father, Mannion's hated enemy. After he has met Margaret and realized that his father will not approve the match, Basil roams the streets with "bitter thoughts" rising in his mind, "bitter thoughts against his inexorable family pride, which imposed on me the concealment and secrecy, under the oppression of which I had already suffered so much" (91). Hence not only does Basil come, like the clerk, to tell "bitter truths bitterly," but he tells these truths secretly, to himself rather than to an audience.

Thus Mannion is an even more frightening double for Basil than are the women because he is a version of the male artist isolated from social and linguistic authority. Mannion's embodiment of transgressive sexuality, and particularly his link with the female sexuality of Margaret, makes him a source both of debased language and of what is socially degraded. Whereas Basil fears that the "honest and pure . . . identity" of his narrative will be contaminated once it leaves his hands (III, 292 [1852]), Mannion's adultery with Basil's wife suggests the adulteration of the male writer's text by the female Gothic that Margaret represents. Again, both the subversiveness and the popularity of the female Gothic are important in this narrative: whatever is subversive in the female Gothic is expressed indirectly, and is thus symbolic of the writer's need to stifle "bitter truths" to sell his or her work in the marketplace.

The category of the "popular" is hence an ambiguous one for the Victorian artist. Whereas writing popular fiction implies that the writer directs his or her work toward "the people," the writer symbolically identifies with the proletariat by selling literature ("bookmongering," as Mannion calls it) to those who can afford to buy it. But at the same time, the reading audience is also associated (surely because literacy and leisure continued to be concentrated in the bourgeoisie and upper classes) with the censorship of the writer and the upholding of social hierarchies. The extent to which popular fiction subverts these hierarchies links it either with lower- and working-class unrest or with covertly rebellious women readers.

The writer's ambivalence about this second meaning of "the popular" is figured through Basil's relationship with Mannion and Margaret. Although Basil chafes against the restraints of veiling his bitterness against his haughty father, he also resents being connected with what is "beneath" him (women, the lower classes) or with what is openly rebellious. Soon after Clara assumes her post as editor, copyist, and reader, he claims that he has "contracted a bad habit of writing at night" (26), thus becoming a Gothic artist who creates during the time of ultimate silence and secrecy. Yet the imagery of contamination implicit in the verb "contracted" invades the latter part of the text to figure the disease of rebellion that must be cured. Margaret catches typhus fever from a patient in the hospital where she visits the disfigured clerk, a fever that literalizes the "pestilence" of Mannion's influence (296). Margaret dies from this fever, and Mannion falls off a cliff in the middle of a storm, losing his balance as he waves his fist in a final maniacally defiant gesture (325–26). The lovers' engulfment by their own febrile transgression (once again, the revolution swallows its children) presumably permits Basil to recover his male identity when he is reunited with his father.

Yet Basil's attempts to rid himself of Margaret and Mannion do not so much cure him of their influence as infect him further. With his attack on Mannion he tries to exorcise this demon, but during this episode his sense of powerlessness is deepened rather than alleviated. Preceding the attack, he listens behind a partition to Margaret and Mannion making love, a voyeurism that, as it isolates him from both action and vision, deprives him of will: "a dream-sensation of being impelled by some hidden, irresistible agency, possessed me" (160).

This dream sensation recalls the dreaminess that overcame him when he first met Margaret: "My ideas were in utter confusion, all my thoughts ran astray. I walked on, dreaming in full day—I had no distinct impressions, except of the stranger beauty whom I had just seen. The more I tried to collect myself . . . the less self-possessed I became" (32). Although this passage illustrates the loss of vision ("no distinct impressions") that afflicts Basil when he meets the "stranger beauty," the important term is "self-possessed." Since social power is linked to possessions—of a paternal name, of money and property, of masculinity itself—Basil literally loses himself from the moment he meets Margaret (herself described as a "stranger"). This loss of self-possession infiltrates the narrative through Basil's allegorical dreams, which, if they figure his "error" in marrying Margaret, also disrupt his narrative: with the dreams "Thoughts and sensations which had been more and more weakly restrained with each succeeding hour of wakefulness, now rioted within me in perfect liberation from all control" (44). This riot is literalized just before Basil discovers the adultery of his wife: as he tries to follow Margaret to the hotel where she meets Mannion, he collides with a crowd that surrounds the scene of a robbery, and his voice is "overpowered" by the noise of a "shouting, struggling mob" (157).

Not only is this mob representative of the lower-class and feminine rebellion figured by Margaret and Mannion, but it prefigures the imagery of the scene that follows. When Basil hears Margaret and Mannion through the partition, his initial dreaminess is followed by something like a negative version of orgasm: "a shivering helplessness in every limb" (161). Yet his next sensation is a "desire for revenge" that takes the form of sexual potency: "a quick vigour leapt hotly through my frame" (161). This hot desire causes him to resemble Mannion, who later claims that his longing for revenge "leaps in my blood like fire" (324). Thus not only is Basil's voice "overpowered" by the riot of the lower classes and of women, but also, despite his desire to escape this transgressiveness, he joins in the violence himself. Although he subsequently regains his masculine potency ("quick vigour"), he loses his class identity, describing himself after his attack on Mannion as a "drunken man" (165) and fleeing from the scene of the crime as a criminal outcast.

This disintegration of social identity accompanies a further disintegration of Basil's narrative. After Basil strikes down Mannion and rushes away from the now hysterical Margaret, bystanders call him "mad" (166), and he himself characterizes his feelings as unintelligible: "no human language ever has conveyed, or will convey [it], in all its horrible reality, to others" (166). Although Basil tries to assure himself that he is "still in possession" of his senses, and thus reassert "mastery" over himself (166), his narrative fragments as "utter oblivion" (167) and a hiatus in the text precede his return to consciousness. Before his fall into unconsciousness, Basil is uncertain whether it is night or day: "Darkness?—*Was* it dark? or was day breaking yonder, far away in the murky eastern sky?" (167). Although by destroying Mannion and rejecting Margaret Basil had tried to reassert the supremacy of the masculine sun over feminine darkness, he now fails to distinguish between the two. An indeterminacy that blurs darkness and light again invades his narrative, as he describes the light he sees before his fall into oblivion as "a blaze of lurid sunshine . . . a hell-blaze of brightness" (167), recalling the lightning that had previously illumined Mannion's face. Using similar imagery, Basil describes his fever as "fierce" and "seething," a "terrible heat" (169), and during his delirium he has to be held down because his "paroxysm of convulsive strength" makes him "dangerous . . . to all about me" (175).

Instead of improving, this feverish inability to control language worsens after Mannion's death, when Basil's text breaks into five fragmentary sections, separated from each other by blank space. As Basil himself claims before his words trail off—an editorial voice explains that the last lines are "illegible" (329)—"the simplest forms of expression confused themselves inextricably in my mind" (328). This delirium plunges Basil ever more deeply into the plot of the feminine carceral by recalling the conflation of insanity with femininity in Gothic and sensation fiction, such as Wollstonecraft's *Maria*, where madness is signified by the fragments of female speech and female silence that make up the text. Significantly, Basil falls into silence as he voices a wish to see his silent sister, Clara: "Oh! if I could only see Clara again . . . Clara!—far from her—nothing but the little book-marker she worked for me—leave it round my neck when I—" (329).

It is appropriate, indeed, that Basil apparently wishes Clara's book-mark to be buried with him. The ghost that haunts him during his delirium is that of a woman whose power, figured synecdochically through her literary influence as a "book-marker," is buried within the domestic circle she inhabits. Basil, who does not die but recovers, is nonetheless buried in this domesticity with his sister; in a letter that forms a brief epilogue to the narrative that ends with his fever, we hear that he lives alone with Clara after his father's death, which occurs several years after their reunion. Although the reconciliation with the father recalls the end of *Antonina*, in *Basil* the return to the patriarch is transformed into a return to the maternal tradition, since brother and sister live on "the little estate" that once belonged to their mother, and which Clara has inherited (341).

Although this rural retreat, like "Morning after a Storm," appears to follow darkness with sunshine, Basil's final letter is written at twilight: "I have done. The calm summer evening has stolen on me while I have been writing to you; and Clara's voice—now the happy voice of the happy old times—calls to me from our garden seat to come out and look at the sunset over the distant sea. Once more—farewell!" (344). Even though Clara's voice is restored to what it once was, she calls her brother to look at the sunset, not at the sun-rise that might appropriately figure the resurrection of the "happy old times." Not only has the summer twilight "stolen" over Basil as he writes—as if it were part of the urban underworld he has just escaped—but also Clara's voice interrupts Basil's writing, causing him to end his narrative. The Gothic tradition associated with the sister and with the mother's "estate" thus reasserts its power both to influence and to silence the voice of the male writer.

Indeed, despite having been written back into the father's book,

Basil does not regain his masculine identity so much as shroud it in feminine obscurity. Although his brother urges him to enter public life like his father, who had been a member of Parliament, Basil claims that he has lost his desire for fame: "I am still resolved to live on in obscurity, in retirement, in peace. . . . The mountain-path of Action is no longer a path for *me*; my future hope pauses with my present happiness in the shadowed valley of Repose" (342).

Stranded in this pointlessly liminal world between action and repose, Basil leaves his feminine retirement only through his writing. The epilogue, a letter to the doctor friend who had attended Margaret in her illness, announces his decision to publish his narrative confession, which he had previously refused to publish while his father was alive, since "I could not suffer a manuscript in which he was represented . . . as separating himself in the bitterest hostility from his own son, to be made public property" (338). The ideological control that the father exerts during his lifetime—Basil's "full and loving" reconciliation with his father (338) does not allow him to publish an account of his rebellion—is sufficiently slackened afterward to allow the narrative to be made "public property." With the death of the aristocratic father, the son can enter the marketplace, yet his anxiety about popular authorship persists; to escape his dependency on "bookmongering," Basil retreats into a domesticity that is stifling because he has purged it of rebellion. The narrative of interrupted maturation suggested by his return to the home figures Collins' inability, at the end of this important and formative novel, finally to do other than to look backward, either to the oppressive and archaic world of the fathers or to the ghost of revolution and the female Gothic.

Four

Writing after Dark: Collins and Victorian Literary Culture

Although Collins' novels after *Basil* continued to engage "modern life," he still wrote historical fiction, returning in the mid-1850s to the subject of revolution that had been thematically important in his earliest works. Recalling the setting of his ghost story about the French Revolution, "Nine O'Clock!" he serialized a lengthy tale about the Reign of Terror, "Sister Rose," in Dickens' journal *Household Words* in 1855, including it the next year in his collection of short stories *After Dark*. In *After Dark*, he embeds this historical fiction within the collection's frame narrative, in which a male artist and his female scribe become both collaborators and rivals in the literary marketplace. This juxtaposition of a tale about revolution with an allegory of the marketplace foregrounds the Victorian writer's relation to history, even as it continues to figure Collins' ambivalent relation to the Gothic genre. Within the frame narrative, the wife, who is an amanuensis, suggests that her husband write for money and then transforms his stories into Gothic narratives, a plot that encodes Collins' anxiety about the female voice and the status of Gothic fiction in the Victorian literary establishment.

Although this narrative about the literary marketplace and the rivalry between male and female artists sounds familiar after *Basil*, both the frame narrative of *After Dark* and the story "Sister Rose" represent a significant development in this plot rather than simply another look backward. Even as the history that the endings of both *Antonina* and *Basil* had tried to repress returns in "Sister Rose" —itself a tale about a kind of resurrection—the subtle shifts between masculine and feminine perspectives in the frame narrative complicate Collins' revision of the female Gothic. Whereas the first-person narrative of *Basil* privileges the male viewpoint (and a misogynist one at that), the frame narrative of *After Dark* is written instead by a figure for the woman writer. Although this narrative strategy does not simply substitute a female for a male perspective, it does render Collins' allegory of the writer in the marketplace more complex, since in his own preface to the work he adopts some of the metaphors for storytelling used by his female narrator. In order to explore why Collins could identify with a female narrator as well as be anxious about that identification, the first part of this chapter will place the relation between writing and gender so often figured in his fiction in the context of Victorian literary culture. In particular, this reading will examine how the development of Collins' career in the 1850s and 1860s intersected with the rise both of the literary marketplace and of a growing gap between "popular" and "serious" fiction. In debates over the status of Victorian fiction, the difference between popular and serious is defined most obviously in class terms—"high" and "low"—but also in gendered terms, contrasting a masculine professional ethos with sensation fiction identified as feminine. Thus before turning to the figuration of Collins' own literary situation in *After Dark*, I will examine the tensions inherent in his desire to identify with masculine professionalism while being identified by his critics with feminine sensationalism.

"No Character at All": The Sensation Novel and Literary Professionalism

At the beginning of the 1860s, the decade that witnessed the craze for and critical debate over the sensation novel, a reviewer wrote about *The Woman in White* that "Like the women in Pope, most of Mr. Wilkie Collins's characters have no character at all."[1] On the surface, this statement endorses an opinion about Collins' fiction that was to become a critical commonplace: his works, like other examples of Victorian sensation or melodramatic fiction, are concerned with plot rather than with character. As this reviewer claims, the readers are "much less interested in the people than in what happens to the people."[2] Yet the argument that Collins "does not attempt to paint character or passion,"[3] although it expels him from the canon of the realist novel, is as much an ideological as an aesthetic judgment. Surely many readers of Collins' fiction would disagree that his characters are any less memorable than those of other Victorian novelists (and if, as the reviewer claims, the figures in Collins' novels have "characteristics, but not character,"[4] those in the works of more securely canonical authors like Dickens and Thackeray are often types rather than psychological portraits).[5] Yet "to have a character" in the Victorian period also meant to have a reputation; when Ezra Jennings says in *The Moonstone*, "I am a man whose life is a wreck, and whose character is gone," he means that he is an outcast because scandalous rumors about his past prevent him from obtaining the written recommendations of character that were a prerequisite for a job.[6] The degraded class status of not having a character may be compared with definitions of femininity as lack or absence. The verse from Pope's "Epistle to a Lady" to which the reviewer of *The Woman in White* refers proclaims that "Nothing so true as what you once let fall / 'Most Women have no Characters at all.'"[7]

Collins' reviewer thus puns on the social, as well as the literary, definition of character, since in *The Woman in White* (as in such later novels as *No Name* and *The Moonstone*) Collins often portrays women and other outcasts who have no "character," because of either their gender or their ambiguous class status (or both, as with the illegitimate daughter who is the central figure in *No Name*). This characterlessness is troped not just through femininity but through a sexually fallen femininity; in Pope's verse, the important word is "fall." Just as the reviewer of *Basil* condemned the novel by exclaiming in horror over its plot of the "adultery of a wife," critics like the reviewer of *The Woman in White* imply that the lack of securely defined social and gender identity among Collins' characters reflects on the aesthetic value of the novels in which they appear. Not only are Collins' characters compared with women without reputation, but he himself is likened to a member of the working class rather than to one of a literary elite; the reviewer from the *Saturday Review*, after claiming that Collins is a "story-teller" rather than a "great novelist," says that "he is, as we have said, a very ingenious constructor; but ingenious construction is not high art, just as cabinet-making and joining are not high art."[8]

To claim that Collins' novels embody the "lowness" of his characters obviously is ironic, since in *Basil* the figure for the male writer tries to escape the contamination of female influence and of Mannion's demonic ressentiment. That Collins returned to *Basil* in 1862 to revise it is appropriate, since the narrative would have been popular in the heyday of the sensation novel, and its story about trying to escape from literary and social "lowness" would have been a compelling one for him amid critical disagreement concerning the value of his fiction.

That fiction deemed sensational should be considered marginal or subliterary attests to a debate about the changing status and definition of Victorian fiction. As Walter Phillips argues in his pioneering study of Dickens, Collins, and Reade as sensation novelists, the Victorian literary marketplace changed drastically during the period in which these writers established their careers. With fiction no longer available only to an elite, the writer became more dependent on appealing to an audience than in the past, a dependency which the demands of serial publication only exacerbated.[9] The previous chapter traced *Basil*'s association of writing for the marketplace with wage slavery and the degradation of aesthetic value. Yet the discourse about the devaluation of fiction in the marketplace that *Basil* reflects appears simultaneously with a new emphasis within the Victorian literary establishment, by writers and critics alike, on the moral and aesthetic value of writing and on the professionalism (not the wage slavery) of the novelist.

The claim that, in the words of a reviewer of *Basil*, the writer has a "high and holy mission"[10] mystifies the economic reality in which that writer creates. This mystification serves to protect and even to enhance the status of the intellectual and, in so doing, to preserve other hierarchies that social and economic changes might threaten. The association of Victorian fiction with democratization, with being available even to the working and lower classes, is countered by a critical discourse that uses aesthetic terms to condemn the content of fiction, particularly if that content is read as subversive of gender and class roles.

Discussing the growing separation between "popular" and "great" literature during the Victorian period, Winifred Hughes notes that "Curiously, some thought ominously, the rise of the sensation genre coincided with the height of the novelist's newly-won prestige, his new presence as a social and ethical force."[11] Yet the timing of the rise of sensation fiction is not curious at all when the genre is viewed as a construction by the literary establishment (reviewers were the first to coin the phrase) of a fiction that contrasts with prestigious, or "great" art. Certainly, the very term *sensation fiction* implies a dichotomy between fiction that, as this label suggests, appeals to the bodily senses—"excitement, and excitement alone, seems to be the great end at which they aim," claimed H. D. Mansel[12]—and that which appeals to the mind. (Would the opposite of sensation fiction be cerebral fiction?) Yet the boundary between high and low reproduces other social dichotomies: male and female, upper class and lower class, even white and nonwhite. A critic for the *Westminster Review* likened the sensation novelist, including Mary Elizabeth Braddon and Collins, to a showman exhibiting a "big black baboon, whose habits were so filthy, and whose behavior was so disgusting, that respectable people constantly remonstrated with him for exhibiting such an animal." According to the critic, the showman's answer was, "If it wasn't for that big black baboon I should be ruined; it attracts all the young girls in the country."[13]

This anecdote conflates all those who are "low" in the body politic: the black baboon, who embodies the racial Other, the showman, an image for the working class, and the young girls whose sexuality is stimulated. In this allegory of the literary marketplace, the writers of sensation fiction (the showman selling a look at his baboon) purvey works that dangerously arouse the sexuality of women—particularly, it is implied, middle-class women, who are supposed to be sexually repressed—the same charge that used to be leveled at writers of earlier Gothic literature. That women were associated with writing and reading such sexually charged fiction (sensation novels, indeed) is evinced by such reviews as the one entitled "Our Female Sensation Novelists." This review, which focuses on women writers like Mrs. Henry Wood, author of *East Lynne*, and Braddon, author of *Lady Audley's Secret*, complains that "the sensation novel . . . is a sign of the times—the evidence of a certain train of thought and action, of an impatience of old restraints, and a craving for some fundamental change in the working of society."[14] This association of women's Gothic writing with revolution is also made by Margaret Oliphant in a lengthy review of sensation novels in *Blackwood's Magazine*, which compares the "hectic rebellion against nature" in the sensation novel with Hester Prynne's adultery in *The Scarlet Letter* and claims that such novels represent "frantic attempts by any kind of black art or mad psychology to get some grandeur and sacredness restored to life—or if not sacredness and grandeur, at least horror and mystery, there being nothing better in earth or heaven; Mesmerism possibly for a make-shift, or Socialism, if perhaps it might be more worthwhile to turn ploughmen and milkmaids than ladies and gentlemen."[15]

Oliphant's link between sensation fiction and frustrated revolutionary aspirations—aspirations that are even millenarian ("nothing better in earth or heaven")—undermines the distinction made between sensation and cerebration by critics of the sensation novel. That sensation novelists crave some "fundamental change in the working of society" implies that they think too much rather than (as their lust for "excitement" presumably suggests) that they do not think at all.[16] Whereas those who believed that fiction should be serious were influenced by Carlyle's vision of the writer as prophet and social critic, popular fiction like the sensation novel was associated with having the wrong type of social vision, or one that blurred social hierarchies. Jonathan Loesberg argues that the debate over the literary status of sensation fiction, by reflecting concerns about the stability of class definition, has many parallels to debates over the parliamentary reforms in the 1850s and 1860s that attempted to expand suffrage.[17] He locates this mid-Victorian "class fear" in such important and highly popular sensation novels as *The Woman in White*, *Lady Audley's Secret*, and *East Lynne*, which all contain socially displaced characters; Collins' Laura Fairlie descends to the level of a working-class woman, Wood's Isabel Vane becomes a governess, and Braddon's central figure rises above her station.[18] Because all these characters are women, however, this anxiety about the miscegenation of classes is also linked to anxieties about gender definition. In this sense, these novels reproduce ideological tensions inherent in the period—"class fear," a fear that women will become insubordinate or lose their "place" —without necessarily being as subversive as they have been called both by their contemporaries and by some recent critics.[19] Still, less important than the radical content of the sensation novel is the perception that it was revolutionary because it depicted types of ambiguity (moral, social, gender) rather than stable and unambiguous ideological definitions.[20] And, equally important, the low status assigned sensation fiction within generic hierarchies reproduces the increasing stratification of literature during the second half of the nineteenth century.

Joining the Gentleman's Club: Collins' Career in the 1850s

Collins' prefaces to his works indicate his desire to be classified as a serious, rather than simply as a popular, novelist. The vehemence of this desire has led critics to describe his prefaces to *Basil* in particular—he revised the original preface for the second edition—as "belligerent," "polemical," and "truculent."[21] Yet if Collins' prefaces in general are, as Sue Lonoff claims, "exercises in self-defense,"[22] they are most importantly a defense against the often dismissive reviews which, like that of *The Woman in White*, impugned his ability to craft "high art." In the 1862 preface to *Basil*, Collins responds to criticism of the novel as both "revolting" and subliterary by repeating a passage from the 1852 edition in which, echoing his father's Romanticism, he depicts himself as a writer who not only exposes social ills but also transforms them into art: "Is not the noblest poetry of prose fiction the poetry of every-day truth?" (xxxvi).

In an admiring review written in the late 1850s, the French critic Emile Forgues, who also translated several of Collins' novels into French, forecast for Collins a career as an author of note and, most significant, as the author who would tell the story of Victorian authors in his fiction: "Who is better qualified than he . . . to depict for us the life of the artist in England and in our period?"[23] Yet it is telling that Forgues compares *Basil*, the novel that concerns the male artist's attempts to differentiate himself from women writers, with the work of Charlotte Brontë and Elizabeth Gaskell. Even though they predate the coining of the term, the novels with which Forgues compares *Basil*—

Jane Eyre and *Mary Barton*—share many of the attributes of sensation fiction: Brontë's novel was condemned for its immorality and, like *Lady Audley's Secret* and *East Lynne*, contains a heroine who rises in class position, whereas *Mary Barton* was criticized for its portrayal of working-class unrest. The comparison between *Basil* and these novels demonstrates a tendency, which was to be emphasized in the debate over sensation fiction, to class Collins' works with those of women writers, and specifically to compare supposedly subversive tendencies in his novels with those in the works of women. Nuel Pharr Davis points out that the comparison of *Basil* with *Jane Eyre* and *Mary Barton*, even in the context of an admiring review, may have galled Collins: "To Wilkie, sensitive about women authors, it must have been irksome to think that the kindest appraisals of *Basil* would call it, as the French critic, Forgues, did, 'quelque chose d'approchant *Jane Eyre*.'"[24]

Davis refers to comments Collins made that resemble Hawthorne's famous line about "scribbling women"; for example, a character in a Collins sketch written for Dickens' periodical *Household Words* in 1858 claims he has been told by "persons of experience in the world of letters" that "Ladies of the present century have burst into every department of literature, have carried off the accumulated raw material under men's noses, and have manufactured it to an enormous and unheard of extent for the public benefit. I am told that out of every twelve novels or poems that are written, nine at least are by ladies."[25] The comparison between writing and manufacturing here, as well as the raw note of rivalry with women, recalls the link in *Basil* between women writers and the degradation of the marketplace in which male writers must now compete. As in *Basil*, too, what is significant about this hostility to women writers is how it expresses in a displaced form anxieties about writing in the marketplace, anxieties that, as Collins' career was being established during the 1850s and 1860s, could only have been exacerbated by the classification of his works with the sensation novel.

In her study of the growth of Victorian literary professionalism, Julia Swindells describes the ways in which the literary establishment was male dominated and male defined; those women who succeeded in obtaining recognition, like George Eliot and the Brontës, did so only after struggles to ingratiate themselves with male patrons or by assuming a masculine professional identity.[26] Swindells refers to literature in the Victorian period as a "gentleman's club,"[27] and Walter Phillips describes the "literary fraternalism" of Dickens, Collins, and Reade.[28] Certainly, this fraternalism may be seen as an attempt to distinguish the gender roles that the rise in the number of women novelists may have threatened. Since professionalism was male defined (as most Victorian women were barred from a career), it was easier to associate "serious" art with male novelists, or with a woman novelist like Eliot who took a male name and conformed to aesthetic standards favored by the male literary establishment. In this context, Collins' relationship with Dickens, who was a formidable embodiment of literary professionalism, may be read as symptomatic of Collins' need to be taken seriously as a professional writer.[29]

Since his career represented many of the same difficulties in professional definition, Dickens was a particularly appropriate model for Collins. As the title of Phillips' study makes clear, Dickens, an enormously popular writer, was classified by some as a sensation novelist. (*Great Expectations*, for instance, was considered an example of sensation fiction.)[30] Yet, more successfully than Collins, he was able to transcend the category of the popular to be recognized as a great novelist and social prophet. In the letter he wrote to Collins about *Basil*, Dickens claimed that it was the seriousness of the younger writer's efforts that pleased him:

> It is delightful to find throughout that you have taken great pains with it [the novel] besides, and have "gone at it" with a perfect knowledge of the jolter-headedness of the conceited idiots who suppose that volumes are to be tossed off like pancakes, and that any writing can be done without the utmost application, the greatest patience, and the steadiest energy of which the writer is capable.[31]

The language of this letter combines elitism with what may be a covert sexism: although the idiots Dickens refers to presumably do not know the difference between a literary work and a product of trade —they are bakers, not writers—to call badly written volumes pancakes implies that such volumes are the product of domestic labor and that the jolter-headed idiots may be women writers. In any event, with the words "utmost application," "greatest patience," "steadiest energy," Dickens demonstrates how, as James Brown has argued, he associates the labors of the professional writer with the apotheosis of industry, thrift, and perseverance that Lukács identifies as characteristic of the "heroic epoch of bourgeois development."[32]

Dickens' praise of Collins' labor and his denigration of those who do not take time to write well echoes the language of the 1852 preface to *Basil*, where Collins claims he is not one of the "mob of ladies and gentlemen who play at writing" (i, xv [1852]). This reference to a "mob of ladies and gentlemen," although it recalls the moment in the text where Basil's voice is literally overpowered by a lower-class mob and symbolically overwhelmed by feminine influence, associates bad writing with a kind of aristocratic decadence. The association of this mob with an aristocratic indolence that the bourgeois writer must overcome is underscored by Collins' objection to these lady and gentleman authors as essentially "holiday authors, who sit down to write a book as they would sit down to a game at cards—leisurely-living people who coolly select as an amusement 'to kill time,' an occupation which can only be pursued, even creditably, by the patient, uncompromising, reverent devotion of every moral and intellectual faculty, more or less, which a human being has to give" (I, xvi [1852]). That Collins identifies writers in the marketplace with effete aristocrats rather than with people struggling for a living is part of a discourse of empowerment for the bourgeois writer, whose hard work does not make him a wage slave but rather guarantees him a professional identity. The casual attitude toward authorship displayed by "leisurely-living people" contrasts with the "humble, work-a-day merit" that Collins claims for his own writing, since he argues that his "painstaking" care (I, xv [1852]) ranks him among those authors who share "the homely but honourable distinction of being workers and not players at their task" (I, xvii [1852]).

The language of a shared literary mission in Dickens' letter and Collins' preface suggests how empowering the relationship between the two writers was to the younger one. Collins' intellectual friendship, and even at times partnership, with Dickens gave him access to the world of literary professionalism in which the elder author had so brilliantly succeeded; during the 1850s Collins first joined Dickens' journal *Household Words* and later (after skillful negotiations on his part) became a staff member. This close bonding between two male artists was reminiscent of that between Collins' father and the Scots painter Sir David Wilkie. Yet the friendship was (at least at first) not so much egalitarian as paternal. Eliza Linton characterized Dickens' relationship to Collins as that of "a literary Mentor to a younger Telemachus,"[33] and in many ways Dickens filled for Collins the place that had been vacated by his father. Although, as a liberal reformer who supported the revolutions of 1848, he was more ideologically congenial to Collins than his father had been, Dickens' career emblematized the rigorous professionalism and bourgeois industry that Collins ascribes to William in the *Memoirs*.

Significantly, however, Dickens' advice to Collins underscored a conflict between politics and professionalism. In *Basil*, the writer in the marketplace is associated both with wage slavery and with the veiling of subversive writing to appeal to an audience. The ideal of professionalism that Dickens and Collins shared may have seemed to elevate the male writer from the position of wage slave, but it did not liberate him from dependency on his readers. In the *Memoirs* Collins describes how his father had claimed that "a painter should choose those subjects with which most people associate pleasant circumstances. It is not sufficient that a scene pleases *him*" (I, 59). In his own role as mentor, Dickens was to advise Collins how to please his audience, even if it meant diluting elements in his fiction that a predominantly middle-class readership would find subversive. As Collins' employer at *Household Words* and *All the Year Round*, Dickens even played the part of censor himself, directing his editor W. H. Wills to delete anything from Collins' articles that might, as he said in one letter, "be sweeping and unnecessarily offensive to the middle class. He has always a tendency to overdo that."[34]

Sue Lonoff suggests that, even given what was positive in his influence, Dickens may have "stunted" Collins' potential by urging him to curb his frank portrayal of sexuality and his critique of the Victorian middle class.[35] Certainly, the very act of writing for Dickens on the staff of *Household Words* may have represented a political choice on Collins' part. Before Collins switched over completely to writing for Dickens' journal, he had been writing for the *Leader*, a socialist journal founded by Thornton Hunt and George Henry Lewes in 1850. Collins contributed to the *Leader* between 1851 and 1856, during the period in which he wrote *Basil* and first began to work for Dickens.[36] Kirk Beetz claims that Collins was a "warm supporter of *The Leader*'s 'Red Republicanism,'"[37] but a sympathy with socialism would not have been unusual among intellectual circles; Dickens called himself a radical during the 1848 revolutions, and even Carlyle, in most ways a political conservative, supported them. Still, the transition during the latter part of the 1850s from writing for a radical journal to writing for middle-class publications like *Household Words*, which spoke to and for bourgeois domesticity, is significant in Collins' career. This choice mirrors the allegories in many of his novels of the male writer's choice between allying himself with radical causes and affirming his identity as part of the bourgeoisie.[38]

Gothic and the Marketplace: The Frame Narrative of After Dark

These tensions in Collins' artistic self-definition are particularly marked in his work of the 1850s and 1860s, the period in which his reputation and his career became firmly established. Even as his revision of Gothic was increasingly associated with "feminine" sensationalism and subversiveness, he was paradoxically placed in a position, like that of Mannion in *Basil*, of having to veil subversive elements in his writing so as not to tell "bitter truths" too bitterly. Yet, if Collins found himself in a position like that of marginalized groups (women and the working classes), who if they were not silent, were criticized for speaking too loudly, he also strove to achieve a voice through a literary professionalism that bespoke masculine and middle-class identity.

Whereas later chapters will discuss this kind of complexity in Collins' most famous works of the 1860s, *The Woman in White* and *The Moonstone*, the short-story collection *After Dark*, published in 1856, is an important early example of a split between a masculine and a feminine perspective. Different works of Collins' enact this tension between strands of masculine and feminine, of being politically engaged or of censoring politics, by embodying different viewpoints: a work with misogynist overtones like *Basil* is followed in 1857 by *The Dead Secret*, which takes as its central, and sympathetically rendered, character a working-class woman with an illegitimate child. Although Collins' novels are famous for their critiques of Victorian women's lack of legal and economic rights, even the most daring have misogynist elements, such as *Armadale* (1866), in which the remarkable and thoroughly Gothic Miss Gwilt attempts to murder her writer husband.

As if to emblematize this multivocal art, the frame narrative of *After Dark*, the collection compiled during the period when he left the *Leader* to write for Dickens, confuses the different voices that define it. In his preface Collins claims that he wishes to provide in the frame narrative "one more glimpse of the artist-life which circumstances have afforded me peculiar opportunities of studying":

> This time I wish to ask some sympathy for the joys and sorrows of a poor traveling portrait painter—presented from his wife's point of view in "Leah's Diary," and supposed to be briefly and simply narrated by himself in the Prologues to the stories. I have purposely kept these two portions of the book within certain limits; only giving, in the one case, as much as the wife might naturally write in her diary at intervals of household leisure; and, in the other, as much as a modest and sensible man would be likely to say about himself and the characters he met with in his wanderings.[39]

Collins asks for sympathy for the "poor traveling portrait-painter" who is the figure for the male artist in the frame narrative. Yet the joys and sorrows of the artist are only "supposed" to be narrated by himself in the prologues to the stories, an uncertainty about the male voice that draws attention to the strength of the female one: it is the wife of the artist whose point of view predominates within the frame narrative itself.

As Collins says, the frame narrative of *After Dark* tells the story of the male artist through excerpts from his wife's journal entitled "Leaves from Leah's Diary." In this diary Leah Kerby describes her husband William's unemployment: an itinerant portrait painter, he is temporarily blinded by an inflammation of the eyes that prevents him from pursuing his trade until he is cured and that threatens to reduce his family to destitution. A benevolent doctor helps the Kerbys find cheap lodging with a farmer's family, but Leah is the one who devises a scheme to make money: she will copy by dictation the amusing stories her husband has gathered from sitters while he paints their portraits, and the resulting book, if popular, will alleviate their financial crisis. Although William Kerby initially resists this plan, he eventually succumbs to his wife's overwhelming enthusiasm, and only the title of the collection remains in doubt. Leah acknowledges that she will not be able to write down the stories until "after dark" (30) because of her daytime chores in the house and the nursery, and the doctor triumphantly seizes on this phrase as the perfect title. When the frame narrative resumes briefly at the end of the stories, the husband has been cured and the book is about to be published.

Since the stories in the collection are tales of mystery and the Gothic, Collins' fictive description of how he came to write them compares his own endeavors with a feminine experience: the interstices of domestic labor are a suitably eerie time in which to create Gothic. Leah's transcribing Gothic stories after dark recalls Basil's reference to how he has "contracted the bad habit of writing at night." The sex of the Gothic writer has been changed, however, for even if Leah only tells her husband's stories, her idea for the title of the narrative she must write at night suggests that she, rather than he, is the originator of the Gothic. Yet Collins' own preface implies that the female perspective becomes central only when male vision fails: William can neither see nor write because he is blinded, so Leah must take his place.

Even as this partnership dilutes female linguistic authority by making Leah an amanuensis, like Clara in *Basil*, it also reduces male power. William Kerby is a diminished version of William Collins: both are painters, yet the homely surname Kerby testifies to the drop in social status between the William of the *Memoirs* and this destitute artist, referred to by his wife pityingly (and with an unintentional pun) as "poor William" on the first page of her narrative (9). This "poorness" is underscored in comically hyperbolic terms during his wife's narrative: "poor William . . . looking so sickly and sad, with his miserable green shade" (17). At another point the husband and children are implicitly lumped together: "the children difficult to manage; William miserably despondent" (21). Yet, despite this pathos, William Kerby does share William Collins' artistic vision. Just as Collins portrayed his father in the *Memoirs* as studying the minutest details to record Nature's truth, so William Kerby claims that portrait painting is "nothing but a right reading of the externals of character recognizably presented to the view of others" (36). In fact, Kerby asks his sitters to tell stories so that he can read their characters correctly, a sequence which implies that fiction making is a form of the father's art.

In the frame narrative's chronology, however, the precondition for fiction making is the male artist's weakness. Kerby's artistic vision is obscured by a blinding that, as a symbolic castration, repeats the imagery of sight and blindness in *Basil*. This image of the blinded male artist, however, recalls a scene within the *Memoirs* themselves, where Collins remembers that William was afflicted near the end of his life by a similar "inflammation of the eyes," which also had a temporarily blinding effect and had to be treated in the same way as William Kerby's malady (II, 165–67).

Whereas William Kerby's situation echoes William Collins', Leah's diary is apparently inspired by one written by Harriet Collins. According to William Clarke, Harriet had shared with her son a diary based on her experiences as an artist's wife, and Collins discussed the possibility of its publication with Dickens, concluding that it would be necessary to "make a story to hang your characters and incidents on."[40] The extent to which Harriet's diary reemerges as Leah's, however, is ambiguous, since Leah's story seems vastly different (William Collins' eye problems came later in life and never reduced the family to the dire straits of the Kerbys). What is significant about Harriet Collins' contribution to the idea of the frame narrative, however, is how it causes Collins to take a role similar to Kerby's. In the frame narrative, Leah is originator of a literary idea for which (since her husband writes the stories) she gets only secondary credit as scribe, a position similar to that of Harriet Collins, who evidently inspired the plot of her son's frame narrative. The status of the mother's writing here recalls the descriptions of Collins' father's paintings in the *Memoirs*, which Collins heard from her though he does not acknowledge this fact, any more than he admits any debt to his mother in his preface to *After Dark* (where he claims that the stories are "entirely of my own imagining" [6]). Whatever the extent of Harriet's contribution to Collins' plot, then, his relation to his mother's writing embodies the anxiety about the male artist's feminine rivals that shapes the frame narrative.

Yet at the same time, the presence of a maternal voice—Leah's if not Harriet's—in the frame narrative enhances the artistic innovation of *After Dark* by replacing Kerby's incapacitated masculine art with an image for feminine art. A narrative strand in the leaves of Leah's diary—which are necessarily fragments broken off by her domestic duties and not completed pieces of writing—records the story of a bead purse that her daughter is sewing, under her supervision, as a present for the daughter of the benevolent doctor-patron who has helped them. The story of the bead purse becomes such a refrain in the entries of Leah's diary—first it is "getting on fast" (15), and then there is a momentary crisis about the steel rings and tassels needed to complete it—that Leah comments when it is done, "So much for the highly interesting history of the bead purse" (17). Leah intends the phrase "highly interesting history" to resound ironically, since she assumes this domestic history would bore anyone not involved in it. Yet this type of history, even if private and domesticated, has a literary significance. The history of the bead purse becomes, like Leah's journal itself, the story of a type of feminine narrative; a craft taught by a mother to a daughter and given to another young girl would seem to symbolize the transmission of creativity between women writers in such feminine genres as the female Gothic, with which Leah, who writes after dark, has already been associated.

Leah's image of netting the bead purse is repeated by Collins in his preface to the collection, where he claims, "I have taken some pains to string together the various stories contained in this Volume on a single thread of interest" (5). This parallel between his own creativity and feminine domestic art—a parallel already suggested by the title *After Dark*—echoes in his own narrative method in the book, since the structure of the collection, with story after story and stories within stories, weaves a multiplicity of voices in place of a strictly linear literary unity. This type of multivoice narrative, a more positive version of the fragmentation of narrative voice in *Basil* because it stresses coherence amid diversity rather than simply a failure of aesthetic unity, anticipates the series of narrators in such later Collins works as *The Woman in White* and *The Moonstone*; in these narratives women and working-class characters often have as significant a voice as do middle-class men.

Yet although it is tempting to read the feminization of the writer in *After Dark* as empowering both for Collins and for the female voices within his works, this feminization, as in *Basil*, still expresses an ambivalence about being an artist in the marketplace. That Leah helps her daughter net a purse for the daughter of a male patron emphasizes the distance in economic status between the two families, since the doctor's daughter would have more to put in the purse than would her own child. That a purse is an image for the woman's text, which we know to be a Gothic one, implies that the genre is itself a commodity: like a woman writer of sensation fiction, Leah hopes that the book bought by her other patrons, the reading audience, will be a popular one so as to garner the most money.

Moreover, read as a symbol for the female genitals, the purse conflates sexual and economic meanings to suggest that selling writing in the marketplace is a form of prostitution. The doctor, who abets the book project, hints at such a reading when he claims that Leah is worth her weight in gold and that she is "all ready to get into the bookseller's scales and prove it" (29). This image of his wife selling herself as well as her book reinforces the emasculation of William Kerby that is suggested not only by his blindness, but also by his wife's ingenuity at making the money he can no longer earn. Although Leah's scheme is formed in response to the doctor's worry that William will fret at "the prospect of sitting idle and being kept by his wife" (15), it strengthens her power within the household, although at the price of her symbolic prostitution in a system of exchange outside the home. Through this image of prostitution, Leah becomes a figure not only for the working woman but also for Victorian anxiety about that figure; as Leonore Davidoff and Catherine Hall have argued in *Family Fortunes*, by laboring outside the home the working woman threatened both domesticity and the class identity of bourgeois men, defined by their ability to provide for women and children.[41]

Although this image of Leah's selling herself for money reveals an anxiety about female economic autonomy, it more specifically targets the autonomy of the woman writer who usurps her husband's role as provider with her "ready pen" (33). The figure of the writer as prostitute, however, represents the degradation of male, as well as female, writing, as Catherine Gallagher argues when she identifies the image of "the author as whore" as one that is "disabling, empowering and central to nineteenth-century consciousness."[42] Although Gallagher, reading *Daniel Deronda*, focuses on attitudes about professional women writers in Victorian England, she claims that the image of prostitute, like that of the Jewish usurer, can also be applied to men: "the activities of authoring, of procuring illegitimate income, and of alienating oneself through prostitution seem particularly closely associated with one another in the Victorian period."[43] Especially since we can read Leah as a figure who is more closely aligned than her husband is with what Collins himself does—she writes for money and she embodies a new type of female Gothic—the prostitution image describes the position of the male writer in the marketplace: if a man is like a woman, it is because what Gayle Rubin calls "the traffic in women," or their sexual barter, becomes an apt metaphor for the Victorian male writer's economic vulnerability.[44]

At the same time that it echoes the image of the mother as harlot in *Antonina*, prostitution in *After Dark* is linked to the theme of declining paternal authority, and the waning power of male literary authority, that Collins had explored in earlier works. Gallagher claims that the figure of literary paternity is associated with the idea of the "procreative Word," unlike prostitution, which becomes an image for "the written word as an arbitrary and conventional sign multiplying unnaturally in the mere process of exchange."[45] Yet just as she also argues that the prostitution image could be "empowering" for the women writers who transform it into a figure for their newfound linguistic creativity, Collins' metaphors for writing in the marketplace are not sheerly negative. For one thing, Leah is associated with a new type of literary generativity. Although she begins her journal by asserting that she is happy she has no more children to feed (9), the book becomes her baby in that its conception, as she says, "originated with *me*" (22). In a domesticated version of Mary Shelley's command in the 1831 preface to *Frankenstein* to her "hideous progeny" to "go forth and prosper," Leah calls the book her "third child," which has "gone out from us on this summer's day, to seek its fortune in the world" (540).

Still, it is uncertain whether Leah's book-baby—which after all is Collins'—is a monster offspring or not. In his preface to *After Dark*, Collins uses the metaphor of procreation to describe his work:

> Let me, once for all, assure any readers who may honor me with their attention, that in this, and in all other cases, they may depend on the genuineness of my literary offspring. The little children of my brain may be weakly enough, and may be sadly in want of a helping hand to aid them in their first attempts at walking on the stage of this great world; but, at any rate, they are not borrowed children. The members of my own literary family are indeed increasing so fast as to render the very idea of borrowing quite out of the question, and to suggest serious apprehension that I may not have done adding to the large book-population, on my own sole responsibility, even yet. (7)

For Collins to call his books "the little children of my brain" does not necessarily feminize him, since the metaphor attests to his masculine potency. (By stressing his originality, it certainly excludes his own mother as coauthor.) Yet Collins' paternal authority may, like William Kerby's, become diluted if he is unable to provide for his "weakly" children who are part of a vast array of books in the marketplace ("the large book-population") that multiply like a Malthusian vision of the lower classes.

In spite of Collins' protests to the contrary, this ceaseless multiplication of books suggests a kind of unoriginality, or repetition of meaning, caused by the need of the writer in the marketplace to produce a "numerous" family. Yet Collins' use at the beginning of the preface of

Leah's image of stringing together threads implies a more positive and innovative version of literary creativity than does his image of literary paternity. Similarly, when the act of generating books within the narrative is associated with Leah's motherhood rather than with William's fatherhood, it signifies a revolutionary originality. Developing the image implicit in her description of how the idea for the book "flashed" upon her, Leah asks: "Did Friar Bacon long to dance when he lit the match and heard the first charge of gunpowder in the world go off with a bang" (25). The violence of this image underscores the inversion of gender roles that Leah's idea has brought about—she is the head of the household now—even as it likens the figure for the woman writer in the marketplace to the "great men" of which Friar Bacon is one (Leah also compares herself to Isaac Newton). Elsewhere, William admits that his wife's idea is "an ingenious idea, and a bold idea" (28). Rather than merely initiating a system of exchange in which signs are arbitrary, Leah's entry into the marketplace thus signifies the advent of radical new ideas.

"Sister Rose": Revolution and the Female Voice

Leah implies that her writing is a revolutionary innovation, and the longest story that her husband tells is a tale about the French Revolution entitled "Sister Rose." Although this story was originally published in *Household Words* in 1855, as the central tale in *After Dark* it reflects the gender and class anxieties expressed in the frame narrative and represents, through the displaced form of the historical narrative, the tensions in Collins' professional self-definition during the 1850s and 1860s.

In particular the tension between masculine professionalism and feminine writing is figured by the confusion between male and female voices in the telling of the story. Within the frame narrative Collins suggests that Leah's voice may overwhelm her husband's, an anxiety about women's writing that resurfaces later. Although William's voice succeeds Leah's as he introduces each story, the tale of Sister Rose is related to him by a woman, a sitter whom he calls the French Governess. In the introduction to "Sister Rose," William explains how he came to tell this feminine narrative after meeting the governess, an employee of an English family who had become a substitute mother to its motherless daughters. As he paints a picture of Mademoiselle as a gift for one of the daughters, who is moving to India, his sitter tells him the story of a woman she calls Sister Rose, whose likeness she wears in a miniature that she insists William reproduce in her own portrait. Although the story of Rose, who is now dead, takes place during the French Revolution, the governess herself is a living embodiment of revolutionary history, quoting *Candide* and mixing her narrative with "outbursts of passionate political declamation, on the extreme liberal side" (117).

That these political outbursts are not repeated within William's version of the governess' tale testifies to his attempt to modulate her voice by imposing his own on it. As he explains, he must modify Mademoiselle's words both because of her political remarks and because of her general manner of telling the tale in "the most fragmentary and discursive manner" (117). Whereas this fragmentary female speech recalls the fragmenting of conventional narrative coherence in the leaves of Leah's diary, William's attempt to retell the governess' tale by "rigidly adhering to the events of it exactly as they were related" (117) substitutes a masculine form of narrative for a feminine one. Yet since we know that Leah rewrites the words her husband repeats, the voice of the male artist is actually sandwiched between those of two women.

These complex concentric circles of narrative add several layers of irony to the tale of Sister Rose. The hidden voice of the female amanuensis undermines the male narrator's attempts to reassert the primacy of his voice over a woman's. Having been pushed to the periphery of the narrative, however, Leah's voice wields its power only from a distance, as does the voice of the governess herself.[46] This marginalization of the female voice is represented through the relation of the miniature of Sister Rose, the female subject of the tale, to the story she inspires. This miniature, bequeathed to the governess who was her "dearest friend" (113), recalls the picture of Caroline Beaufort in *Frankenstein* willed to Elizabeth Lavenza. As in Shelley's novel, a legacy transmitted from one woman to another is intercepted by a male figure who here repaints the miniature in his own portrait of the governess. This symbolic appropriation of the female voice by the male artist anticipates the struggle for primacy between male and female voices within the story itself.

The story that the French governess tells is not, as its title might imply, about a nun, but about a woman named Rose Danville, who is the sister of the major male character, Louis Trudaine, who promises to look after her at their dying mother's request. Trudaine, a scientist, even rejects an offer from the French Academy for an important position because he is concerned about Rose's mistreatment by her haughty aristocratic husband, Charles Danville. The story begins in 1789, on the verge of the outbreak of the revolution, and continues during the period just before the end of the Reign of Terror in 1794, when Danville, who resents Trudaine's influence over his sister, denounces him to the revolutionary tribunal. Unbeknown to Danville, however, the suspicious behavior of Trudaine and Rose that he has observed and intends to use as a way of revenging himself on his wife's brother represents their joint efforts to help Danville's mother, an unabashed royalist, escape to safety outside France. Although Trudaine and Rose are arrested and condemned, they are saved from the guillotine by a former servant of the Danvilles named Lomaque, who has become a major official in the secret police but retains a loyalty to Trudaine, whose father helped his own, and to Rose, who was once kind to him. In a final confrontation after the Terror, Trudaine denounces Danville, who is unwittingly about to commit bigamy because he assumes that his wife and brother-in-law perished during the revolution. When the full extent of Danville's treachery is revealed (he helped to convict Rose and Trudaine by pretending that he knew of the plot to save his mother and acted as a fervent patriot by informing on her rescuers), his mother rejects him and the father of the woman he was about to marry kills him in a duel. The story ends with Rose, Trudaine, and Lomaque—adopted by the grateful pair he has saved—living together as one family.

In its focus on an incestuously close relationship between a brother and a sister, this narrative is indebted most obviously to *Basil*, but also through that novel to *Frankenstein*, with its plot concerning the bond between Frankenstein and his sisterlike spouse, Elizabeth Lavenza.

The figure of Lomaque also recalls both Frankenstein's monster and Mannion; his "wrinkled, haggard face" (142) is reminiscent of the seamed face of Shelley's monster, but Lomaque's ressentiment of his servile status determines his later allegiance to the revolution. Yet Lomaque is a revision of the kind of monstrous outcast embodied both by the monster and by Mannion because he domesticates revolution, betraying the revolutionary government he serves to save a family. His situation reverses Mannion's because he saves the son of a man who had been kind to his father (rather than, like the earlier character, revenging himself on the son of a man who hadn't). Moreover, Lomaque is touched by the kindness Shelley's monster never receives: he helps Rose for no other reason than because she once kept a cup of coffee hot for him.

Lomaque, however, is not the only male character whose rebellion against the family is tamed, since Trudaine himself is a domesticated Frankenstein figure. Although he is an "amateur professor of the occult arts of chemistry" (127), whose research Danville sneeringly characterizes as a search for the "Elixir of Life," Trudaine is not, like Frankenstein, so much a figure for the revolutionary metaphysician as he is for an emergent bourgeois professionalism. His devotion to chemistry, which causes him to be courted by the French Academy, recalls Collins' description in the original preface to *Basil* of professional writers as those who "follow Literature as a study and respect it as a science" (I, xvii [1852]). Yet Trudaine, who claims that the best elixir of life is the "quiet heart" and "contented mind" he has found in his sister's company (127), abandons professional ambitions to live, like Basil, in the private world of women.

This decision, although it indicates the extent of Trudaine's allegiance to domesticity, is implicitly emasculating. Although Trudaine claims that he has learned to feel toward his orphan sister "more as a father than as a brother" (134), fulfilling his mother's deathbed promise—"Be all to her, Louis, that I have been" (145)—has placed him in a feminine role. His assumption of his mother's position, in fact, makes him like the French governess, who tells his sister's story and who is a "second mother" to the motherless daughters in her charge (108). The most dramatic way that Trudaine's association with the feminine effaces his career, however, is through his rescue from the guillotine. Lomaque borrows a chemical formula from Trudaine to erase the names of both brother and sister from the death list, an erasure that symbolizes how Trudaine's profession and his masculinity have been made into a blank. This blankness in turn links him with the femininity associated with absence and blankness through Rose, whose gentle self-effacement embodies an idealized femininity.

Yet, as in the female Gothic, the power of women is as terrifying to men as their powerlessness. Although Rose is terrorized by her marriage to a brutal aristocrat, the revolution that triumphs over the aristocracy liberates her from that marriage to transform her, albeit temporarily, into a symbol for the Terror itself. Her nervousness, a signifier for the female Gothic plot of imprisonment and claustrophobia that engulfs her, blossoms into a shrill and hysterical voice during her imprisonment and trial. Trudaine's arrest in her husband's presence causes Rose to resist her cruel husband openly for the first time, as she seizes his arm in the "recklessness of terror . . . with both hands—frail, trembling hands—that seemed suddenly nerved with all the strength of a man's. 'Come here—come here! I must and will speak to you!'" (174). The outbreak of both Rose's violence and her voice coincides with the eruption of a revolution associated with women as well as with figures for class ressentiment like Lomaque. At Rose's trial the major part of the audience are women: "all sitting together on forms, knitting, shirt-mending, and baby-linen-making, as coolly as if they were at home" (183).

While she is defending herself, Rose's voice resembles that of this female audience, which often shrilly interrupts the proceedings. Although her brother does not want her to talk and further incriminate herself (even claiming that her efforts to speak reflect a temporary madness), Rose becomes an image for the revolutionary virago as she speaks over his voice, which had momentarily "overpowered" her own (190): "Her hair lay tangled on her shoulders; her face had assumed a strange fixedness; her gentle blue eyes, so soft and tender at all other times, were lit up wildly. A low hum of murmured curiosity and admiration broke from the women of the audience" (190). This female audience even clears the way for Rose's voice: "'Let her speak! let her speak!' exclaimed the women" (191). Earlier the "winning gentleness of her voice" (166–67) had been described as Rose's most remarkable feature, but that voice now is conflated with that of the Terror.

After the trial, however, Rose is silenced, "her head sunk on her bosom, her hands crossed listlessly on her lap" (206). Collins ascribes this silence to "that spirit of resignation, which is the courage of women in all great emergencies" and which now seems like "the one animating spirit that fed the flame of life within her" (213–14). This transformation of Rose's feminine flaming eloquence into feminine silent resignation prepares for her brother's assuming the role of her savior: she does not even know of Lomaque's plan to save their lives until some time afterward. This attempt to contain the female power associated with the revolution is mirrored by the way the revolutionary women themselves are relegated to signifiers of domesticity. Although the female audience seem to be monstrous mothers as they sew baby linen at the revolutionary tribunal, they are horrified by Danville's boast that he would inform on his own mother: "the fiercest woman-republican on the benches joined cause at last with the haughtiest woman-aristocrat on the platform. Even in that sphere of direst discords . . . the one touch of Nature preserved its old eternal virtue, and roused the mother-instinct which makes the whole world kin" (201).

This invocation of a universal feminine nature dovetails with the mission of the journal that first serialized the story, *Household Words*, which similarly valorized domesticity as the ideology that, although bourgeois in origin, nonetheless spoke to and united all classes. Still, in "Sister Rose," even the "mother-instinct" that allies "the fiercest woman-republican" with the "haughtiest woman-aristocrat" escapes from the boundaries of a conventional domesticity to threaten men. Besides the unnervingly dangerous makers of baby linen at the trial (predecessors of Dickens' *tricoteuses*),[47] the story's figure for a disruptive rather than an angelic mother is Madame Danville, Rose's mother-in-law, disapprovingly called "that passionate woman" by Trudaine (145). Madame Danville's voice, however, is silenced by terror: paralyzed with fear at the end of the story when she spots Rose, whom she thought dead, "She neither spoke nor moved" (255). She is stricken by the evidence of her son's perfidy with an illness that "affects her mind more than her body" (260), a mental imbalance that recalls the hysterical near-madness that Trudaine ascribes to Rose when she wants to speak at the trial.

This diagnosis of femininity as disease associates masculinity with the diagnostic power of reason. Unlike Basil, who could not see, discriminate, or know, Trudaine, for all his association with feminine blankness, is nonetheless possessed of a knowledge that saves both himself and his sister from the guillotine. Similarly, the crabbed police agent Lomaque, despite the belatedness for which he castigates himself —"too late to speak—too late to act—too late to do anything!" (136) —becomes the tale's figure for detection and plotting, uncovering the "impenetrable mystery" of Madame Danville's escape and planning Trudaine and Rose's. The rise of this figure for male detection, Collins' most important narrative innovation and one he would develop in such later novels as *The Woman in White* and *The Moonstone*, represents an attempt to reassert male authority by emphasizing men's analytical power and their ability not only to be differentiated from, but also to read and control the feminine. In "Sister Rose," however, this strategy is only partially successful, for though it silences Rose, both Trudaine and Lomaque (whose "weakness of the eyes" suggests the tenuous nature of his reading skill and recalls the weakened figure of William Kerby) end their days with Rose in a domestic obscurity that banishes history.

By effecting what by now seems to be Collins' trademark ending—a containment both of female power and of history—"Sister Rose" apparently invokes revolution in order to extinguish it. This pattern is emphasized by two of the tales that surround "Sister Rose" in *After Dark*, which are even more conservative parables about the French Revolution. In "A Terribly Strange Bed," the first story of the collection and one of Collins' most extraordinary mystery tales, an Englishman is almost robbed and murdered by a group of charlatans who arrange for the canopy of a bed to descend upon him in his sleep—an image that suggests sexual suffocation. It is telling that one of the architects of the murderous plan is a veteran of Napoleon's army, and hence a relic of the threat the French Revolution posed to the English. (Not surprisingly, it is the English narrator's skill at detecting the danger of his situation that saves him.) Although "Gabriel's Marriage," the second story after "Sister Rose," is told by a female narrator, it similarly celebrates the Catholic reaction against the French Revolution in a plot about the reconciliation of fathers and sons. The mingling of different types of discourse about revolution in these tales mirrors the mixture of male and female voices in the frame narrative and tales like "Sister Rose."

In spite of her silencing, however, the figure of Sister Rose in some sense bridges the ideological gaps within *After Dark* and, particularly, within the story that bears her name. The pun implicit in Rose's name—she rises from the dead to confront her oppressive husband—suggests that the ghostly presence of revolution in *After Dark* persists despite its attempted erasure. William Marshall sees Rose's apparent resurrection as an example of the theme of "the return to life of those presumed by someone to be dead," which repeats itself continually in Collins' fiction, most famously in *The Woman in White*, where Laura Fairlie must reestablish her legal identity after her double is buried in her place.[48] In "Sister Rose," this resurrection of the dead is a return of the repressed, since Rose's story, told by the French governess, provokes a resurrection both of feminine power and of revolutionary history.

As if haunted by these ghosts, William Kerby ends his retelling of Rose's story by confessing that he finds it difficult to end:

> I linger over these final particulars with a strange unwillingness to separate myself from them, and give my mind to other thoughts. Perhaps the persons and events that have occupied my attention for so many nights past have some peculiar interest for me that I cannot analyze. Perhaps the labor and time which this story has cost me have especially endeared it to my sympathies, now that I have succeeded in completing it. However that may be, I have need of some resolution to part at last with Sister Rose, and return, in the interests of my next and Fourth Story, to English ground. (263–64)

As if he finds the spell of Rose's femininity particularly compelling, William admits to needing masculine "resolution" in order to leave her story. The trancelike hold of the story, however, paralyzes even his ability to choose another to tell, precipitating his wife to make that decision "on her own responsibility" (264). Since we know that his wife is writing down the story of Sister Rose and that the "labor" in crafting the story is partly hers, this resurrection of a female voice renders ironic both Kerby's relief at returning from the foreign ground of the story to comfortable English safeness, and the attempt within the story to contain female power.

Yet William Kerby's lingering over the story of Sister Rose is important not just for the resurrection of female power that this moment implies. That William claims he cannot analyze the attraction the story has for him suggests that he refuses to do so, possibly because the narrative is compelling for him as an artist who has (albeit unwillingly) entered the marketplace. As a story that, through Lomaque, contains a narrative about class ressentiment, "Sister Rose" might be a compelling tale for a male artist who is economically marginalized. The juxtaposition of a historical fiction about revolution with the frame narrative, which so obsessively figures the blurring of gender and class boundaries in the marketplace, underscores how "Sister Rose" figures the ambiguous status of the Victorian male writer. The Gothic governs this symbolic narrative: William ponders on the story that he, like his wife, has told after dark—"for so many nights past." The writing of Gothic again represents the ideological choices available to the male writer. Within the story Rose's voice, like Leah's, figures kinds of subversive feminine narratives, yet if the figure for the male artist (Trudaine or William) does not identify himself with this revolutionary voice, he nonetheless resembles women in their economic and social vulnerability. When Leah's voice resumes the frame narrative at the end of *After Dark*, she does not describe the restoration of her husband's power with the cure of his blindness. Instead she reveals a dependency on the marketplace that causes the narrative to end in a limbo only emphasized by the final reference to Gothic obscurity: "Oh, Public! Public! it all depends now upon you . . . our future way in this hard world is to be smoothed for us at the outset, if you will only accept a poor painter's stories which his wife has written down for him After Dark!" (543–44).[49]

Five

The Woman in White: Portrait of the Artist as a Professional Man

The spectacular popular success of *The Woman in White* in 1860 was the most triumphant moment in Collins' career. More completely than any of his earlier works, this novel transformed him from a promising young protégé of Dickens into an author of established reputation and one of the most popular novelists writing in English during the nineteenth century. Not surprisingly, this popularity translated into economic security: Collins was able to negotiate a lucrative contract for his next novel, *No Name*, on the strength of the reception of *The Woman in White*, and his income from his writing remained high during the rest of his career.[1] Even as this monetary success attests to Collins' attainment of a secure position in the marketplace, it is also evidence of the marketplace's power to transform both text and author into a seemingly endless series of commodities: while his best-selling novel was reproduced as Woman in White perfume, bonnets, and quadrilles, Collins reproduced himself, with the reissue of such early works as *Basil* and *Hide and Seek*, as "the author of *The Woman in White*."

It was, however, the novel's very status as commodity—not merely as a best seller but as a rage, a sensation, a stimulating food to be "devoured" in one sitting[2]—that contributed to its mixed reception as a work of art. Although many critics admired it, both positive and negative notices codified the reading of the aesthetic value of Collins' fiction that was destined to become as canonical as the fiction was not. According to most critics, *The Woman in White* demonstrated that Collins was a master of construction but deficient in the portrayal of character; one of the most hostile, calling him a "manufacturer of stories," dismissed his plots as a type of soulless modern machinery. The *Saturday Review*, though using a less industrially coded metaphor, likened the novel's plot to ingenious "cabinet-making and joining," and pronounced its "mechanical talent . . . not enough to entitle a man to a rank as a great artist."[3] Having disparaged the canonicity of Collins' art, this critic made the comment, to which I referred in the previous chapter, that Collins' characters, like Pope's women, have no character at all.

It is ironic, if appropriate, that these events surrounding the publication of *The Woman in White* replicate the tensions within the text itself. The novel that achieved such success in the marketplace is animated by an ambivalence about the marketplace and its process of commodification; the work that provoked a comparison of its author's art to feminine fallenness and invisibility revolves around the attempts of a male artist to detach himself from the world of women and their blank "whiteness," or lack of social identity. Although *The Woman in White* is named after one of its female characters, its central figure is Walter Hartright, a drawing master of impoverished gentility who gradually rises in social status to become securely established in his profession and, finally, even a member of the landed gentry. This emphasis on the rise of the artist is reinforced by his literary significance within the text: not only does Hartright's narrative begin and end the novel, but he is also the editor of the other first-person accounts that compose it, a role as guardian and interpreter of the "truth"[4] of the conspiracy against Laura Fairlie that has led one critic to identify him as the novel's "rhetorical hero."[5]

This attempt to endow a character who begins his career as a wage slave with both economic and literary power represents an important development of the tale of the male artist in the marketplace that Collins conceived in such works as *Basil* and *After Dark*. Yet the significance of *The Woman in White* in Collins' canon rests on more than its revision of the familiar male plot in his fiction. The novel also develops and foregrounds the feminist elements in Collins' earlier works, such as the theme of women's oppression in *Basil* and the tales of outcast women with illegitimate children in *Hide and Seek* and *The Dead Secret*, the latter particularly noteworthy for its female Gothic narrative of the daughter who is reunited with her lost mother. As the most fully realized of these Gothic narratives, and the one most firmly structured by a critique of women's legal and economic inequality in Victorian Britain, *The Woman in White* is at once an extraordinarily feminist, as well as a Radcliffean, work.

It is the intersection, and indeed the collision, of the male and female plots of the novel that constitutes its aesthetic and ideological complexity. Anne Catherick, the woman in white, marks the analogy between the story of the novel's oppressed women and that of Walter Hartright, the artist as wage slave, who resembles the women in his lack of a clearly defined masculine and middle-class identity within the marketplace. Anne Catherick also embodies the tension, however, between these masculine and feminine narratives; as a figure for the confusion of gender and class boundaries, she is the locus of Collins' ambivalence about the male artist's association with women. The resolution of the novel, in fact, is devoted to redefining the gender and class distinctions that she disrupts in its attempt to instate a domestic ideology where the professional man prospers in the marketplace by distinguishing himself from women, who in turn are relegated to the private sphere where they safeguard and reproduce the fruits of men's labor.

Female Gothic and Feminine Experience in The Woman in White

The feminist elements of *The Woman in White* have often been noted by critics, who call attention to how the novel expresses a strong critique of Victorian women's disadvantaged economic and legal position, especially within marriage.[6] The weapon that allows Percival Glyde and Fosco to launch their conspiracy against Laura Fairlie is a marriage settlement that deprives her of power over her inheritance, a plot that emphasizes the lack of legal control Victorian wives had over their money prior to the Married Women's Property Acts of 1870 and 1882. Anne Catherick, the woman in white, embodies the social invisibility that renders women blank pages to be inscribed by men. In the case of Laura, Anne's double, this is effected by the law of the father, who wills her engagement to Percival Glyde as his dying wish. The creaky yet purposeful archaism of this plot—for Laura's hyperbolic lack of choice about her marriage partner invokes an earlier era —has two important narrative functions. First, it suggests that women's disenfranchised position is anachronistic (it is, after all, a nearly dead patriarch who exerts such control over his daughter's life), and second, it underscores the novel's generic indebtedness by setting in motion all kinds of melodramatically Gothic machinery.

The Woman in White is, indeed, of all Collins' novels the one most steeped in the conventions of the female Gothic. Henry James identified the presence of these conventions in the novel at the same time he characterized the difference between Collins and his most important female predecessor, "Mrs. Radcliffe's mysteries were romances pure and simple; while those of Mr. Wilkie Collins were stern reality."[7] This comment underscores the compelling contemporaneity of female Gothic in *The Woman in White*, but underestimates how much Collins is indebted to Radcliffe precisely for her figuration of domesticity as nightmare. Percival Glyde's attempts to force Laura to sign away all remaining control over her money are patently modeled on Montoni's similar efforts in *Udolpho* to compel his wife to abdicate control of her wealth; that Laura only narrowly escapes Madame Montoni's fate, being hounded to her death for her fortune, draws attention to the rapaciousness of the Victorian legal and economic system concerning women. Blackwater Park, the gloomy site of Glyde's oppression of his wife, is Collins' nod to Radcliffe's Udolpho as well as, one suspects, to Brontë's Thornfield, the house in which a wife is (as Laura will be) incarcerated as a madwoman. "Suffocated" by trees (177), the claustrophobic Blackwater represents women's experience in true Gothic style as a kind of stifling prison sentence; it is here that Marian Halcombe laments she is "condemned to patience, propriety, and petticoats, for life" (178). Not surprisingly, Marian is imprisoned by Fosco in the most crumbling and Gothic section of the mansion while Laura is sent to London to take Anne's place.

Within this carceral world, Collins represents the family romance as a Radcliffean narrative in which the daughters share the mother's invisibility; the novel's most central symbolic site is the grave of Laura and Marian's mother, which functions as an image for women's lack of identity. Mrs. Fairlie shares her grave with Anne Catherick, the adoptive daughter who wears white at her behest; engraved on the "fair" and blank whiteness of their tombstone is the inscription that falsely identifies Anne as Laura, causing Laura to be symbolically buried alive.

Anne Catherick thus concentrates the novel's female Gothic imagery and indeed acts as a walking signifier for that genre's claustrophobic narrative. Her imprisonment in an asylum by the man who will become Laura's oppressive husband updates the classic Radcliffean plot as a specifically Victorian version of Gothic that encodes contemporary concerns about the treatment of the insane, particularly of mentally ill women who were subject to unjust incarceration.[8] Anne, however, is more than simply the victim she initially appears to be. With her cry to Walter Hartright—"I have been cruelly used and cruelly wronged" (19)—she also embodies the radically feminist version of the female Gothic plot, an allusion strengthened by the resemblance of her story to that of Wollstonecraft's Maria, that icon of the "wrongs of woman." In her escape from the asylum, and thus from the female Gothic narrative that encloses her, Anne represents the "resistance" (272) to male rule that Marian, the novel's most obviously rebellious woman, vows to undertake when Percival Glyde abuses his wife.

Male Insecurity and Walter Hartright's Story

The story of Marian's resistance is concentrated in her lengthy journal entry written at Blackwater Park, which is also the most female Gothic portion of the novel. In her entries at Blackwater as well as the earlier ones written at Limmeridge, Marian describes the Gothic oppressiveness of her sister's situation while interjecting her criticism of women's situation and her defiance of men. Whereas her journal entries before Laura's marriage record her objection to men's role in marriage —"They are the enemies of our innocence and our peace—they drag us away from our parents' love and our sisters' friendship" (162)—her narrative at Blackwater reports her threat to Glyde and Fosco: "There are laws in England to protect women from cruelty and outrage. If you hurt a hair of Laura's head, if you dare to interfere with my freedom, come what come may, to those laws I will appeal" (267).

Yet even if, as Peter Brooks points out, Marian's narrative of resistance at Blackwater lies "at the center of the text,"[9] *The Woman in White* has a doubled focus since Walter Hartright's narrative constitutes, as William Marshall has said, the "structural center" of the novel.[10] As in *After Dark*, with its male and female narratives, the major voices in *The Woman in White* are Hartright's and Marian's perspectives on the conspiracy against Laura. Yet even though Marian's voice has a greater centrality than Leah's did in *After Dark*, where the female voice was on the margins of the text, Walter Hartright's voice has a greater textual significance. It is Hartright who claims the right to "guide" the reader (379) and to unravel the "tangled web" of the conspiracy against Laura, since it is he who is editor as well as author. As editor-in-chief of the novel's many narratives, Hartright has the power to solicit writing from other characters, to arrange the order of the narratives, and even to delete what seems extraneous; we hear in one of his editorial notes, for example, that passages from Marian's diary having nothing to do with the conspiracy have been omitted (145). This position as what U. C. Knoepflmacher has called "the prime orderer"[11] of the novel extends to the Adamic power of naming; toward the end of the narrative we hear that Hartright has renamed the characters to safeguard their anonymity. In a novel so concerned with the importance of identity, Hartright's power to determine identity supports his interpretation of characters in his narrative; as Knoepflmacher claims, Hartright's naming his wife Laura makes him her Petrarch and writes her firmly into the role of silent object of his devotion.[12]

As in *After Dark*, then, there is an obvious tension between the male and female voices in *The Woman in White*. Hartright, who will later join the staff of a periodical, becomes a figure for the Victorian professional artist who, like Dickens and his periodicals, is author and editor at the same time. In this role as a male voice of authority, he has as much at stake in controlling the novel's female voices as Glyde and Fosco, the more obviously chauvinistic figures, have in taming the novel's women.

At the beginning of the novel, however, there is more congruence than dissonance between Hartright's and the women's experiences.

Like the women, who are linked by the "whiteness" of their lack of social identity, Hartright is a powerless figure in the period comprising his first narrative. This powerlessness stems from a crisis of class definition, as Hartright uses the rhetoric of professionalism to describe what is in fact an economically marginal existence. At the time the story begins Hartright remarks that, for his own "poor part," he is out of spirits, and in the next sentence he attributes his mood having "not managed my professional resources as carefully as usual" (2). The ambiguous class status suggested by this genteel poverty undercuts the professionalism he claims to have inherited from his father, a figure who sounds very familiar after the *Memoirs*. That Hartright's father had been "a drawing master before me" and that "his exertions had made him highly successful in his profession" (2) recall not only Collins' description of William Collins, but also how the father in the *Memoirs* represents the successful transition from Romanticism to the Victorian era, in which the artist is businessman.

Hartright's narrative, in fact, begins with his tribute to his father's professionalism:

> His exertions had made him highly successful in his profession; and his affectionate anxiety to provide for the future of those who were dependent on his labours, had impelled him, from the time of his marriage, to devote to the insuring of his life a much larger portion of his income than most men consider it necessary to set aside for this purpose. Thanks to his admirable prudence and self-denial, my mother and sisters were left, after his death, as independent of the world as they had been during his lifetime. I succeeded to his connexion, and had every reason to feel grateful for the prospect that awaited me at my starting in life. (2–3)

As in *After Dark*, however, the artist's situation in *The Woman in White* has become economically degraded. Having insisted that his artistic prospects are good, Hartright's description following this of the "quiet twilight . . . trembling" (3) around London underscores the elegiac, rather than the hopeful, note in his eulogy to the father whose professional "connexion" he has supposedly inherited. His own artistic prospects are obviously clouded by the poverty that makes it difficult for him to attain even the modest professional status of his father. Moreover, Hartright's description of his father imperfectly conceals that it took him a lifetime of "self-denial" to bequeath even a genteel poverty to his dependents.

This mention of self-denial also suggests an insecure gender, as well as class, status: Walter praises in Marian Halcombe the "sublime self-forgetfulness *of women*" (504; my emphasis), and it is evident that Marian's self-denial is one of her feminine (rather than masculine) traits. In Hartright's father, this feminine self-denial might appear to be its masculine antithesis, the kind of diligence and ambition that secures the elder Collins' status as patriarch in the son's biography. Yet the term "self-denial" points to what is nebulous both in the professional ideal and in the ideology that reinforces it, the Victorian cult of manliness. The father might appear to be manly by supporting women, leaving his wife and daughter "independent of the world," and thus preserving the division between a rigorously isolated domestic unit and the work place that was essential to the ideology of the bourgeois family. Yet the difficulty with which the son maintains this division is suggested when he faces the prospect of returning to his mother's home for part of the week in order to live economically (2). Hartright's narrative, which begins with his biweekly visit to his mother's cottage (3), demonstrates how easily the son can come to share the status of women—the mother and sister with whom he associates —rather than supporting a wife and children of his own.

This symbolic emasculation of the male artist is continued at Limmeridge House, where the drawing master is not master of his fate. That role is assumed by Hartright's aristocratic employer, Frederick Fairlie, a man whose "haughty familiarity and impudent politeness" (37) are resented by his employee. Hartright's employment at Limmeridge House once again casts him into the company of women, namely Marian, Laura, and Mrs. Vesey, whose "female amiability" was defined by her extreme passivity: "Mrs. Vesey *sat* through life" (38). The account of Mrs. Vesey's hyperbolic passivity, which amounts to downright paralysis, follows Hartright's description of the difficulty with which he himself acts and underscores his resemblance to the novel's women. On the first page of his narrative, he emerges from a state of near-torpor: "I roused myself from the book I was dreaming over rather than reading, and left my chambers to meet the cool night air in the suburbs" (2). Ironically, this attempt to rouse himself only leads to the scene at his mother's cottage where, told by Pesca he has the position at Limmeridge House, he admits to an "inexplicable unwillingness within me to stir in the matter" (11).

This language of impotence foreshadows the position in which Hartright finds himself at Limmeridge, where his economic degradation is mirrored by his inability to express his love for his employer's niece. In describing how in the past he has had to repress any sexual feelings he may have for his female charges, Hartright explains, in a significant phallic image, that he habitually leaves "the sympathies natural to my age in my employer's outer hall, as coolly as I left my umbrella there" (54). Such repression, he adds, makes him a "harmless domestic animal" (55), a pointed allusion in a novel that often makes the Wollstonecraftian equation between women's lot and that of pet dogs.[13] At Limmeridge, Hartright's illicit passion for Laura recalls the Héloïse and Abélard story that Basil alludes to in his instruction of Margaret (102). Yet Hartright, in his position as the poor teacher of a woman who belongs to a higher class, resembles Basil less than he does Mannion, the hack writer and monster of ressentiment.[14]

Revolution and the Multivalence of the Woman in White

The most obvious and dramatic point at which these stories of female and male disempowerment intersect is when Anne Catherick first startles Hartright on the road from Hampstead to London in a moment of sheer Gothic terror: "in one moment, every drop of blood in my body was brought to a stop by the touch of a hand laid lightly and suddenly on my shoulder from behind me" (15). That Hartright should meet this spectral figure on the night before he departs for Limmeridge underscores the analogy between the situation of the "cruelly wronged" woman and himself, about to enter yet another form of genteel wage slavery. The female Gothic story that Anne embodies crosses with a kind of male Gothic narrative of the marketplace. Hartright begins his narrative with an image of urban anomie, when immured in his chambers in London "the small pulse of the life within me and the great heart of the city around me seemed to be sinking in unison, languidly and more languidly, with the sinking sun" (2); on the night on which he meets Anne Catherick he flees the "gradual suffocation" of London's heat (14), anticipating Marian's description of stifling Blackwater Park and underscoring the smothering nature both of women's oppression and of the site of the marketplace. Choosing the long way back to the city in order to enjoy nature, Hartright takes a symbolic detour from the marketplace to assume temporarily the persona of the Romantic artist. It is on this Wordsworthian "night-walk" (14) that Hartright sees Anne Catherick in an iconic position pointing to the site of his own particular landscape of imprisonment: "There, in the middle of the broad, bright high-road—there, as if it had that moment sprung out of the earth or dropped from the heaven—stood the figure of a solitary Woman, dressed from head to foot in white garments; her face bent in grave inquiry on mine, her hand pointing to the dark cloud over London, as I faced her" (15).

Readers might find that the portentous allegory of this scene is dissipated by Anne's childishness and disorientation in her brief exchange with Hartright. Acknowledging that without Anne's "oracular imaginations" Collins' novel could not exist, Nina Auerbach argues nonetheless that Anne is an "addled prophet and victim" whose "half-witted" behavior parodies the proper feminine vacuity exhibited by her double, Laura.[15] What I would suggest, however, is that the "solitary Woman" is a multivalent figure who enables multiple, yet linked, levels of reading. Far from being simply the blank page that her "whiteness" evokes, Anne is a palimpsest on which are inscribed the traces of symbolic meanings that encompass not only gender but also class and history itself.

I have already mentioned that Anne embodies not just the Radcliffean Gothic but a specifically Victorian Gothic narrative constructed by concerns over the treatment and institutionalization of women mental patients. Certainly, as Barbara Fass Leavy and Jenny Taylor have shown, Anne Catherick becomes a clearly legible figure in light of Victorian medical discourses about madness in which women were given an important symbolic role. Elaine Showalter has shown in

The Female Malady that in such discourses madwomen synecdochically represented madness, and madness metaphorically defined femininity as potentially chaotic, mysterious, and even dangerous, in a view that predated and underlay the Victorian ideal of the Angel in the House.[16] Whereas Anne's nervousness and "agitation" (16) in her meeting with Hartright evoke the figure of the female hysteric, her sexually suggestive gestures recall the belief that mental instability in women reveals their libidinous (not virginally white or passionless) nature. Anne lays her hand on Hartright's shoulder in that first arresting gesture, and then she feels "obliged to steal after . . . and touch" him (16); in her appeal to him to help her, she places her hand "with a sudden gentle stealthiness" on his breast (17). Anne's very presence alone at night on the road prompts Hartright's protest, provoked by his awareness of this likely interpretation, that she is not a prostitute: "The one thing of which I felt certain was, that the grossest of mankind could not have misconstrued her motive in speaking, even at that suspiciously late hour and in that suspiciously lonely place" (16).

Hartright's relief at hearing the "first touch of womanly tenderness" (17) in Anne's voice when she thanks him recalls the fear implicit in Victorian medical discourses that maintained that women patients (hysterics, women in childbirth under anesthesia) were not womanly but in fact unwomanly.[17] In her initial meeting with Hartright and in her later one in the Limmeridge churchyard, Anne reveals, in addition to these traces of feminine desire, a repressed and apparently dangerous anger. Both displays of rage are provoked when he mentions the "Baronet" who incarcerated her:

> "Will you tell me his name?"
> "I can't—I daren't—I forget myself, when I mention it." She spoke loudly and almost fiercely, raised her clenched hand in the air, and shook it passionately; then, on a sudden, controlled herself again, and added, in tones lowered to a whisper: "Tell me which of them *you* know." (18)

A most extraordinary and startling change passed over her. Her face, at all ordinary times so touching to look at, in its nervous

> sensitiveness, weakness, and uncertainty, became suddenly darkened by an expression of maniacally-intense hatred and fear, which communicated a wild, unnatural force to every feature. Her eyes dilated in the dim evening light, like the eyes of a wild animal. She caught up the cloth that had fallen at her side, as if it had been a living creature that she could kill, and crushed it in both her hands with such convulsive strength that the few drops of moisture left in it trickled down on the stone beneath her. (91)

Anne's "maniacally-intense hatred and fear" seem "unnatural" to Hartright because the erase the signs of neurasthenic femininity ("nervous sensitiveness, weakness, and uncertainty") that apparently construct her character. Both passages, however, expose Anne's ability to be a Medusa figure who paralyzes men—a power suggested when her first touch causes the blood to "stop" in Hartright's body (15)—once her childlike surface vanishes.

In these quick flashes Anne is transformed from "half-witted" victim into a full-fledged Madame Defarge figure, a likeness underscored by the way that both hysterical outbursts are provoked by Hartright's mention of the oppressive aristocrat Sir Percival Glyde. Anne's "wild" and animal-like hatred, the clenched fist she shakes "passionately" in the air, transform her into an iconic figure for the revolutionary woman, of which Madame Defarge is but one example, an earlier version being Collins' Goisvintha and an earlier one yet Burke's revolutionary viragos. Indeed, Dickens himself suggested this context when he claimed that the two most dramatic moments in nineteenth-century literature were Carlyle's description of the march of the market women on Versailles in *The French Revolution* and the first meeting between Hartright and Anne in *The Woman in White*.[18]

The Woman in White was published initially in serial form in *All the Year Round*, following the serialization of Dickens' *A Tale of Two Cities*, which drew its own picture of the revolutionary woman from Carlyle—and probably from Collins' *Antonina* and "Sister Rose" as well. Collins' novel was announced in Dickens' periodical with the remark that it would pass "into the station hitherto occupied" by *A Tale of Two Cities*.[19] Collins' novel does seem an appropriate sequel to *A Tale of*

Two Cities, which Collins calls, in the preface to the book version of *The Woman in White*, "the most perfect work of constructive art" that Dickens ever produced (xxix). As a novel set in the 1848 period of revolutionary activity across Europe, *The Woman in White* is a historical novel that addresses the question of the male artist's relation to revolution in the Victorian period.

Collins alludes to the historical events of the period in which he sets his novel most obviously through his references to the revolutionary Italian Brotherhood, thus setting Laura's struggle to regain her identity, as Peter Caracciolo claims, "against the epic back-cloth of the Continental struggle to assert national and class identities in the 1848 revolutions and their aftermath."[20] Yet Collins' interest in the theme of revolution here, as in *Basil* and "Sister Rose," is in the issue of the intellectual's implication in revolution, with which Hartright symbolically collides with when his path crosses that of the woman in white. In this sense, *The Woman in White* responds to Dickens' thematization of this question in *A Tale of Two Cities*. Although the plots of both novels revolve around doubles who are substituted for each other, in Dickens' novel the doubles are split aspects of the male intellectual. Charles Darnay is an aristocrat who, repulsed by his oppressive family, rejects their name and title to seek an alternative identity as a member of the bourgeoisie, entering into the requisite domesticity with Lucie Manette and earning his bread—like Collins' Professor Pesca—as a teacher of his own language in London. Like Doctor Manette, his father-in-law and a former Bastille prisoner, however, Darnay retains an ambiguous relation to the revolution; rebelling in oedipal fashion against his aristocratic "fathers," he distances himself from revolutionary violence. That he himself becomes a target of this violence when his aristocratic origins are held against him waives the question of the rebellious son's implication in revolution, although this issue then resurfaces through two other characters, Doctor Manette and Darnay's double, Sydney Carton. Although Doctor Manette's rediscovered manuscript with its final cry of ressentiment against Darnay's family convicts his son-in-law, Darnay is saved by the efforts of Carton, a kind of rebel manqué, a bohemian outcast who embodies the irreverent and unconventional traits denied the staid Darnay.

Following *A Tale of Two Cities*, Collins' novel preserves not only the plot of the intellectual's relation to revolution but also the equation in Dickens' novel between the revolutionary plot and a plot of sexual transgression. Carton's love for Lucie Darnay, chaste and sublimated as it is, is a potentially adulterous one, a possibility averted when Carton sacrifices himself for the good of domesticity by saving Darnay. In *The Woman in White*, this plot of potential transgression resurfaces in Hartright's love for Laura, betrothed and then married to another man. Once again, this implicitly transgressive love is presented in as inoffensive a manner as possible—Laura, for example, dutifully locks away her sketchbook when she marries Sir Percival—but Collins is more daring than Dickens in suggesting a possible defense of adultery. Because of Glyde's hyperbolic villainy and Laura's apparent insipidity, it becomes easier for the Victorian reader to accept a wife's defense of her passion for another man: "From that time, Marian, I never checked myself again in thinking of Walter Hartright. I let the memory of those happy days, when we were so fond of each other in secret, come back, and comfort me. What else had I to look to for consolation? . . . I know it was wrong, darling—but tell me if I was wrong, without any excuse" (234–35). This type of sexual plot is a figuration, on the domestic front, of revolutionary discourses in the political realm. More so than the one-sidedness of Carton's unrequited love for Lucie, the love between the married Laura and Hartright reproduces in Collins' narrative the structure of the Romantic triangle, a plot associated with radical defenses of free love in such works as Wollstonecraft's *Maria* and Percy Bysshe Shelley's *Epipsychidion*.

Viewed against this climate of radical ideas, the figure of Anne Catherick as she first appears to Hartright—pointing to the "dark cloud" over London—suggests an entire context of radical discourse. When *The Woman in White* is read as a novel about 1848, Anne Catherick evokes not just the female Gothic but its radical antecedents as well. I have mentioned how her claim to have been "cruelly wronged" echoes Wollstonecraft's *Wrongs of Woman*, and indeed the novel alludes to Wollstonecraft's inspiration of the nineteenth-century discourse "Rights of Women" (210), which Marian refers to in connection with its former devotee, Countess Fosco.[21] Most significant, however, Anne embodies a signifying system where gender and class figure each other: she resembles not only Wollstonecraft's Maria, but also her Jemima, a character who suggests an analogy and interconnection between gender and class oppression. Of working-class origins (her mother was a servant), Anne is striking for the ambiguity of her class position; when Hartright encounters her, he does not know how to place her because her manner is not that "of a lady, and, at the same time, not the manner of a woman in the humblest rank of life" (15). By making this figure for the wrongs of woman not "exactly" (15) a lady, Collins, as Nicholas Rance says, "suggests parallels between class oppression and the oppression of women."[22] In terms of the novel's feminist allegory, the way that Laura and Anne come to be interchangeable suggests their fundamental likeness, despite their class difference. The habit of dressing in white that Mrs. Fairlie teaches Anne apparently effaces her origins by garbing her in the costume of a virginal bourgeois femininity, but this very indeterminacy of class underscores the link between women of various classes. Anne and Laura are both Glyde's victims, and when the woman of privileged background is thought to be Anne Catherick she is reduced to sharing the "struggle for existence" (397) of the poor in the East End of London.

Anne's status as a figure for revolution comes not just from her signification of gender and class oppression, but also from her being the voice of the rhetoric of dissenting Christianity, which as historians such as E. P. Thompson and Barbara Taylor have documented was popular in nineteenth-century working-class, as well as feminist, movements.[23] Anne's first allegorical appearance as a "solitary Woman, dressed from head to foot in white garments . . . pointing to the dark cloud over London" suggests her embodiment of the apocalyptic and prophetic rhetoric of radical dissenting politics; Anne in fact recalls the "woman clothed with the sun" from Revelation 12:1, a favorite text in radical rhetoric. (It is presumably to this prophetic character, indeed, that Nina Auerbach refers when she comments on Anne's "oracular pronouncements.") Anne also assumes this apocalyptic role in sending an anonymous letter warning Laura of Glyde's villainy. As E. P. Thompson notes, the anonymous letter has been in many cases a populist genre.[24] The biblical allusiveness of Anne's letter—"See what Scripture says about dreams and their fulfilment" (67)—recalls the dissenting tradition, linked in several historical periods (including the French Revolutionary era and that of the growth of Chartism) with radical political movements. (It is perhaps no accident that during their first meeting Hartright walks with Anne past a symbol of Methodism, the "new Wesleyan College" [19].) In the anonymous letter that begins "abruptly, without any preliminary form of address" (67), Anne disdains middle-class proprieties and assumes the rhetoric of revelation. In the dream-vision she describes, her tears are transformed into "two rays of light" that read the truth of Glyde's "inmost heart" (67). Just as the discourse of radical millenarianism informed both working-class and feminist movements during the nineteenth century, so Anne's language of revelation is tied to the issue of women's resistance of their disempowered position, since she writes to warn Laura not to marry Glyde. Even during her second meeting with Hartright, when Anne tells him she wishes to be buried with Mrs. Fairlie—"Oh, if I could die, and be hidden and at rest with *you*!" (90)—her desire expresses not feminine passivity so much as what could be called feminine millenarianism. As she explains to Laura in an overtly apocalyptic passage, she envisions after death a woman-centered heaven: "oh! if I could only be buried with your mother! If I could only wake at her side, when the angel's trumpet sounds, and the graves give up their dead at the resurrection!" (254–55).

Hartright's meeting with Anne Catherick thus signifies his confrontation with the types of radical and revolutionary contexts she embodies. It is significant that he should meet a woman he obliquely associates with prostitution, given his own symbolic prostitution in the marketplace, where he has to sell his services to the highest bidder. Hartright's meeting with Anne has been identified by D. A. Miller as a "primal scene," where Anne's sexually fraught overtures to Hartright symbolize the contagion of femininity.[25] According to Miller, what Hartright fears about Anne is the infection of her femininity, which he symbolically catches from her along with her, and Laura's, nervousness.[26] Drawing upon the nineteenth-century diagnosis of male homosexuality as a "woman's breath caught in a man's body," Miller reads Hartright's meeting with Anne as a moment where this homosexual threat is figured as a dissolution of the boundaries between masculinity and femininity.[27] Miller's reading is an illuminating one, and same-sex networks are important to the novel in a way I shall explore later. But in this scene sexuality does not simply represent itself but figures economics—since it is the marketplace that makes Hartright "like a woman"—as well as the historical context evoked by Anne's embodiment of radical rhetoric.

What Hartright most notably "catches," indeed, is the ressentiment that Anne displays during her eruptions into Madame Defarge-like ire. When Anne presses Hartright to recite the names of baronets he knows, he lists the titles of previous employers.

> I could hardly refuse to humour her in such a trifle, and I mentioned three names. Two, the names of fathers of families whose daughters I taught; one, the name of a bachelor who had once taken me a cruise in his yacht, to make sketches for him.
> "Ah! you *don't* know him," she said, with a sigh of relief. "Are you a man of rank and title yourself?"
> "Far from it. I am only a drawing-master." As the reply passed my lips—a little bitterly, perhaps—she took my arm with the abruptness which characterised all her actions.
> "Not a man of rank and title," she repeated to herself. "Thank God! I may trust *him*." (18)

Although Miller's reading implies that Anne externalizes something that Hartright fears to find within himself, that something seems to be not only the "woman's breath" within his body, but also the way that a woman's voice echoes his own bitterness about his class position ("As the reply passed my lips a little bitterly, . . . she repeated to herself").

It is not surprising that after only one meeting Hartright seems to have been infected by Anne's bitterness, toward "men of rank and title" in general, and to Sir Percival Glyde in particular. Anne's anonymous letter is an embarrassingly influential text for him, as Marian herself notes: "Mr. Hartright! I hope you are not unjust enough to let that infamous letter influence you?" (71). Yet the letter gives

Hartright an excuse to distrust the man who is his rival for Laura's affections:

> I began to think, with a hateful eagerness of hope, of the vague charges against Sir Percival Glyde which the anonymous letter contained. . . . I have tried to think, since, that the feeling which then animated me began and ended in pure devotion to Miss Fairlie's interests. But I have never succeeded in deceiving myself into believing it. . . . The feeling began and ended in reckless, vindictive, hopeless hatred of the man who was to marry her. (70)

Hartright's hatred of Sir Percival Glyde, which he characterizes elsewhere as "blind hatred and distrust" (71), is the mirror image of Anne's hatred for Glyde; similarly, Hartright's "vindictive" hatred of the landed gentry allies him with the women's campaign to vindicate their rights as he takes their part in helping to prove Laura's identity.

Rewriting the Enterprise I: Homoeroticism and Failed Romanticism

That Walter Hartright meets the woman in white at a crossroads—"that particular point in my walk where four roads met" (14–15)—figures the juncture in his career where he must choose between identifying himself with the masculine, and middle-class, discourse of professionalism, or with the radical discourses associated with revolution. Although Hartright devotes himself to restoring Laura's stolen identity, and thus symbolically to the cause of rectifying women's weakened legal status, his path tends away from a total identification with the disenfranchised. Indeed, Collins' ambivalence about the revolutionary politics he so frequently invokes is expressed by his efforts to consolidate his male protagonist's position as a professional man, efforts reinforced by the narrative's resolution in accordance with the dictates of domestic ideology.

Since domestic abuses are the cause of women's disadvantaged position in the novel, this reassertion of domesticity proves particularly problematic for the women characters, who increasingly are written into stereotypically feminine and disempowered roles. In this way, Collins redefines and delimits the gender and class boundaries that he had confused by juxtaposing the women's assumption of powerful and prophetic roles with Hartright's weakened, feminized position. In *Family Fortunes*, their study of the emergence of the English middle class, Leonore Davidoff and Catherine Hall trace how middle-class identity was defined through the "enterprise," a term that suggests the interdependence of seemingly separate spheres. Within the family enterprise, men "must act" by entering the work place, but the "hidden investment" of women's role in the private sphere is the necessary backbone of men's actions (even though women's work is, in the words of another critic, that classic paradox, "labor that is not labor").[28] The major contribution of Davidoff and Hall's study, which is influenced by marxist-feminist scholarship, has been to integrate gender and class concerns, and indeed to show how, for the Victorian bourgeoisie, gender and class identities wrote and reinforced each other, since middle-class identity is defined through the dependency of women and children on men. In *The Woman in White* Collins turns to the enterprise of the Victorian professional (a group particularly invested in reproducing domestic ideology) as the solution to the problem of masculine identity that was a major concern in works like *Basil* and *After Dark*. The resolution of the mystery in *The Woman in White* functions as a textbook example of defining the enterprise in the ways that Davidoff and Hall describe, as Hartright, despite his initial resemblance to and alliance with the novel's oppressed women, seeks to distinguish himself from them and hence to clarify his hitherto ambiguous class position. This definition of the enterprise of the Victorian professional is linked to the triumph of a liberal ideology that, while it defeats a corrupt aristocracy, also diffuses the novel's radical thematics and the Romanticism associated with them.

Collins' valorization of the twin ideologies of domesticity and professionalism is accomplished through a classic deployment of what Roland Barthes calls "neither-nor" doctrine: to be defined as a member of the "middling" class, Walter Hartright is identified neither with the rebellious lower classes nor with a reactionary and oppressive aristocracy.[29] This neither-norism is plotted through a weakening of the same-sex networks that represent these radical and reactionary poles, the "sisterhood" of Marian, Laura, and Anne, and the friendship between the aristocrats Fosco and Glyde.

In the context of domestic ideology, same-sex friendships are potentially subversive: although the politics of the male friends are antithetical to those of the female friends, these relationships are defined not through heterosexuality, but homosociality, and even, as D. A. Miller argues, homosexuality.[30] Because of the subversion such sexuality poses to domesticity, it is not surprising that Collins uses types of homoeroticism to figure radical politics that are equally dangerous to convention. Embodying the stereotype of the lesbian as mannish woman, Marian threatens domesticity by transforming female friendship—the "female world of love and ritual," as Carroll Smith-Rosenberg calls it[31]—into a sisterhood that resists the domination of men, who tear women from "our sisters' friendship" (162).

While Marian is a figure for the lesbian, Fosco and Glyde are the kind of male couple who represent, as Eve Sedgwick has said, the Victorian perception of homosexuality as aristocratic decadence.[32] In this context, the effeminate bachelor Fairlie's relationship with his valet may also be covertly homoerotic; Fairlie's repeated references to Louis as an "ass" (35, 310) are part of this joke, as is his opinion of Laura's maid's name: "the name (in my opinion a remarkably vulgar one) was Fanny" (310). As in his portrayal of Fosco and Glyde, Collins associates Fairlie's decadence with the oppressiveness of the aristocracy. Fairlie's remark when he first comes to Limmeridge, "So glad to possess you at Limmeridge, Mr. Hartright" (33), is both sexually and economically suggestive; to be possessed at Limmeridge means to be economically sodomized—indeed, Hartright's position at the house recalls Fairlie's use of Louis as a "portfolio stand" (141) to display his art works.

Yet Fairlie is not just the decadent aristocrat but the Romantic as aesthete and dilettante. In appearance, in fact, Fairlie is a caricature of Percy Shelley; contemporary descriptions of the radical poet as effeminate—a "weakly, yet intellectual-looking creature," with a "most feminine and gentle voice" that was also described as shrill[33]—fit the invalid Fairlie, whose voice combines "a discordantly high tone with a drowsily languid utterance" (33). Although Fairlie professes, in true

Shelleyan style, to recognize the importance of the artist, he applies this "liberal social theory" (34) by treating Hartright more like a wage slave than ever.

As the embodiment of a hypocritical Romanticism, Fairlie resembles Count Fosco, who is the novel's major figure for a radicalism that has betrayed its revolutionary origins. Because Collins himself is so taken with Fosco's energy and cynical disregard of propriety, it is easy to see this character, as U. C. Knoepflmacher does, as the novel's hidden hero, the Romantic outsider who rises above stifling social conventions.[34] Yet Fosco is allied not only with the Victorian "counterworld," but also with the oppressiveness of the ruling classes. Although he joined the revolutionary Italian Brotherhood in his youth, Fosco is a double agent who dies, as his wife puts it in her hagiographic biography, to uphold "the rights of the aristocracy, and the sacred principles of Order" (582). His "daring independence of thought" (199) includes a remarkably Wollstonecraftian speech denouncing marriage as a type of legal prostitution (213), but Fosco's feminist sentiment is rendered ironic by being delivered in the presence of the woman who has abjured "the Rights of Women" (210) to become his subservient wife.

This characterization of Fosco as a revolutionary turned counterrevolutionary is strikingly similar to Mary Shelley's depiction of Frankenstein, who, like Fosco, recalls the imperialist Napoleon. Collins conspicuously underlines this reference to Mary Shelley's novel when he makes Fosco "one of the first experimental chemists living" (199). We hear, moreover, that Fosco's great contribution to science is his discovery of a "means of petrifying the body after death, so as to preserve it, as hard as marble, to the end of time" (199). The Count's talent for turning people into objects—his tamed wife is as "cold as a statue, and as impenetrable as the stone out of which it is cut" (195)—is similar to Frankenstein's disregard for the autonomy of his creature. Fosco himself boasts of the totalitarian nature of his scientific interests: "Chemistry, especially, has always had irresistible attractions for me, from the enormous, the illimitable power which the knowledge of it confers. Chemists, I assert it emphatically, might sway, if they pleased, the destinies of humanity" (560). By recalling Frankenstein, Fosco embodies a Romanticism that has betrayed the feminist and egalitarian ideals of the revolution. Like Dickens' figure of Harold Skimpole in *Bleak House*, to whom a reviewer of *The Woman in White* immediately likened him,[35] Fosco is a Romantic gone to seed, a fat Shelley who discourses on the beauties of nature (261) while dominating women.

Collins' gallery of pseudo-Romantics in *The Woman in White* records on one level the sense of loss common among Victorian intellectuals at the failure of Romantic ideals to survive into the Victorian period. Still, what is most striking about this Victorian *Big Chill* narrative is that it reads Romanticism as an outmoded and above all (in a period that elevates domesticity) sterile ideology; Frederick Fairlie, for example, frequently voices his unwillingness to have children. Because the women's radical "sisterhood" and the men's "brotherhood" threaten domesticity and the discourse of professionalism, both are disabled.

The men's network is a brotherhood that encompasses not just Fosco and Glyde's relationship, but also the revolutionary Brotherhood to which Hartright's friend Professor Pesca belongs. The excessively diminutive Pesca ("the smallest human being I ever saw, out of a show-room" [3]), who serves such masters as the wealthy manufacturer he dubs "the golden Papa" (8), is a parody of the kind of wage slave Hartright is in the early part of the narrative; yet he is also a closet terrorist. Like Anne Catherick and the novel's women, then, he hides a secret, more rebellious self that makes him a mirror of what Hartright might become; indeed, when Hartright bests Fosco he enlists Pesca's help as a member of the Brotherhood, and leads the secret society's agents, bent on assassinating Fosco as a traitor, to their target.

Rewriting the Enterprise II: Restoring Class and Gender Legitimacy

Even though Hartright temporarily joins forces with the terrorist Brotherhood, during the latter part of the novel he acts not to challenge convention but to restore its legitimacy. Hartright's discovery of Percival Glyde's "secret" is an important step in this process, and another moment where Collins targets radical politics. Since Glyde emblematizes male tyranny, the reader might expect that his secret is linked to his signification of oppression. Instead, however, his secret is his illegitimacy, a status that ironically makes him resemble Anne Catherick, the woman he incarcerated, who is herself an illegitimate daughter. In general, Collins portrays illegitimacy as a figure for types of social exclusion and disenfranchisement; in *The Dead Secret*, written several years before *The Woman in White*, one major character is a servant who had borne an illegitimate daughter, and in the novels after *The Woman in White* (*No Name* and *Armadale*) illegitimacy and disinheritance are central, and sympathetically portrayed, themes.[36] In *No Name*, indeed, the plight of illegitimate daughters denied the right to inherit money and property is the linchpin of the plot. In this context it is ironic that *The Woman in White* condemns an illegitimate son whose crime is the desire to be "legitimate," and hence accepted by society.

This negative portrayal of illegitimacy is explicable, however, when it is linked to Collins' disavowal of radical politics. Not only did Glyde's father, Sir Felix Glyde, suffer "under a painful and incurable deformity" (420), but he left college with the reputation of being "little better than a revolutionist in politics and an infidel in religion" (421). The combination of Sir Felix's deformity and his radical politics (the first seeming to trope the second) forced him to live abroad, so that Percival was born on the Continent; the Glydes are thus associated with revolution and like Fosco, the "Italian," are linked to the invasion of "foreign" ideas.

Whereas Sir Felix Glyde, the infidel aristocrat in exile, is a type of Shelley figure, Percival's mother is a Wollstonecraftian figure. The couple lived abroad not just because of Sir Felix's deformity, but also to conceal the fact that they were not married. This story is related to Hartright in a letter from Mrs. Catherick, the novel's fallen woman, a Fosco-like pragmatist who herself rebels against the constraints of her gender and class position. According to Mrs. Catherick, Percival's mother "was really a married woman, married in Ireland, where her husband had ill-used her and had afterwards gone off with some other person" (491). This ill-used wife who consents to an adulterous union becomes a figure for free love and its context of nascent feminism; she is another version of Wollstonecraft's Maria in a novel that resembles *Maria* in its plot of an ill-used wife shut up in an insane asylum, since she, like Wollstonecraft's heroine, flouts convention to flee an unhappy marriage and live with her lover.

Hartright's strategy against Glyde thus becomes an attack against his radical parents, and particularly against his mother. Hartright's discovery of an entry in the Knowlesbury register verifying the marriage of Percival's father and mother disappoints him: "What progress had I made towards discovering the suspected stain on the reputation of Sir Percival's mother? The one fact I had ascertained, vindicated her reputation" (463). Since Percival's forgery, as Mrs. Catherick says, "made an honest woman of his mother, after she was dead in her grave" (492), Hartright's exposure of this crime indicts not just the son but also the mother, who had chosen to live with her lover.[37]

Such a plot is a conservative revision of the Radcliffean female Gothic narrative, where the daughter often searches for her lost mother, discovering in the process the secret of the mother's oppression. Although Percival's mother "dead in her grave" is the counterpart of that other significant dead mother, Mrs. Fairlie, whose story is connected with the novel's oppressed women, this story is not the Gothic plot of a daughter seeking a lost maternal heritage. Instead, the story here is of the son's fraudulent erasure of his mother's history, a plot that discredits the notion of a maternal lineage by revealing it to be a shameful deviation from a patrinomial line. The male tyrant Glyde is in fact associated with "the mother's side," as Mrs. Catherick calls it, of his "great family" (451)—the side linked not with the oppressive aristocracy, but with social marginality and radical discourse. Of equal importance is that this association of radical politics with the novel's villains contains the potential transgressiveness of the Romantic triangle plot surrounding the love between Hartright and Glyde's wife, Laura. Hartright's exposure of Glyde leads to the restoration of aristocratic property rights and primogeniture, thereby restoring the legitimacy of conventional gender and class positions rather than—as in the earlier, more feminist portion of the novel—criticizing them. In a moment that invokes images of revolution as the destruction of social order, Glyde dies when he tries to destroy the evidence of his crime and accidentally sets fire to a church.

Collins' restoration of legitimacy prepares for the redefinition of gender roles toward the end of the novel. In narrative terms, one form this redefinition takes is the containment of Marian's voice, which is associated with the most feminist portion of the narrative. Initially, this textual containment of the feminine is associated with the characters most antithetical to the women's interests. In an action critics have identified as a violation of her text,[38] Fosco signifies his defeat of Marian's resistance by reading and writing on her journal after she is stricken with typhus:

> Yes! These pages are amazing. The tact which I find here, the discretion, the rare courage, the wonderful power of memory, the accurate observation of character, the easy grace of style, the charming outbursts of womanly feeling, have all inexpressibly increased my admiration of this sublime creature, of this magnificent Marian. The presentation of my own character is masterly in the extreme. (308)

Fosco's language here is that of a male critic commenting on the work of a woman writer. Although he calls Marian's writing "strong," he also patronizingly characterizes it as feminine, since it expresses "tact," "discretion," "grace," the "charming outbursts of womanly feeling." This colonization of Marian's voice is particularly villainous, but it is only a more obvious version of Hartright's own strategy for containing Marian's narrative energy.

Hartright's tendency in fact is to treat Marian as a character rather than as a writer. This tendency is most marked when, once his narrative succeeds hers, he writes her into the role of the self-abnegating, rather than powerful, woman who illustrates the opening line of the novel: "This is the story of what a Woman's patience can endure, and of what a Man's resolution can achieve" (1). The division of labor implicit in this sentence anticipates the tendency to differentiate gender roles in the resolution of the novel. Marian, the masculine woman who describes herself as a devil—"In short, she is an angel; and I am —Try some of that marmalade, Mr. Hartright, and finish the sentence, in the name of female propriety, for yourself" (27)—is now, perversely, the "good angel" of the story (584). Meanwhile, the once feminized Hartright returns to face the situation in England "as a man should" (374), after having "tempered . . . [his] nature afresh" (373) on an expedition to Central America. Imperialism, as in other Victorian narratives, proves the rejuvenation of a hitherto vitiated manhood, and Hartright returns to England to deal, not just with the foreign menace Fosco, but also, as it turns out, with the "gipsy" Marian, who had first appeared to him in the character of an enigmatic Dark Continent.

This resurgence of manhood provides the solution to the problem of female power Hartright had confronted in that first meeting with Marian, where, as the authors of *Corrupt Relations* note, his disgust at her dark female Otherness ("The lady is ugly!" [25]) is ludicrously hyperbolic.[39] As Nina Auerbach has argued, Hartright's calling Marian ugly "characterizes himself as much as it does 'the lady,'" since her embodiment of dark Pre-Raphaelite beauty "would no doubt appal a drawing-master like Walter, who sees and works by the rules."[40] To Hartright, the rules are those not only of conventional art but also of conventional gender roles; Marian is distressingly "masculine" in his eyes, and her expression is "altogether wanting in those feminine attractions of gentleness and pliability, without which the beauty of the handsomest woman alive is beauty incomplete" (25). Hartright's relief when Marian's expression becomes "womanly" (26) is similar to his reaction when Anne Catherick thanks him, in the meeting that only slightly precedes this scene, with "the first touch of womanly tenderness that I had heard from her" (17).

Although for modern readers Hartright's preference for the insipid and infantile Laura over the infinitely more admirable Marian is clearly ironic, Collins' narrative works to control the female power represented by Marian's voice, her dark sexuality (much more threatening, indeed, for being feminine than "masculine"), and her writing. After she daringly eavesdrops on Fosco and Glyde, she falls into a "burning fever" (327) that causes her to lose control over her text. Wandering about her room with the pen in her hand, "incapable" of communicating with the housekeeper (327) or of writing Laura's name in her journal, Marian proves her failure as a woman writer. Writing subsequently becomes a masculine domain when Fosco takes up the pen and inscribes the woman's text in a "man's handwriting, large, bold, and firmly regular" (307).

Fosco's similarity to Hartright, however, is underscored when Hartright, as the second editor of Marian's text, writes on her text after Fosco does, and, like Fosco, also functions as a critic. As the editor of the collection of narratives, it is presumably Hartright who identifies Marian's journal as a work that at its conclusion "ceases to be legible," ending instead in "fragments of words only, mingled with blots and scratches of the pen" (307). That Fosco's silencing of Marian prepares for Hartright's is emphasized by Marian being not only the text's female writer, but also its female detective. It is following her detection of Glyde's and Fosco's villainy, an act that requires all her resourcefulness and courage, when she is stricken into silence by the fever, and thus incapable of communicating her knowledge of impending danger to Laura. Marian's detection represents the moment where she obtains knowledge of male oppression, paralleling the moment in *The Mysteries of Udolpho* when Emily lifts the veil that evokes the mystery of the mother's oppression. Like Emily, however, who is denied a chance to attain this knowledge, Marian is deprived of the opportunity to use it, a deprivation that makes her resemble Anne Catherick, who, the reader discovers, never knew the secret she spends half the novel trying to communicate.

This denial of Anne's knowledge trivializes, with apparent gratuitousness, her importance within the text, suggesting that the pursuers who claimed she was simply a half-wit were right. The ease with which Hartright believes Mrs. Catherick, the only source for whether Anne knew Glyde's secret, is the more puzzling because the voice of the mother, whose contempt for her daughter colors her speech, is scarcely an authoritative one. This belittling of Anne, however, becomes comprehensible when, after she and Marian have been debarred from knowledge, Hartright's acquisition of knowledge becomes the focus of the text: it is Hartright who takes up the search at which Anne and Marian have failed, bringing the buried knowledge of Percival Glyde's secret to light at the appropriately named Knowlesbury.[41]

The devaluation of female knowledge speeds Hartright's professional career. While he champions Laura's cause, Hartright works as an "obscure, unnoticed man," engraving for the "cheap periodicals" without "patron or friend to help me" (379). Yet he manages to avoid, even in this exile, the emasculation that this association with women, and their economic deprivation, might suggest. Not only does he use this period as a chance to succeed in the role of detective at which both Anne and Marian have failed, but he also becomes the breadwinner on whom Marian and Laura are dependent. This assertion of his "manliness" in establishing a pseudofamily (for all it looks like the Romantic triangle's ménage à trois) reverses the situation at the beginning of the novel, when he was forced to share the genteel poverty of his mother and sister.

In *Family Fortunes*, Davidoff and Hall underscore how important it was to the family enterprise that women not work outside the home, since such labor compromised not only gender but also middle-class identity. During the Victorian period the regulation of women's paid labor in the work place thus became extremely urgent.[42] Although Marian's assumption of the household domestic chores in the East End flat apparently compromises class identity—since she does not hire a servant to help with the more strenuous tasks—her labor within the home prevents her from venturing "outside" (as she did in the eavesdropping episode) and keeps her inside, in her proper gendered position: "What a woman's hands *are* fit for . . . early and late, these hands of mine shall do" (398).[43] That this is her proper place is underscored by the image of Hartright literally holding her back when she wants to go with him to confront Fosco with the evidence of his crime:

> She held me by both hands . . . "I see!" she said, in a low eager whisper. "You are trying the last chance to-night."
>
> "Yes—the last chance and the best," I whispered back.
>
> "Not alone! Oh, Walter, for God's sake, not alone! Let me go with you. Don't refuse me because I'm only a woman. I must go! I will go! I'll wait outside in the cab!"
>
> It was my turn, now, to hold *her*. She tried to break away from me, and get down first to the door. (542)

Circumscribing the independent Marian's behavior is accompanied by another dramatic regulation of women's work, this time specifically of paid labor. When Laura complains that she feels useless because she is not contributing to the support of the household, Hartright deceives her: telling her that he is selling her drawings, he pays her out of his own purse and hides the works he privately thinks worthless. "I set aside a little weekly tribute from my earnings, to be offered to her as the price paid by strangers for the poor, faint, valueless sketches, of which I was the only purchaser" (442). This moment is reminiscent of Fosco's patronizing comments on Marian's writing, and the relentless diminution of Laura (a "little weekly tribute" is all the wage she gets) recalls Fosco's chauvinist claim that women are "nothing but children grown up" (295). Laura, for whom Hartright has provided a "little box of colours" (400), is the house pet and child relegated to domestic space: "She spoke as a child might have spoken; she showed me her thoughts as a child might have shown them" (403). When Hartright prevents Laura from selling her pictures, the clearest figuration of a rivalry between a male and a female artist in the novel, he asserts his manliness by ensuring that a woman is dependent on him. It is after this episode that Hartright marries Laura, and he considers the "poor," "valueless" sketches "my treasures beyond price" (442), since they are mementos of the curious courtship that reinforces his role as head of the household.

Not surprisingly, following this crisp delineation of gender roles Hartright is transformed from an impoverished professional into a successful one. He learns of Fosco's death in Paris, where he has been sent on business that will determine his financial destiny: "if I acquitted myself of my commission as I hoped I should, the result would be a permanent engagement on the illustrated newspaper, to which I was now only occasionally attached" (578). Once he has performed his commission and been given a permanent position with the newspaper, Hartright becomes affiliated with the landed gentry. When the effeminate aesthete Mr. Fairlie dies, symbolically enough of "paralysis" (583), Hartright's "resolution" (445), which he had resurrected to overcome his earlier inability to act, is rewarded. He and his family move to Limmeridge, and the narrative ends with the celebration of the primogeniture he has defended: Marian playfully introduces his son to him as "one of the landed gentry of England . . . *the Heir of Limmeridge*" (584).

The final paradox of the novel, however, is the lingering instability of masculine identity. A novel about confused identities ends with a moment of confusion, as Marian introduces Hartright to his son as if he does not know who the baby is. "Do you know who this is, Walter?" she asks (583–84). "'Even *my* bewilderment has its limits,' I replied. 'I think I can still answer for knowing my own child.' 'Child!' she exclaimed . . . 'Are you aware, when I present this illustrious baby to your notice, in whose presence you stand? Evidently not!'" (584). Hartright's inability to recognize his son as a member of the landed gentry underscores the tensions inherent in his union with the upper classes. As James M. Brown argues, during the Victorian period the bourgeoisie's partnership with and continued dependence on the upper classes threatened to undermine the ideology that justified middle-class hegemony by distinguishing it from the rule of the aristocracy.[44] Hartright's quest for a bourgeois manliness defined as virtuous independence from the gentry is rendered ironic when he becomes the occupant of Limmeridge House not through his own industry, but through inheritance from the gentry.

This uneasy marriage between the bourgeoisie and the gentry is predicated on a last confusion of gender roles: it is not Hartright who inherits Limmeridge House, but Laura. If the joke seems to be on Hartright, however—who has worked so hard to differentiate gender roles, only, in the end to be "kept" by his wife—Laura's inheritance of Limmeridge also attests to the diffusion of the more radical elements in the novel's feminist critique. The reparation of women's disadvantaged legal and economic status only affects wealthy landowners, not working-class women like Anne Catherick. Anne and Laura, formerly doubles, are finally distinguished when Laura is recognized by her tenants after being displayed among the proper class markers. Yet Laura's economic power is still only the traditional power of being a conduit to her son, who will inherit the estate.

Even Hartright's economic power is deferred, however: like Laura, his identity as a landowner will also be validated only through his son, the heir of Limmeridge. This curious alienation from his own success suggests that the issue of the male artist's status in the marketplace has, finally, not been resolved. Hartright's momentary inability to name his son mirrors the reader's incredulity at the fairy-tale ending, which, by hyperbolically elevating the poor artist's status, elides the cash nexus that lies outside this magic circle. The novel thus mystifies economic reality, but the way Hartright's confusion draws attention to this maneuver reminds us of the professional writer's continued "need to earn from writing."[45] Although the theme of the bourgeoisie's alienation from the aristocracy thus is important in itself, it also figures the larger issue of the artist's alienation in the marketplace. Hartright's inability to control his success—the move to Limmeridge is, like his meeting with Anne Catherick, as unreal as a dream—mimics his inability to control his poverty earlier in the narrative. Similarly, his momentary alienation from his "product"—his son—figures an alienation from the process of production that has determined his position in the marketplace. This ambivalence about his "need to earn" from his art is also signified by Hartright's position at the end of the novel. Whereas his status as head of the household apparently represents his authority over the women and children, and women-as-children, whom Fosco claimed need male control, the novel also ends as it began, with Hartright in the company of women—here, the very ones the novel has silenced, Laura and Marian.

It is symptomatic of this ambiguous closure that Marian's words "the Heir of Limmeridge" are followed by a hiatus, and then Hartright's final words: "So she spoke. In writing those last words, I have written all. The pen falters in my hand; the long, happy labour of many months is over! Marian was the good angel of our lives—let Marian end our Story" (584). Although Hartright has reasserted his manhood in this novel to an extent denied to Basil, these final lines of *The Woman in White* recall the last image in the earlier novel, where Basil, retired to the "valley of Repose," is called away from his writing by Clara. If the pen is, as Sandra Gilbert and Susan Gubar have called it, a "metaphorical penis"[46] (and we know that it is here because Marian, the figure for the woman writer, couldn't control this phallic signifier), then Hartright loses his manhood in these final lines when the pen falters in his hand. Moreover, by bequeathing his faltering pen to a woman who now symbolizes, like Anne, Laura, and the novel's dead mothers, an absence of power, Hartright reintroduces the Gothic into the text. As a figure for the editor, Hartright attempts to impose order and coherence on the narrative and hence to exorcise the female Gothic, which Marian's journal imitated when it trailed off into unintelligibility and silence. Yet Hartright's own writing ends with a Gothic void. If his "let Marian end our Story" refers back to Marian's words "the Heir of Limmeridge," then the last line of the novel underscores the male writer's alienation from his own economic power. If, however, he expects Marian to speak further, the silence after this line emphasizes the irony of his expecting to speak through a woman who has been silenced. Either way the novel that has attempted to assert the potency of the male writer ends with a blank.

Six

Blank Spaces: Ideological Tensions and the Detective Work of *The Moonstone*

In Collins' *The Moonstone* (1868), which T. S. Eliot called "the first and greatest of English detective novels,"[1] the major feat of ratiocination is performed not by Sergeant Cuff, the inspector from Scotland Yard, but by a freakish-looking outcast and doctor's assistant, Ezra Jennings. Jennings proves what others already know—that Franklin Blake stole the Moonstone. More important, though, Jennings figures out that Blake did this to protect his cousin Rachel and that he acted in a trance caused by a dose of opium administered without his knowledge. Jennings' method for arriving at this conclusion vindicates not only Blake but the process of detection itself. Piecing together the "broken phrases"[2] spoken in a delirium by the doctor, Mr. Candy, who slipped Blake the dose of laudanum, Jennings demonstrates the power of reason and of reading. He shows both that in delirium the "superior faculty of thinking" continues despite the apparent "incapacity and confusion" of language (415), and that the person who tries to interpret this confusion can extract intelligibility and coherence from what is fragmentary and unintelligible.

Ezra Jennings' version of detection, however, is riddled with gaps and silences. Since the only clues he has are broken words surrounded by empty spaces, the narrative he reconstructs, as Ross Murfin argues, may not be the truth of what happened so much as a fictional account arrived at by guesswork.[3] Moreover, the zeal with which Jennings fills in gaps is equaled only by his determination that his own story remain "a blank" (511). Such paradoxes show how in *The Moonstone* detection defers rather than fixes meaning, uncovering mysteries only to suggest that others stay covered up.

This chapter argues that Jennings' ambiguous act of detection emblematizes how *The Moonstone* is Collins' great cover-up. With greater subtlety and complexity than the works that preceded it, this novel written at the end of the decade of his greatest achievement simultaneously expresses and suppresses the ideological and generic tensions that had animated his fiction from the beginning of his career. Critics have praised *The Moonstone* as Collins' most seamless transformation of the Gothic into the detective novel, a genre that brings to light and banishes the buried secrets so prominent in the Gothic. This genealogy, in which feminine genres are the matrix for the male-dominated detective novel, locates *The Moonstone* as the triumphant finale to Collins' revision of his female predecessors. Yet this critical tradition tends to ignore how the novel that "fathered" detective fiction[4] resembles the female Gothic in the thematics of blankness and silence that puncture its narrative of revelation and rational interpretation.

The tension between Gothic and detective fiction in the novel is symptomatic of Collins' continued and heightened ambivalence about his literary project. *The Moonstone*, written near the close of the decade that began with *The Woman in White*, followed two novels that critics considered particularly shocking and sensational (*No Name* and *Armadale*), mainly because they place at center stage fallen women who embody a bold critique of Victorian conventions and gender roles. In both novels, however, these women are chastened by being married off (*No Name*) or killed off (*Armadale*). By the time he wrote *The Moonstone*, then, Collins, whose enormous popularity relied on his being a kind of literary outlaw, had apparently strained to the limit the expression of radical impulses in his fiction. Setting most of *The Moonstone* in the same revolutionary period of 1848–49 that he had chosen as the backdrop for *The Woman in White*, he creates a narrative that self-reflexively focuses on the fate of subversive fictions.

The central image in this narrative, the theft of the Moonstone, represents an exposé of Victorian culture that recognizes the links between types of domination—of the colonizers over the colonized, of men over women, and of the upper over the lower classes. Yet the novel also papers over the traces of its own exposé, an erasure attested to by its obsession with images of buried writing. Rosanna Spearman, the servant who sinks her love letter to Franklin Blake in the quicksand that is the site of her suicide, spectacularly introduces this theme, which culminates when Ezra Jennings requests that his writing—letters, journals, and his daring unfinished book on the "intricate and delicate subject of the brain and the nervous system" (414)—be buried with him. The buried writing of these outcasts—particularly that of Jennings, who becomes Collins' figure for his own project—is a synecdoche for the novel's tendency at once to diffuse its social criticism and to draw attention to its own self-censorship.

Anatomies of Empire: Reading the Theft of the Moonstone

Readings of the mystery plot of *The Moonstone* have tended to focus on the psychosexual symbolism of Franklin Blake's stealing Rachel's jewel from her boudoir at night.[5] This Freudian reading of the theft as a "symbolic defloration"[6] associates detection with the analyst's work of interpreting a psychological and familial narrative, since Blake's unconscious motivations are bound up in his role as his cousin's suitor. Another influential reading, however, argues that the novel's criticism of imperialism makes its emphasis more political than domestic: John Reed claims that Britain's exploitation of its "jewel," India, symbolized by Colonel Herncastle's greedy plunder of the diamond, is the central target in Collins' indictment of an "oppressive society."[7]

The psychosexual and historical readings of the novel have yet to be fully integrated. The novel itself, however, is structured around a comparison between the private world of English families and the public dimension of imperialism. The parallels Collins draws between the two thefts of the diamond—the first in India, the second in England—demonstrate the interpenetration of the realms of empire and domesticity by showing how the hierarchies of gender and class that undergird British culture replicate the politics of colonialism.

Imperialism is, then, both an important subject in *The Moonstone* and a thematic bridge between the foreign and English worlds in its narrative. The novel is framed by its references to imperialism, tracing a history of British rule in India that begins with the storming of Seringapatam in 1799, a crucial moment in consolidating the sway of the East India Company, and ends with the restoration of the jewel to its temple by the Indians. Although this final act of native resistance recalls the Indian Mutiny of 1857, Collins' response to such rebellion differs from that of most of his contemporaries by locating the source of violence in imperialism itself. This is not to say that the novel is unmarked by British paranoia in the wake of the Mutiny and other colonial uprisings; unabashedly Orientalist, *The Moonstone* portrays the conspiratorial Indians as shady and sinister Others, a colonial version of the terrorist Brotherhood in *The Woman in White*.[8]

Yet the novel also breaks down the terms of the imperialist ideology represented by Gabriel Betteredge's comment "here was our quiet English house suddenly invaded by a devilish Indian Diamond" (36). Betteredge, whose Bible is that classic imperialist text *Robinson Crusoe*, voices the naive Orientalism that opposes inside to outside, English to foreign, and good to evil. *The Moonstone*, however, blurs these polarities, an effect Dickens noticed when he described its narrative as "wild, and yet domestic."[9] Dickens' comment suggests how the seemingly opposed realms of exotic (wild) and English (domestic) permeate each other: what is wild is still domestic, yet what is domestic may also be wild. Whereas the Indians are motivated by an apparently "English" sense of justice, Englishmen like Blake appear, to the horrified eyes of Betteredge, to have turned foreign. Indeed, the distinction between English and Indian, orderly interiors and disorderly exteriors, is most radically disrupted by the revelation that Blake stole the Moonstone.

Although making the decadently foreign Blake the thief reinforces the novel's Orientalism (particularly since he takes the gem under the influence of the Eastern drug opium), Collins' decision to have a second Englishman steal the Moonstone becomes the linchpin for his radical reading of British culture. Just as the history of imperialism becomes a family story—the revelation of Herncastle's guilt is "extracted from a family paper" (1)—so the "strange family story" (7) of Blake's theft mirrors the larger narrative of imperialism. By juxtaposing the plots of courtship and colonialism, Collins suggests an analogy between sexual and imperial domination.

Both thefts resemble a symbolic violation: Rachel's loss of her jewel, read by many critics as her virginity, echoes the plunder of the Moonstone, which had originally graced the statue of an "inviolate deity" (2). That Rachel is dark underscores her likeness to the Indians: "Her hair was the blackest I ever saw. Her eyes matched her hair" (58). These repeated parallels imply that, like colonial possessions, femininity is a Dark Continent to be explored and ultimately controlled; Blake's searching the drawer in Rachel's Indian cabinet echoes the eroticized language of empire that Mr. Bruff uses when he claims that Murthwaite, the authority on India, is intent on returning there and "penetrating into regions left still unexplored" (313). Moreover, just as a colonized territory loses its sovereignty when it is subordinated to an imperial power, so Blake's theft of the jewel anticipates Rachel's loss of autonomy within Victorian marriage. Indeed, the theft symbolically corrects Rachel's desire for independence. As male characters in the novel are all too happy to point out, her main "defect" (58) is her tendency "to shut herself up in her own mind" to think (303)—an image that suggests that the jewel (which also has a single flaw) signifies not merely her virginity but what Bruff calls her "self-dependence" as well (303).

Even the way that Blake's act is finally defended reinforces the analogy between Victorian ideologies of gender and imperialism. Ezra Jennings' experiment clears Blake, not of the act of the theft, but of a bad motive for the act: he is free of moral responsibility not simply because he stole the jewel in an unconscious state, but because even while unconscious he wished to protect Rachel from the threat of the Indians lurking outside the house. Blake's fears, reminiscent of the paranoia about female chastity whipped into hysterical fury by the Mutiny, also reveal how his "innocence" is a social and rhetorical construction. Blake's reason for stealing the jewel mirrors the rationalization of imperialism as "the white man's burden," protecting people who presumably cannot take care of themselves. That Blake appropriates the jewel Rachel had insisted on placing in an unlocked drawer is a sign of how marriage "locks up" women's independence and desire, transferring their possessions to their husbands with the blessings of an ideology that assumes wives need such protection.

The character of Rosanna Spearman adds another level to this analysis of types of domination by introducing the issue of class. If the question of Blake's moral responsibility is raised most insistently concerning the theft, it is suggested also by Rosanna's suicide, since what comes between her and Blake is not so much a literal as a metaphorical "plainness," her working-class status. The lack of communication between Rosanna and Blake shows how members of the working class are invisible to those they serve. In the letter she leaves for him, Rosanna describes Blake's indifference—"I tried—oh, dear, how I tried—to get you to look at me" (349)—and notes how he ignored her labor when she straightened his room: "You never noticed it, any more than you noticed me" (352). Blake himself unwittingly supports Rosanna's claim when, responding to her accusation that he deliberately snubbed her, he says, "The writer is entirely mistaken, poor creature. I never noticed her" (362).

Because she is a woman as well as a servant, however, Rosanna's story also links the issue of class to that of gender. Just as Rachel's story demonstrates the analogy between Victorian ideologies of gender and imperialism, Rosanna's narrative shows how gender and class are mutually reinforcing categories. That her domestic labor in cleaning Blake's room is also a labor of love suggests how Victorian wife and Victorian servant were both, in Leonore Davidoff's words, "mastered for life."[10] (Rosanna signs her letter to Blake "your true lover and humble servant" [368].) Although Rosanna and Rachel appear to be rivals for Blake's affections, these women from vastly different class backgrounds thus are also doubles, linked by a desire to serve the man they love that ensures their silence about his role in the theft.

Resistance on the Margins: The Symbolism of the Shivering Sand

Sergeant Cuff also sees a bond between Rachel and Rosanna, but he believes this to be partnership in crime. Even though he is mistaken in his belief that the two women sold the jewel to pay Rachel's debts, his theory reveals that the novel is not just about types of domination but also about types of resistance, of which female insubordination is the most important. The novel that recalls the Indian Mutiny also alludes to a notorious criminal case that was read by contemporaries as an example of female mutiny against male law. Sergeant Cuff, who tries to track down criminal women, is modeled on an Inspector Whicher, who investigated the Road Murder of 1860, in which a nightgown stained with blood linked a young girl, Constance Kent, to the murder of her stepbrother. Cuff's suspicions about Rachel reflect the paranoia about female rebellion expressed in accounts of the Road Murder; Constance Kent's father claimed that his daughter's criminality stemmed from her wish "to be independent," a claim paralleling men's uneasiness about Rachel's "defect" of "self-dependence" in *The Moonstone.*[11]

The imagery of defect or disfigurement to describe women's "self-dependence," or resistance to conventional roles, links Rachel to other rebellious female characters. Rosanna's deformity—one shoulder higher than the other—images her desire to "get above herself" through her love for an upper-class man.[12] And Rosanna's closest friend, Limping Lucy, another female character associated with both rebellion and disfigurement, expresses the independence she shares with her friend in her denunciation of Blake as Rosanna's "murderer" (205) and in her rejection of heterosexuality ("if she had only thought of the men as I think, she might have been living now" [206]). Like Marian Halcombe's passion for Laura in *The Woman in White*, the erotic intensity of Lucy's love for Rosanna represents an alternative to the novel's heterosexual plot. But the shattering of Lucy's dream of living in London with Rosanna "like sisters" (206) evokes from her a protest, not just against men, but against class privilege: "Ha, Mr. Betteredge, the day is not far off when the poor will rise against the rich. I pray Heaven they may begin with *him*" (207).

Lucy's cry, the novel's clearest allusion to the revolutionary period of 1848 that is its setting, shows how women's rebellion also can symbolize other types of resistance; like women, Indians and the working class are not just subdued victims but possible troublemakers and instigators of revolt. That Limping Lucy voices this cry, however, also demonstrates how the thematics of revolution that are so important to *The Woman in White*, set in the same period, here have been moved from center stage. Not only is Lucy a more minor figure than Anne Catherick, the character in the earlier novel she most resembles in her resentment of the wrongs of women and of the lower classes, but this diminished status mirrors the marginality of other images of resistance. The Indians are voiceless presences lurking on the margins of the text, and even the letter that finally gives Rosanna a narrative voice must first be rescued from burial in the Shivering Sand.

The Shivering Sand, which hides both Rosanna's body and her letter, becomes Collins' central image for a resistance that is reduced to a trembling beneath the surface of the text:

> The sand-hills here run down to the sea, and end in two spits of rock jutting out opposite each other, till you lose sight of them in the water. . . . Between the two, shifting backwards and forwards at certain seasons of the year, lies the most horrible quicksand on the shores of Yorkshire. At the turn of the tide, something goes on in the unknown deeps below, which sets the whole face of the quicksand shivering and trembling in a manner most remarkable to see, and which has given to it, among the people in our parts, the name of the Shivering Sand. (24)

A Gothic site of what is "most horrible," the Shivering Sand represents everything that the novel has identified as being "below" in the body politic. It is an image for the female body, with a "face" that at the turn of the tide "dimple[s] and quiver[s]" (136) like, as Albert Hutter says, "some grotesque coquette."[13] Since it hides the secret of Rosanna's transgressive desire, it is also appropriate that it is a female sexual symbol, lying between "two spits of rock" and deriving its name from its parody of female orgasm, its "shivering and trembling in a manner most remarkable to see." But the face of the Sand is specifically described as a "broad brown face" (28), thus linking it not only to women but also to the Indians. Moreover, Rosanna Spearman's comment to Betteredge that the Sand reminds her of "hundreds of suffocating people . . . all struggling to get to the surface" (28) suggests the lower classes struggling (as she does) to rise above their "place." Unlike Lucy, however, who insists that the poor will successfully rise up, Rosanna identifies this struggle as a failed one: those who seem to rise only sink "lower and lower in the dreadful deeps" (28).

The burial of resistance in the Shivering Sand only emphasizes its resemblance to the female Gothic text, where women's rebellion is similarly submerged and hidden. The tension in the novel between the genres of detection and the Gothic is coded by the scenes where male detectives try to penetrate the secrets of the marginal and feminine space of the Sand. Sergeant Cuff, who dogs Rosanna's footsteps as she goes back and forth between her "hiding-place" on the Sand (174), is a major figure for this male project, as well as being, with his love of roses and eye for trifling clues, a déclassé version of William Collins, the Romantic artist who had been portrayed in the *Memoirs* as an inveterate detective of Nature ("his power of observation . . . thus regulated, it was seldom that the smallest object worthy of remark escaped its vigilance" [*M* II, 310]). Although Collins' father had successfully interpreted Nature, however, Sergeant Cuff's efforts to track down Rosanna (his "rose") are frustrated; in one of the most wildly Gothic scenes in the novel he traces her footprints to the Sand to discover that, by committing suicide, she is beyond his grasp.

The more crucial clash between female Gothic and male detection, however, occurs in the scene where Blake confronts the quicksand face to face to retrieve from it Rosanna's letter and the stained nightgown:

> In this position, my face was within a few feet of the surface of the quicksand. The sight of it so near me, still disturbed at intervals by its hideous shivering fit, shook my nerves for the moment. A horrible fancy that the dead woman might appear on the scene of her suicide, to assist my search—an unutterable dread of seeing her rise through the heaving surface of the sand, and point to the place—forced itself into my mind, and turned me cold in the warm sunlight. I own I closed my eyes at the moment when the point of the stick first entered the quicksand. (343)

The eroticized terms in which detection is described here—the phallic stick penetrating the Sand's *vagina dentata*—represents interpretation as male virility that controls the mystery of femininity. Having "penetrated the secret which the quicksand had kept from every other living creature" (345), Blake makes two erotic discoveries: the stained nightgown, which is evidence for his symbolic violation of Rachel, and the letter, which contains the secret of Rosanna's desire. This mysterious feminine desire recalls related types of mysterious Otherness in the novel; the Sand's "fathomless deeps" and its "false brown face" (342) resemble the "unfathomable" and "yellow deep" of the Indian diamond (68) and, synecdochically, of the East. Like Mr. Murthwaite's travels "penetrating into regions left still unexplored," detective work maps and colonizes these Dark Continents.

Although critics have read this scene in psychoanalytic terms as Blake's confrontation with the id, or "a threatening second self,"[14] he in fact discovers not so much the Other within himself as the Other outside it. As in earlier descriptions of the Sand, female sexuality figures the unruly rebellion that is potentially beyond the control of the Englishman. At the site of Rosanna's buried desire Blake witnesses the return of the repressed, the reawakening of feminine sexuality signified by the "hideous shivering fit" of the quicksand. A sense of the threat (already vividly conveyed by the name Spearman) that this female sexuality poses to his masculine identity pervades the language he uses to describe his reaction to the Sand. Not only are his nerves shaken, as if he were a neurasthenic woman, but he confesses to overpowering fear at the moment he penetrates the quicksand: "I own I closed my eyes." Blake's triumph as a detective—when he finds the box he is "throbbing with excitement from head to foot" (343)—dispels both this sexual fear and the Gothic narrative represented by his fantasy that he is haunted by Rosanna's ghost.

Male Detectives and Silent Women: The Double Voice of The Moonstone

Although Blake's detective work appears to overpower the Gothic, the discovery there of his apparent guilt leads him to confront the woman who embodies both the repression and the potential unruliness of the Gothic text. The stillness of the Shivering Sand, that site of all that is hidden and buried, is a mirror for the novel's central Gothic silence—Rachel's silence, around which its mystery plot is structured. The scene on the Sand is a prelude for the climactic scene where a male detective penetrates female secrets; hoping she can prove his innocence, Blake arranges a surprise meeting with Rachel in order to induce her to tell him what she knows.

Collins' staging of this scene makes it clear that the battle to break women's silence is, like the scene on the Shivering Sand, a battle over the control of knowledge. In Foucauldian terms, this knowledge is understandable as a form of power; Blake's role as a detective, his search to repossess Rachel's knowledge, reinforces the control over women that Victorian gender ideology gave to men within courtship and marriage. In an exchange that reads as both a love scene and an interrogation, Blake gets answers to his insistent questions by assuming once more the role of Rachel's suitor: "while her hand lay in mine I was her master still" (383). When he boasts that after more of this persuasion "she willingly opened her whole mind to me" (384), he implies that Rachel's willingness to open her mind obligingly reverses her previous unwillingness to have the drawer opened and her jewel stolen.

Rachel's hysteria not only unmans her lover but also subverts the language of Victorian courtship and marriage. Castigating Blake with a "cry of fury" (388), she accuses him of duplicity: "he wonders I didn't (382) provokes the revelation most damaging to his case—that she saw him take the diamond—his reproach of her silence ("if you had spoken when you ought to have spoken") causes him decisively to lose his "influence" over her: "the few words I had said seemed to have lashed her on the instant into a frenzy of rage" (388). So powerful are Rachel's angry words ("The hysterical passion swelled in her bosom—her quickened convulsive breathing almost beat on my face" [393]) that they provoke a reaction in Blake similar to the near-hysteria he had felt on the Shivering Sand. He had said earlier, "I roused my manhood" (379) before going in to see Rachel, but by the end of the scene he is reduced to tears (393).

Rachel's hysteria not only unmans her lover but subverts the language of Victorian courtship and marriage. Castigating Blake with a "cry of fury" (388), she accuses him of duplicity: "he wonders I didn't charge him with his disgrace the first time we met: 'My heart's darling, you are a Thief! My hero whom I love and honour, you have crept into my room under cover of the night, and stolen my Diamond!'" (389). In this passage, a woman's "heart's darling" is in fact a thief; her "hero," who like a husband receives "love and honour," practices deception and sexual violation. In this sense, Rachel's words express the critique of marriage implicit in Collins' figuration of the theft as the domination of women.

The introduction of the thematics of hysteria, however, causes the scene to convey an increasingly reductive message about gender. Although Rachel's "hysterical passion" at first blurs gender roles by making the manly detective cry, the references to hysteria work more strongly to reinscribe the notion of sexual difference. As in *The Woman in White*, to label woman's speech a symptom of hysteria defines it as defective and normalizes male speech.[15] In *The Moonstone*, medicine provides the greatest help of all professional languages in charting, and controlling, the Dark Continent of femininity (it is no accident that at the birthday dinner Rachel is seated between the explorer Mr. Murthwaite and the doctor Mr. Candy).[16] Rachel's power to voice the novel's hidden critique of bourgeois marriage is weakened as she is transformed into the object of diagnostic scrutiny. The hysterical symptoms written on her body (her angry words, her "convulsive breathing" [393]) invite an interpretation that undercuts the authority of her subversive reading of the events surrounding the theft.

In the nineteenth-century medical discourses of which Freud's is the culminating example, hysteria is a sign of women's fruitless rebellion against the things they secretly desire but will not acknowledge: heterosexuality and the subordination to men that its institutionalization represents. As Hélène Cixous explains, the hysteric's initial resistance to male law is transformed into acquiescence: "She asks the master 'What do I want?' and 'What do you want me to want, so that I might want it?'"[17] In *The Moonstone*, the narrative that consists of an interrupted and then resumed courtship is the "master" text that teaches Rachel to want the man she accused of symbolically violating her; indeed, her learning to acknowledge this need is as important a revelation as any other in the mystery plot. Just as Cixous says that "silence is the mark of hysteria,"[18] so Rachel's silence is not just her way of protecting her lover but a sign of pathology, of her difficulty in voicing her need. During the period of her estrangement from Blake, both her silence and her hysterical outbursts suggest her sexual frustration at the separation, as she herself admits when she reveals her thwarted love to Godfrey Ablewhite and then asks, "Is there a form of hysterics that bursts into words instead of tears?" (262). The exchange with Blake is the climactic scene where her anger against him may in fact be read as the mark of her hidden desire for him. That her protests signify the opposite of what they supposedly mean is demonstrated not only by her starting to return Blake's kisses when he first enters the room, but also by the way she lets him hold her "powerless and trembling" hand while saying, with obvious lack of conviction, "Let go of it" (383).

The symptomatology of hysteria thus neutralizes the power of what had seemed most threatening about women: their words and their sexuality. The deviant and defiant women of the novel are explained by a single etiology that assigns them the status of various hysterical types: in her letter Rosanna "bursts into words" to reveal her unrequited love for Blake, and even Limping Lucy's hysterical cries of ressentiment signal the defectiveness of her desiring a woman rather than a man. The centrality to the novel of this reading of femininity is embodied in the figure of the only woman assigned a narrative, the evangelical spinster Miss Clack, whose hysteria is coded by her failure to acknowledge her desire for Godfrey Ablewhite. After watching from behind a curtain as Godfrey proposes to Rachel, Miss Clack attributes her voyeurism to "suppressed hysterics" (263). The very inaccuracy of her diagnosis points, ironically, to the underlying hysteria of her text; the reader must become the analyst who perceives how her hypocrisy in cloaking her feelings renders her narrative inauthentic, a meaningless "clacking" that emblematizes the fate of female language in the novel.[19]

The Moonstone's use of the discourse of hysteria to invalidate women's voices supports D. A. Miller's Foucauldian reading of the text. For Miller, the detective work in Collins' novel is another example of how Victorian novels in general are implicated in the operations of surveillance and social policing that secure bourgeois hegemony. He argues that the tendency of the multiple narratives in *The Moonstone* to endorse Blake's version of what happened—some, like Miss Clack's, by being transparently "wrong"—demonstrates how the novel stifles dissent and establishes instead a "master-voice that corrects, overrides, subordinates, or sublates all other voices it allows to speak."[20]

Yet despite the way *The Moonstone* silences women's voices, the model of a master voice is finally not as useful for understanding the text as is the theory of the double voice that feminist critics have used to describe the subversive undercurrent, conveyed by irony and indirection, that underlies the conventional plot in nineteenth-century women's writing.

It may seem in itself ironic to locate such a feminine strategy in a novel that deauthorizes female language. Yet since women's voices (Rachel's, Rosanna's, and Limping Lucy's) convey the novel's social criticism, for Collins to silence their dissent is also to silence his own. Although this containment of radical tendencies is not new in Collins' fiction, it is even more pronounced than it is in *The Woman in White*, where ideological conflict is also reflected in the conflict between men's and women's voices. Unlike Marian Halcombe, though, Rachel has no narrative of her own, so Blake's narration in the scene of their meeting can more effectively rewrite her protest as acquiescence. Yet this type of voice-over attests, finally, not to the "monological" nature of the text, as Miller claims,[21] but to the continued ideological doubleness that causes the novel to speak in two voices, one of which, according to the double voice theory, is a palimpsest. Paradoxically, even as Collins' art becomes more masculine in *The Moonstone*—more allied with the male science of detection—it becomes increasingly more feminine, fissuring the official version of what happened with ironies and indirections. In this way, the feminine and Gothic space of the Shivering Sand, where resistance trembles beneath the surface, becomes a symbol for the novel itself.

One scene where this double voice of irony and indirection is particularly apparent is that where Franklin Blake reads Rosanna's letter after discovering the evidence of his guilt in the Sand. Blake's narration portrays this scene as one more painful step in his detective safari from "the darkness to the light" (369). Rosanna's text is stranded in "darkness" because she (like Rachel and Miss Clack) does not correctly interpret what she sees; all these women either suspect or know that Blake took the diamond, but they turn out to be wrong about why he took it. Although this devaluation of female knowledge is typical of detective work, Rosanna's letter, by representing one of the novel's more subversive analyses of gender and class, shows that in this regard she is more knowing than Blake. When he refuses to finish reading Rosanna's letter, handing it to Betteredge half-read, the novel draws attention to how Blake continues not to "notice" Rosanna or her narrative, which is a criticism of class privilege.

As an allegory of reading, this scene comments on the fate of Collins' own art. That Blake puts aside the letter he finds offensive demonstrates the fate of texts that offend the middle-class reader, even when the text's author is trying (like Rosanna, the faithful servant) to please. As the detective plot of *The Moonstone* unfolds, Collins does not so much offend as he does what Rosanna does with her letter before Blake reads it: buries his social criticism so deep that the reader can only with difficulty dig it out again. This transformation of the radical elements in the text into a subtext explains why, as detection works to disclose all, the novel becomes obsessed with images of alienated writers who censor themselves. Whereas Rosanna's jumping into the quicksand that buries her letter is *The Moonstone*'s most dramatic image of self-erasure, Ezra Jennings, the detective who solves the mystery yet obstinately refuses to tell his story, becomes the novel's main figure for authorial self-censorship.

Buried Texts and the Victorian Romantic: The Role of Ezra Jennings

As a figure for the double impulse of the text toward revelation and self-censorship, Ezra Jennings embodies the ideological and generic contradictions in *The Moonstone*. Entering the novel by interrupting the reading of Rosanna's letter, he signals simultaneously the outcast status he shares with her and the way he will become the male detective who leads Blake "from the darkness to the light." This doubleness is inscribed on his body, making him a walking set of contrasts:

> Judging him by his figure and his movements, he was still young. Judging him by his face, and comparing him with Betteredge, he looked the elder of the two. His complexion was of a gipsy darkness; his fleshless cheeks had fallen into deep hollows, over which

> the bone projected like a penthouse. His nose presented the fine shape and modelling so often found among the ancient people of the East, so seldom visible among the newer races of the West. His forehead rose high and straight from the brow. His marks and wrinkles were innumerable. From this strange face, eyes, stranger still, of the softest brown—eyes dreamy and mournful, and deeply sunk in their orbits—looked out at you, and (in my case, at least) took your attention captive at their will. Add to this a quantity of thick closely-curling hair, which, by some freak of Nature, had lost its colour in the most startlingly partial and capricious manner. Over the top of his head it was still of the deep black which was its natural colour. Round the sides of his head—without the slightest gradation of grey to break the force of the extraordinary contrast—it had turned completely white. The line between the two colours preserved no sort of regularity. At one place, the white hair ran up into the black; at another, the black hair ran down into the white. (358–59)

With the most obvious contradiction in Jennings' appearance, the colonial plot of the novel resurfaces. In this passage the disjunction between youth and age is not as riveting as the mingling of black and white in Jennings' piebald hair, which signals, as Blake puts it, "the mixture of some foreign race in his English blood" (411). The references to Jennings' "gipsy complexion" and the "fine shape and modelling" of his nose are signifiers leading to this final image of miscegenation ("The line between the two colours preserved no sort of regularity").[22]

This physical "freak of Nature" symbolizes the transgression of the boundary between colonizer and colonized that permitted Jennings' birth: "I was born, and partly brought up, in one of our colonies. My father was an Englishman, but my mother—We are straying away from our subject, Mr. Blake . . ." (411). This passage shows how Jennings, who blends the identities of English "gentleman" (410) and colonial Other, nonetheless feels a tension between these origins. The man whose detective work in the novel consists of filling in blanks resolutely leaves a blank after "my mother" because of his desire to cloak the racial background that would account in part for why he is distrusted. (Betteredge, for example, refers contemptuously to him by the signs of racial difference, "the man with the piebald hair, and the gipsy complexion" [359].) That Jennings prefixes "colonies" with "our" attests to his desire to identify not with his native mother but with white men—his father and Blake, to whom he is speaking. When Jennings does note his affinity with women, he emphasizes that this is an undesirable attribute. Confessing that he burst into tears after saving Mr. Candy's life, he offers Blake a "bitterly professional apology": "An hysterical relief, Mr. Blake—nothing more! Physiology says, and says truly, that some men are born with female constitutions —and I am one of them!" (414).

Jennings' diagnosis of hysteria draws attention to what Jenny Taylor calls his "double role."[23] The novel's most able practitioner of the male science of detective work, he appropriately is a doctor. Yet, paradoxically, Jennings speaks with the voice of male professionalism to diagnose his own powerless and feminized position (at one point he even claims that it is "useless to appeal to my honour as a man" [420]). This confusion in gender roles also manifests itself as a generic confusion: the novel's most scientific detective, Jennings is also its most Gothic figure, not just in his flamboyantly weird appearance but in his embodiment of the Gothic plot of silence and potential subversion. In the same conversation with Blake where he diagnoses himself as female, he becomes an image for a potentially dangerous radicalism. When Blake tries to gain access to Jennings' notes, he commands him to stop:

> I looked at him in astonishment. The grip of some terrible emotion seemed to have seized him, and shaken him to the soul. His gipsy complexion had altered to a livid greyish paleness; his eyes had suddenly become wild and glittering; his voice had dropped to a tone —low, stern, and resolute—which I now heard for the first time. The latent resources in the man, for good or for evil—it was hard, at that moment, to say which—leapt up in him and showed themselves to me, with the suddenness of a flash of light. (419)

The flash of light illuminates Jennings' resemblance to other Gothic images of ressentiment—Mary Shelley's monster, whom he resembles in his freakish appearance and outcast state, and also Collins' version of that monster in *Basil*'s Mannion, whose history of being blacklisted because of his scandalous past anticipates that of Jennings. Jennings' threatening expression, in fact, recalls the scene in the earlier novel where Basil sees Mannion's look change from deference to maniacal hatred as a flash of lightning reveals his face.[24]

Unlike these Gothic predecessors, however, Jennings almost immediately contains his subversive energy. He not only attributes his extraordinary reaction to self-hatred rather than to hatred of Blake (whom he does not wish to expose to someone whose "character is gone"), but he also admits he wants to help the more privileged man in order to stifle his bitterness about social inequality: "A man who has lived as I have lived has his bitter moments when he ponders over human destiny. You have youth, health, riches, a place in the world, a prospect before you. You, and such as you, show me the sunny side of human life, and reconcile me with the world that I am leaving, before I go" (422). As Jennings becomes (appropriately enough in this novel that alludes to *Robinson Crusoe*) a kind of Friday who serves the upper-class Blake, he also becomes an image of the writer who reconciles himself to the social order instead of challenging it.

In this context, Jennings' wish for amnesia—"Perhaps we should all be happier . . . if we could but completely forget" (410)—expresses the novel's own impulse to erase its origins in the Gothic and in radical Romanticism. The script that Jennings writes for the "experiment" that exonerates Blake is the novel's climactic example of how it erases both its subversiveness and its generic antecedents. Jennings' reenactment of the theft begins as a Gothic narrative, casting him in the role not only of Frankenstein's monster but also of Frankenstein himself, the daring scientist whose theories provoke, as Jennings puts it, "the protest of the world . . . against anything that is new" (463). Jennings convinces hostile witnesses like Bruff and Betteredge that he is right, and he persuades Rachel's exceedingly proper chaperone Mrs. Merridew that he is not so disruptive a force as she had feared, causing Blake to comment that "there is a great deal of undeveloped liberal feeling in the world, after all" (480). Yet Mrs. Merridew's fears about Jennings are revealing: she is sure that his experiment will set off an explosion that, presumably, would literalize his association with a revolutionary "flash of light." She is mollified, however, because, as she explains after the experiment, "Explosions . . . are infinitely milder than they were" (480).

What makes this comment so funny, of course, is the reader's knowledge that there was no explosion. This absence of disruption implies that the writing of the Victorian Romantic is not "explosive," like that of his predecessors, but instead serves domestic ideology. Jennings is not the Frankenstein, or Frankenstein monster, who attacks families but the physician who cures their ills. In this role he resembles Dickens, Collins' great model for this kind of literary activity, whose domestic fiction diagnoses social disease by stabilizing the family and normalizing gender roles. By reuniting Rachel with Blake, the experiment replaces the hysteria that "bursts into words instead of tears" with conventionally feminine language. Jennings describes her response to his letter explaining the circumstances of the theft as "A charming letter! . . . She tells me, in the prettiest manner, that my letter has satisfied her of Mr. Blake's innocence" (442). This charming and pretty female text is a paean to romantic love: "the rapture of discovering that he has deserved to be loved, breaks its way innocently through the stoutest formalities of pen and ink" (442).

This channeling of female writing into the expression of heterosexual desire precedes the reenactment of the theft in which Rachel reprises her role as silent witness of Blake's theft: "She kept back, in the dark: not a word, a movement escaped her" (473). Whereas Blake's theft had represented men's domination of women, this repeat performance stages the ritual with the woman's consent to her own invisibility. Unlike her horrified silence during the original theft, Rachel's silence during the experiment expresses her happy anticipation of her impending marriage. Watching Blake sleep off the effects of the opium, she reverses the effects of her hysteria by bursting into tears instead of words: "She looked at him in a silent ecstasy of happiness, till the tears rose in her eyes" (477).

Yet Jennings, who engineers this happy ending, never makes it to the wedding of Franklin Blake and Rachel, when for the duration of the festivities he was to have been a "guest in the house" (479). Even though he has been a figure for the writer of domestic fiction who pleases his readers with scenes of married bliss, Jennings dies before he himself can enter the "house," or the terms of the domestic ideology he has served so well. If in life the Romantic he evoked was Thomas De Quincy, whose *Confessions of an English Opium Eater* he lends to Blake, in death he resembles the Romantic figure most closely associated with buried writing. The language in Mr. Candy's letter, which describes Jennings' death, echoes the account of the death of John Keats written by his friend Joseph Severn.[25] In particular, Severn's line "the letters I put into the coffin with my own hand"[26] is echoed by Mr. Candy's account of how, at his friend's request, he buried his letters and other writing with him ("'Promise,' he said, 'that you will put this into my coffin with your own hand; and that you see that no other hand touches it afterwards'" [512]). All that was buried with Keats were other people's letters, but Jennings requests that the "locked volumes" (511) of his journal and his unfinished book be buried with him as well. As if to mimic this total erasure of his writing, Jennings begs that no tombstone mark his grave—a namelessness even more profound than that of Keats, who requested as an epitaph "here lies one whose name was writ in water."[27]

That the Victorian version of Keats buries his writing in an even more hyperbolic fashion than his predecessor had comments on the fate of Romanticism in the Victorian period. Writing about Charlotte Brontë's *Villette*, Mary Jacobus claims that the image of the buried letter symbolizes for the Victorians the "divorce of the Romantic imagination from its revolutionary impulse."[28] Similarly, Jennings' buried writing records a grim fable about the suppression of radical Romanticism, which becomes, like his journal, a locked volume. All that remains of Jennings' writing is the conventional domestic narrative of the experiment, not his projected daring book on psychology. This narrative about the suppression of Romanticism is based on the recognition that the radical writer will meet with critical disapproval. The Victorian mythologies of Keats's death attributed it to the harsh attacks of critics, an account echoed by Jennings' history of being hounded, until his death, by mysterious slanders. In making Jennings a Keats-like figure, Collins represents his anxieties about the critical hostility that greeted his own Romantic and unconventional impulses.[29]

In this way, Ezra Jennings becomes the novel's most important mirror of its author. Collins and his creation have obvious similarities: both are opium addicts who live on the margins of respectability, and both respond satirically to convention (hence Jennings' scathing remark that there is a "wonderful sameness in the solid expression of the English face" [464]). Like Collins, Jennings becomes a figure for the noncanonical writer, dismissing the classics of "Standard Literature" in Blake's bedroom as boring (464). Both Collins and Jennings, however, try to muffle their unconventional tendencies in order to write domestic fictions that will win the approval of their audience. In the preface for the revised edition of 1871, Collins describes his struggle to complete the novel, despite severe attacks of gout and grief over the death of his mother, in terms that echo Jennings'. Like his character, who struggled despite his illness to bring the experiment to its happy conclusion, Collins claims that he overcame "merciless pains" and "useless tears" in order not to disappoint his "good readers" (xxxiii). For Collins, the result of these efforts, which recall the stereotypical sufferings of the Romantic artist, is triumph in the Victorian marketplace: "Everywhere my characters made friends, and my story roused interest" (xxxiv). Yet the fate of Jennings, who finally makes some friends but never publishes his writing, provides an ironic counterpoint to Collins' tale by implying that the price of this popularity is self-suppression. Whereas Jennings figures the aspect of Collins that prevented him from being considered sufficiently respectable by the critics, the burial of Jennings' writing and his death represent Collins' attempts to achieve this respectability.

In light of Collins' erasure of Romanticism in *The Moonstone*, it is only fitting that he later claimed to have been so dazed by the influence of opium that he did not remember writing the end of the novel! Although this self-mythologizing narrative is Coleridgean in its plot of drug-induced inspiration, it suggests the suppression of Romantic artistry. By claiming that he wrote the end of the novel unknowingly, Collins writes himself into the role of Blake, who stole the Moonstone in a drugged trance. But, unlike the erstwhile bohemian Blake, whose dark secret is his most unrespectable moment, Collins suppresses the secret of the self-suppression he undertook in the interest of respectability. Forgetting that he created Jennings, he achieves in parodic fashion Jennings' goal of forgetting everything. In the stage version of *The Moonstone*, Collins takes this willful amnesia to an even more remarkable extreme, excising Ezra Jennings, Rosanna Spearman, the Indians, and even opium, and attributing Blake's sleep-walking to a fit of indigestion.[30]

The novel, however, does not forget its ideological doubleness but rather underscores it; like Jennings and Collins—the author within the text and the author outside it—*The Moonstone* never manages to be respectable enough. The narrative ends twice, once in England, the second time in India. The relation between these two endings reflects the tensions within the novel's double voice. The English ending is the finale to the novel's suppression of all that is outcast and Other. The death of Godfrey Ablewhite, killed by the Indians while he is in blackface, represents the novel's most horrifying image of what happens when white men go native (as Miss Clack says, "How soon may our own evil passions prove to be Oriental noblemen who pounce on us unawares!" [222]). That this character with a double life is punished only emphasizes how Blake, who has led a similarly bohemian bachelor existence, is now a family man. The novel, however, moves from the warm contentment of English domesticity (with Rachel expecting a child, her new jewel) to the foreign, dark, and impersonal realm of the colonial Other, where the Moonstone is finally restored to its temple. Although described by a Westerner, the explorer Murthwaite, the Indian ending opens up possibilities closed down when Gabriel Betteredge says he is going to "shut up" the English part of the story (515). Even though, in Murthwaite's narrative, the Indians who have recaptured the gem disperse amid "dead silence" (521) to become outcasts, the end of the novel promises a repetition of the historical cycle in which repression is followed by resistance. In choosing to conclude on the margins of resistance, Collins thus resists the falsely comfortable closure of the English narrative to end instead with the riddling ambiguity of a question mark: "So the years pass, and repeat each other; so the same events revolve in the cycles of time. What will be the next adventures of the Moonstone? Who can tell?" (522).

EPILOGUE: THE HAUNTED NARRATIVE

An eerie image of a woman's tortured writing from Collins' *The Haunted Hotel* (1879) serves as an emblem for the fate of female Gothic in his later work. *The Haunted Hotel* is dominated by one of Collins' grand Gothic villainesses, Countess Narona, who poisons her husband for his money. Driven by a need to confess the crime, the Countess tries again and again to write a play that describes the murder in only slightly veiled form; unable, despite compulsive scribbling, to finish the manuscript, she starts it over before succumbing to an illness that causes her words, before she dies, to trail off (like Marian Halcombe's in *The Woman in White*) into illegible fragments. Just as she had been obsessively compelled to write, the Countess stubbornly and paradoxically lives on after her death, continuing to draw breath in a way the doctor describes as "purely mechanical."[1]

Many readers would claim that this image of the animated corpse is all too symbolic of Collins' career after *The Moonstone*. Like his early works, Collins' later novels merit more critical attention and respect than they have generally received either during his lifetime or since. Yet a decline in the quality of his fiction after the 1860s is unquestionable. This decline has been attributed, plausibly enough, to many causes: his poor health and opium addiction; the continued demands of serial publication, which compelled an author to write, like Countess Narona, more or less mechanically; the death of Dickens and with it the symbolic passing of the literary generation with which Collins was most intimately connected. Yet the deterioration in Collins' fiction after *The Moonstone* also occurs in a dialectical relation to the deterioration of his reputation. Sue Lonoff has argued that, in the decades following Dickens' death, Collins lost touch with the taste of his audience, many of whom, despite the continued popularity of his work, became interested in other types of fiction than he provided.[2] This argument suggests that Collins' late writing suffered even more than his early work from changing critical norms. Certainly, the critical devaluation that dogged Collins' career in the 1860s accelerated in the last two decades of his life; this may be ascribed to the low quality of the fiction, but it is as likely that the decline in the quality of the fiction is linked to the decline in the value placed on it, both by critics and by the culture more generally. The intensified dismissal of Collins' work, due to the shift in literary taste to which Lonoff refers, reflected such changes in the literary marketplace as the heightened stratification of culture into highbrow and lowbrow, the increased emphasis on realism as a criterion for literary excellence, and, concomitantly, on codes of aesthetic value, exemplified in the work of writers like Eliot and James, that move away from melodrama toward an emphasis on psychological "roundness" and irony.

Collins' later works often seem to have been written as if he had his by-now securely lowbrow status in mind. Liberated from the pressure of trying to be read as a serious writer, he takes the Gothic and sensational elements in his fiction to such an extreme as to seem surreal. In *Poor Miss Finch,* the disfigurement of the hero, a typical Collins grotesque, is (as in the case of Ezra Jennings) an image for racial difference. Yet though the issue of race is implicit, it is no longer represented with any sort of realism: the hero is not black but, in a reaction to medicine he has taken, blue.[3] As if to assure us that such bizarre things do happen, Collins includes a scene where another blue man wanders nonchalantly onto the beach of a seaside resort. Such scenes suggest that one direction Collins' later work takes is to stray so far from realism as to enter (in a manner reminiscent of works like *Armadale*) the realm of fantasy. Like the Gothic, the genre of fantasy, developed in the work of such late-nineteenth-century writers as Robert Louis Stevenson and Jules Verne, allows its authors the freedom to imagine other worlds—which, in Collins' case, are worlds of Others.

Another important way in which Collins articulates his characteristic themes of social marginality in the late works is to engage, more strenuously and explicitly than ever, in writing polemical fiction. To some critics, this choice was added reason for his decline; as Swinburne put it, "What brought good Wilkie's genius nigh perdition? / Some demon whispered—'Wilkie! Have a mission!'"[4] Such a comment, like those of critics in the earlier part of Collins' career, suggests that aesthetic judgments can also be ideological ones; in his treatment of the causes he espoused in the later novels—reform of marriage laws in *Man and Wife*, antivivisection (a reform movement often supported by women) in *Heart and Science*, the rehabilitation of fallen women in *The New Magdalen* and *The Fallen Leaves*—Collins is often as critical of convention, and as daring in his representation of issues of gender and sexuality, as he had been in works like *Basil*, *No Name*, and *Armadale*.[5] Yet, since polemical fiction tends to be defined as subliterary, Collins' choosing to write this kind of work is another index of his resignation to his low status.[6] Certainly, in novels that are openly didactic—that un-bury, as it were, the subversive subtexts of his fiction—Collins moves away from the irony created by the tension between surface and hidden meaning that makes a novel like *The Moonstone* delight readers trained to read the presence of such nuance as a sign of aesthetic value.

In becoming more transparent about his political concerns, however, Collins did not necessarily resolve the tension between the desire to be subversive and the desire to be respectable that animates the fictions of the first twenty years of his career. His efforts to render his representation of delicate sexual issues palatable to his audience causes a novel like *The New Magdalen* to be riddled by the same wariness about how far it can go that marks earlier works like *Basil* and *No Name*. This desire at once to challenge and to placate his audience can, as Collins became less adept at aesthetic innovation, lead to the aesthetic awkwardness of a novel like *The Fallen Leaves*.

Of course, that Collins conveys his representation of themes of gender and sexuality through his characteristic, and sensational, version of female Gothic is one more reason for his fiction's apparent outmodedness. Despite his important innovation in transforming Gothic into detective fiction in *The Moonstone*, Collins left the task of developing that genre to those influenced by him—including his most important successor, Arthur Conan Doyle, who launched his career as detective writer (with *A Study in Scarlet* in 1887) as Collins neared the close of his. Often, as in Doyle's case, post-*Moonstone* detective stories focus on masculinity against a backdrop of male bonding to the extent of marginalizing, if not excluding, female characters. Yet in the fiction that Collins himself wrote after *The Moonstone*, he returns faithfully, and even obsessively, to the stories about femininity told by the female Gothic. *Man and Wife*, the novel he wrote after *The Moonstone*, is his purest example after *The Woman in White* of the feminine carceral. *The Law and the Lady*, one of Collins' most aesthetically and ideologically complex mystery tales, centers on a female, not a male, detective, in a narrative that rewrites the Radcliffean plot of the potentially murderous husband.

This return to the Gothic indicates Collins' need to return to the issue—the tension between feminine marginality and male professionalism—that animated his earlier fiction. I have spoken of how Collins continues to cloak subversive impulses in his fiction to please his audience, but, more centrally, the nervousness about going too far in his later works indicates his own continuing ambivalence about his relation to both female rebellion and marginality. As in his early work, the female Gothic narratives of his later years are structured by the desire at once to identify with rebellious women and to contain their rebellion through narratives of male professionalism. Thus, in *The Haunted Hotel*, Countess Narona is subjected in the novel's first scene to the gaze of a male physician; after her death the male readers of her play—figures for critics—consign it to the flames. Since Collins, by killing off his anti-heroine, participates in taming her energy, he allies himself with these figures for the male diagnostician of female deviance; as in *The Woman in White*, however, his writing is also identified with that of this marginalized character. Since the Countess claims that she is writing her play because of a desperate need for money, like Leah Kerby in *After Dark*, she represents the popular author, and the fate of her Gothic melodrama is a grim commentary on the critical reception of the Victorian sensation writer.

Finally, Collins' inability to go any further than he had in *The Moonstone* in his representation of gender and power causes his later novels to have a quality curiously reminiscent of the Countess Narona's mechanical breathing and writing. In his earlier work Collins carefully returns to important themes and characters to revise and develop them; Ezra Jennings of *The Moonstone*, that figure for the marginalized Victorian Romantic, is the culmination of this process. He embodies, in a more emblematic fashion than Collins ever realized again, the central theme in his fiction of the conflict for the Victorian writer between subversion and repression. In his later work, however, as if he were aware there was no place else to go with this narrative, the process of revision often seems like repetition, producing a pastiche of fragments, stitched together like Frankenstein's monster, that no longer have the vitality and coherence of earlier incarnations. In *Heart and Science*, for example, a nearly identical version of the Ezra Jennings story appears at the end of the novel almost as an afterthought, at once more marginalized and less securely moored to the narrative than the analogous plot is to *The Moonstone*, where Jennings' marginality is a central concern.

This inability to resolve his narratives of professionalism can scarcely be blamed on Collins' lack of vision. Since professionalism tends to be defined by the exclusion and control of women, it is not as if Collins could easily resolve his desire to be professional with his subversive and feminist impulses. Nor could he possibly imagine an ending for the larger historical problem of the writer's contested and ambiguous status—a status that has remained in dispute. In the decades following Collins' death, the rise of literary Modernism—a reaction not only against Victorian familial ideology but also against the reliance of authors on a popular audience—would be a twentieth-century response (if one often hostile to women) to the questions about the writer's status that Collins raises. For Collins himself, however, his inability to resolve the tensions in his representation of gender and the writer provokes a problem of closure both in his fiction and in his career. In the later works the careful balance of *The Moonstone*—between female Gothic and male detection, marginality and professionalism, resistance and suppression—crumbles, and Collins, like the Countess with her play, returns to the same story without being able to finish it.

NOTES

Introduction

1 Wilkie Collins, *The Dead Secret* (New York: Dover, 1979). All references will be to this edition and are cited by page in the text.

2 Wilkie Collins, *The Moonstone*, ed. Anthea Trodd (Oxford: Oxford University Press, 1982), 414.

3 See, e.g., Claire Kahane, "The Gothic Mirror," in *The (M)Other Tongue: Essays in Feminist Psychoanalytic Interpretation*, ed. Shirley Nelson Garner, Claire Kahane, and Madelon Sprengnether (Ithaca: Cornell University Press, 1985), 334–51, and Tania Modleski, *Loving with a Vengeance: Mass-Produced Fantasies for Women* (1982; reprint, New York: Methuen, 1984), 59–84.

4 Sandra M. Gilbert and Susan Gubar, *The Madwoman in the Attic: The Woman Writer and the Nineteenth-Century Literary Imagination* (New Haven: Yale University Press, 1979), especially 336–71.

5 Dorothy L. Sayers, introduction to *The Moonstone*, by Wilkie Collins (London: Dent, 1944), vii, quoted in Sue Lonoff, *Wilkie Collins and His Victorian Readers: A Study in the Rhetoric of Authorship* (New York: AMS Press, 1982), 26; Maurice Richardson, introduction to *The Woman in White*, by Wilkie Collins (New York: Dutton, 1972), vii; Robert Ashley, "Wilkie Collins Reconsidered," *Nineteenth-Century Fiction* 4 (1950): 271.

6 Richard Barickman, Susan MacDonald, and Myra Stark, *Corrupt Relations: Dickens, Thackeray, Trollope, Collins, and the Victorian Sexual System* (New York: Columbia University Press, 1982), 111.

7 Ibid., 113.

8 Joanna Russ, "Somebody's Trying to Kill Me and I Think It's My Husband: The Modern Gothic," in *The Female Gothic*, ed. Juliann E. Fleenor (Montreal: Eden, 1983), 31–56.

9 Two recent studies examine gender in Collins' work: Philip O'Neill, *Wilkie Collins: Women, Property and Propriety* (Totowa, N.J.: Barnes, 1988); and Jenny Bourne Taylor, *In the Secret Theatre of Home: Wilkie Collins, Sensation Narrative, and Nineteenth-Century Psychology* (London: Routledge, 1988).

10 Lonoff, *Wilkie Collins and His Victorian Readers*.

11 John R. Reed, "English Imperialism and the Unacknowledged Crime of *The Moonstone*," *Clio* 2 (1973): 281–90; Albert D. Hutter, "Dreams, Transformations, and Literature: The Implications of Detective Fiction," in *The Poetics of Murder: Detective Fiction and Literary Theory*, ed. Glenn W. Most and William W. Stowe (New York: Harcourt, 1983), 230–51; D. A. Miller, "From *roman-policier* to *roman-police*: Wilkie Collins's *The Moonstone*," *Novel* 13 (1980): 153–70.

12 Review of *The Woman in White*, by Wilkie Collins, *Saturday Review*, 25 August 1860, in *Wilkie Collins: The Critical Heritage*, ed. Norman Page (1974; reprint, London: Routledge, 1985), 83.

13 Review of *The Moonstone*, by Wilkie Collins, *Nation* 7, no. 168 (September 1868): 235.

14 [Margaret Oliphant], review of *No Name*, by Wilkie Collins, *Blackwood's Magazine* 94 (August 1863), in *Critical Heritage*, ed. Page, 143.

15 [H. F. Chorley], review of *Armadale*, by Wilkie Collins, *Athenaeum*, 2 June 1866, in *Critical Heritage*, ed. Page, 147.

16 Gaye Tuchman, with Nina E. Fortin, *Edging Women Out: Victorian Novelists, Publishers, and Social Change* (New Haven: Yale University Press, 1989).

17 The phrase "period of invasion" is Tuchman's; see her definition in *Edging Women Out*, 7–8, and chap. 6, 120–48.

18 Edmund Yates, "W. Wilkie Collins," *Train* (June 1857), in *Critical Heritage*, ed. Page, 67.

19 For the rise of professionalism and its link to domestic ideology, see Leonore Davidoff and Catherine Hall, *Family Fortunes: Men and Women of the English Middle Class, 1780–1850* (Chicago: University of Chicago, 1987); for relevant recent studies on the nineteenth-century professionalization of literature in England and America, respectively, that address gender politics, see Julia Swindells, *Victorian Writing and Working Women: The Other Side of Silence* (Minneapolis: University of Minnesota Press, 1985), and Richard Brodhead, *The School of Hawthorne* (New York: Oxford University Press, 1986).

20 Taylor, *In the Secret Theatre of Home*, 25.

21 For another comparison between Collins and his Gothic sources, see Keith Brown Reierstad, "The Demon in the House: or, The Domestication of Gothic in the Novels of Wilkie Collins" (Ph.D. diss., University of Pennsylvania, 1976).

22 Harold Bloom, *The Anxiety of Influence: A Theory of Poetry* (New York: Oxford University Press, 1973), and Gilbert and Gubar, *Madwoman in the Attic*, 187–212.

Chapter 1. Reigns of Terror

1 Michael Sadleir, *The Northanger Novels: A Footnote to Jane Austen*, English Association Pamphlet no. 68 (Oxford: Oxford University Press, 1927), 4. Other readings of the Gothic (though not from a feminist perspective) that link the genre to ideological currents during the period of the French Revolution are David Punter, *The Literature of Terror: A History of Gothic Fictions from 1765 to the Present Day* (London: Longmans, 1980), and Ronald Paulson, *Representations of Revolution (1789–1820)* (New Haven: Yale University Press, 1983), 215–47.

2 Edmund Burke, *Reflections on the Revolution in France*, ed. Conor Cruise O'Brien (Harmondsworth, Eng.: Penguin, 1968), 121.

3 Mary Wollstonecraft, *A Vindication of the Rights of Men* (1790), ed. Eleanor Louise Nicholes (Gainesville, Fla.: Scholars' Facsimiles and Reprints, 1960), 100.

4 There has been a great deal of feminist criticism of the female Gothic, of which I cite here several of the most formative and important sources. Ellen Moers used *Frankenstein* as her original example of female Gothic in *Literary Women: The Great Writers* (New York: Doubleday, 1976; reprint, New York: Oxford University Press, 1985), 90–110; she expands this definition in her exploration of the Radcliffean tradition (see "Gothic for Heroines," 122–40). Margaret Anne Doody argues that the tradition of female Gothic fiction accuses the "real world" that women inhabit of "falsehood and deep disorder" in "Deserts, Ruins, and Troubled Waters: Female Dreams in Fiction and the Development of the Gothic Novel," *Genre* 10 (1977): 529–72. Claire Kahane examines the mother-daughter narrative of the female Gothic from a psychoanalytic perspective in "The Gothic Mirror," in *The (M)Other Tongue: Essays in Feminist Psychoanalytic Interpretation*, ed. Shirley Nelson Garner, Claire Kahane, and Madelon Sprengnether (Ithaca: Cornell University Press, 1985), 334–51. Kate Ellis uses a historicizing marxist-feminist framework to explore the works of both male and female writers of Gothic in *The Contested Castle: Gothic Novels and the Subversion of Domestic Ideology* (Urbana: University of Illinois Press, 1989). For essays that usefully summarize the tradition of

feminist criticism of the genre, see Juliann E. Fleenor, ed., *The Female Gothic* (Montreal: Eden, 1983). For a reading of female Gothic and Radcliffe relevant to this chapter, see also Eugenia C. DeLamotte, *Perils of the Night: A Feminist Study of Nineteenth-Century Gothic* (New York: Oxford University Press, 1990), 29–35, 149–92.

5 Edmund Burke, *Letters on a Regicide Peace*, in *Works* (London: George Bell, 1884–89), V, 210.

6 Burke, *Reflections*, 86. For more on male writers' fascination with the monstrous woman as a figure for revolution, see Neil Hertz, "Medusa's Head: Male Hysteria under Political Pressure," *Representations* 4 (Fall 1983): 27–54.

7 Burke, *Letters on a Regicide Peace*, in *Works*, V, 155.

8 The literary genealogy that links the female Gothic to the novel of sensibility is explored in Jane Spencer, *The Rise of the Woman Novelist* (New York: Blackwell, 1986), especially 192–210.

9 Ann Radcliffe, *The Mysteries of Udolpho: A Romance, Interspersed with Some Pieces of Poetry*, ed. Bonamy Dobrée (Oxford: Oxford University Press, 1966), 381. All references will be to this edition and are cited by page in the text.

10 Ann Radcliffe, *The Italian, or the Confessional of the Black Penitents: A Romance*, ed. Frederick Garber (Oxford: Oxford University Press, 1981), 84.

11 Doody, "Deserts, Ruins, and Troubled Waters," 562.

12 Sandra M. Gilbert and Susan Gubar discuss double meanings and concealment of subversion in women's writing in *The Madwoman in the Attic: The Woman Writer and the Nineteenth-Century Literary Imagination* (New Haven: Yale University Press, 1979), 71–83. The guiding metaphor of their study—Brontë's incendiary madwoman hidden in, and periodically escaping from, the attic where she is guarded by her husband—is one in which the Gothic expresses this plot of "self-division" on the part of women writers who desire "both to accept the strictures of patriarchal society and to reject them" (78).

13 Elaine Showalter, "Literary Criticism," *Signs* 1 (1975): 435.

14 Ann Radcliffe, *A Sicilian Romance* (London: Hookham and Carpenter, 1796), II, 158–59. All references will be to this edition and are cited by volume and page in the text.

15 See Kahane, "Gothic Mirror," 334–40, especially her reading of Radcliffe, which complements my own.

16 Mary Wollstonecraft, *A Vindication of the Rights of Woman*, ed. Carol H. Poston, 2d ed. (New York: Norton, 1988), 177. All references are to this edition and are cited as *VRW* and by page in the text.

17 Tania Modleski, *Loving with a Vengeance: Mass-Produced Fantasies for*

Women (1982; reprint, New York: Methuen, 1984), 68.

18 Mary Poovey, "Ideology and *The Mysteries of Udolpho*," *Criticism* 21 (1979): 319.

19 Marilyn Butler, "The Woman at the Window: Ann Radcliffe in the Novels of Mary Wollstonecraft and Jane Austen," in *Gender and Literary Voice*, ed. Janet Todd (New York: Holmes and Meier, 1980), 133.

20 For more on this sexual plot, see Cynthia Griffin Wolff, "The Radcliffean Gothic Model: A Form for Feminine Sexuality," in *Female Gothic*, ed. Fleenor, 207–23.

21 See especially Foucault's first volume of *The History of Sexuality*, trans. Robert Hurley (New York: Vintage, 1980).

22 One good example of the double function of terror—at once to express and to contain feminine sexuality—may be found in Charlotte Smith's Jacobin Gothic *Desmond* (1792). Smith's *Emmeline* (1788) was one of the early female Gothics, and an influence on Radcliffe. (The scene where Count Morano sneaks into Emily's bedchamber at Udolpho is strikingly similar to scenes in *Emmeline* where the virtuous heroine's importunate aristocratic suitor keeps popping out of the conveniently dark and twisting corridors of the family estate to woo her.) An argument in favor of the early progress of the French Revolution that refutes Burke's "elaborate treatise in favor of despotism," *Desmond* is perhaps the most explicit of female Gothics in comparing the status of the oppressed French people under the ancien régime to that of women; Smith deploys Gothic conventions to express not only the outmodedness of the French class system, but also her heroine's enslavement in a miserable marriage. (In this way, the novel reads as a fictionalization of Wollstonecraft's *Vindication of the Rights of Woman*, published in the same year.) Into this political Gothic Smith inserts a sexual plot reminiscent of the adultery theme surrounding the Marchioness and Signora Laurentini in Radcliffe's *Udolpho*. Lionel Desmond, a young English Jacobin, is in love with the married heroine, Geraldine, and Smith subtly suggests that sexual frustration for both men and women is one pernicious effect of the corrupt present system of marriage and gender politics. At the same time, however, like Radcliffe, she seeks to diffuse the radical implications of her narrative about the liberation of feminine sexual desire. Although Geraldine is presumably also attracted to Desmond, she cannot show this adulterous feeling; instead, in a memorable sequence where Desmond gallantly saves her from counterrevolutionary brigands in France, her terror at her danger codes her concealed sexual desire (she is so frightened she allows Desmond to put his arm around her waist!). Although terror here, as Kate Ellis argues, expands the "sphere of permissible action" for the heroine ("Charlotte Smith's Subversive Gothic," *Feminist Studies* 3 [1976]: 52), it also limits the boldness of her sexuality and her voice; like Smith's Emmeline

and Radcliffe's heroines, Geraldine is finally terrorized into a state of silence and confusion that makes her emotionally dependent on her male rescuer. I have explored Smith's use of the Gothic in *Desmond* in "Feminism, Gothic, and the French Revolution: The Case of Charlotte Smith's *Desmond*" (paper presented at the MLA convention, Washington, D.C., 29 December 1989).

23 Honoré de Balzac, *Les paysans*, vol. 9 of *La comédie humaine* (Paris: Gallimard, 1978), 161. "Le peuple, les femmes et les enfants se gouvernent de même, par la terreur. Ce fut là le grand secret de la Convention et de l'Empereur." I am indebted to Roddey Reid for drawing my attention to this reference.

24 See, e.g., Tania Modleski's discussion of the female Gothic as a paranoid genre in *Loving with a Vengeance*, 59–84.

25 Douglas Hay, "Property, Authority and the Criminal Law," in Douglas Hay et al., *Albion's Fatal Tree: Crime and Society in Eighteenth-Century England* (New York: Pantheon, 1975), 17–63. For Foucault's theories on discipline, see especially *Discipline and Punish: The Birth of the Prison*, trans. Alan Sheridan (New York: Vintage, 1979).

26 The phrase is from a contemporary criticism of Radcliffe entitled "Terrorist Novel Writing," *Spirit of the Public Journals* 1 (1797): 227; quoted in Elizabeth Napier, *The Failure of Gothic: Problems of Disjunction in an Eighteenth-Century Literary Form* (Oxford: Oxford University Press, 1987), 20.

27 Mary Wollstonecraft, *Maria, or The Wrongs of Woman*, ed. Moira Ferguson (New York: Norton, 1975), 23. All references will be to this edition and are cited by page in the text.

28 Janet Todd and Mary Poovey address the Utopian potential of female solidarity in *Maria* in, respectively, *Female Friendship in Literature* (New York: Columbia University Press, 1980), 208–26, and *The Proper Lady and the Woman Writer: Ideology as Style in the Works of Mary Wollstonecraft, Mary Shelley, and Jane Austen* (Chicago: University of Chicago Press, 1984), 104.

29 For more on women during and after the French Revolution, see Claire Tomalin, *The Life and Death of Mary Wollstonecraft* (1974; reprint, New York: Meridian-NAL, 1983), 147–62; Olwen Hufton, "Women in Revolution, 1789–1796," *Past and Present* 53 (November 1971): 90–108; and Margaret H. Darrow, "French Noblewomen and the New Domesticity, 1750–1850," *Feminist Studies* 5 (1979): 45–65. Mary Poovey usefully discusses anti-Jacobin reaction in England and the affirmation of domestic ideology in *Proper Lady and the Woman Writer*, 30–35.

30 That the woman's Gothic narrative is a story of madness is implied by Sophia Lee's *The Recess* (1787), an early historical Gothic whose use of jour-

nal entries anticipates *Maria*'s first-person narratives. In Lee's novel, about two daughters of Mary Queen of Scots, the journal of one daughter who goes mad resembles Wollstonecraft's evocation of Maria's "scattered thoughts." The aesthetic implications of this theme of madness in female Gothic—whether it causes the text to disintegrate into meaninglessness or powerfully critiques the culture that has declared rebellious women "insane"—is explored in several readings of *Maria*. See, e.g., Mary Jacobus, "The Difference of View," in *Women Writing and Writing about Women*, ed. Mary Jacobus (London: Croom Helm, 1979), 15–16, and Poovey, *Proper Lady and the Woman Writer*, 257 n. 20.

31 My discussion of ressentiment is indebted to Fredric Jameson, *The Political Unconscious: Narrative as a Socially Symbolic Act* (Ithaca: Cornell University Press, 1981), especially pp. 185–205, for his reading of Gissing.

32 Moers, *Literary Women*, 90–110.

33 Mary Shelley, preface to *Frankenstein; or, The Modern Prometheus*, ed. M. K. Joseph (Oxford: Oxford University Press, 1980), 10. All references will be to this edition of the 1831 text and are cited by page. For gender and textuality in *Frankenstein*, see Gilbert and Gubar's chapter "Horror's Twin: Mary Shelley's Monstrous Eve," in *Madwoman in the Attic*, 213–47, and Margaret Homans, *Bearing the Word: Language and Female Experience in Nineteenth-Century Women's Writing* (Chicago: University of Chicago Press, 1986), 100–119.

34 Paulson, *Representations of Revolution*, 215–47; Lee Sterrenburg, "Mary Shelley's Monster: Politics and Psyche in *Frankenstein*," in *The Endurance of* Frankenstein: *Essays on Mary Shelley's Monster*, ed. George Levine and U. C. Knoepflmacher (Berkeley: University of California Press, 1979), 143–71. For more on the political dimensions of Shelley's novel, see Chris Baldick, *In Frankenstein's Shadow: Myth, Monstrosity, and Nineteenth-Century Writing* (Oxford: Clarendon, 1987).

35 Sterrenburg, "Mary Shelley's Monster," 163–64.

36 Gilbert and Gubar, *Madwoman in the Attic*, 673 n. 30.

37 Edmund Burke, *A Letter to a Noble Lord*, in *Works*, V, 141.

38 Mary Poovey, "'My Hideous Progeny': Mary Shelley and the Feminization of Romanticism," *PMLA* 95 (1980): 332–47, reprinted as chap. 4 in *Proper Lady and the Woman Writer*, 114–42.

39 Andrew Griffin, "Fire and Ice in *Frankenstein*," in *Endurance of* Frankenstein, ed. Levine and Knoepflmacher, 59. Frankenstein echoes the rhetoric of his teacher M. Waldman, who claims in similar sexual imagery that scientists "penetrate into the recesses of nature, and show how she works in her hiding places" (47).

40 Marc Rubenstein, "'My Accursed Origin': The Search for the Mother in *Frankenstein*," *Studies in Romanticism* 15 (1976): 175.

41 Barbara Johnson, "My Monster/My Self," *Diacritics* 12 (1982): 7.
42 Rubenstein, "'My Accursed Origin,'" 192.
43 See William Veeder, *Mary Shelley and* Frankenstein: *The Fate of Androgyny* (Chicago: University of Chicago Press, 1986), 192–93, for a similar reading of the scene of Elizabeth's death: "She is killed . . . by the male principle in its extreme, monstrous form."
44 Edmund Burke, *Letters on a Regicide Peace*, in *Works*, V, 220.
45 Rubenstein, "'My Accursed Origin,'" 173.
46 Nancy Armstrong, *Desire and Domestic Fiction: A Political History of the Novel* (Oxford: Oxford University Press, 1987). Sterrenburg's "Mary Shelley's Monster" also addresses the psychologicization of politics in *Frankenstein* that reads class rebellion not as itself, but as a sign of moral and familial dysfunction.
47 D. A. Miller coins the term *feminine carceral* to describe the female Gothic plot in his "*Cage aux Folles:* Sensation and Gender in Wilkie Collins's *The Woman in White*," *Representations* 14 (1986): 120.

Chapter 2. Becoming an Author in 1848

1 W. Wilkie Collins, *Memoirs of the Life of William Collins, Esq., R.A., With Selections from His Journals and Correspondence* (1848; reprint, Wakefield, W. Yorkshire: EP Publishing, 1978), II, 311. All references will be to this edition, a facsimile of the original two-volume edition, and are cited by both volume and page. Since Collins dropped the initial "W." in most of the books he published after the *Memoirs*, I refer to him in all subsequent citations of his works as Wilkie Collins.
2 Wilkie Collins, "Memorandum, Relating to the Life and Writings of Wilkie Collins" (1862), in Morris L. Parrish and Elizabeth V. Miller, *Wilkie Collins and Charles Reade: First Editions (with a Few Exceptions) in the Library at Dormy House, Pine Valley, New Jersey* (London, 1940; reprint, New York: Franklin, 1968), 4. This brief autobiographical sketch is printed in its entirety on pp. 4–5.
3 Verlyn Klinkenborg, "Wilkie Collins's *Memoirs of the Life of William Collins*: The Creation of His Portrait of the Artist," typescript, 5.
4 See Nuel Pharr Davis, *The Life of Wilkie Collins* (Urbana: University of Illinois Press, 1956). This biography has proved understandably controversial, since unfortunately Davis supports his case that there were violent disagreements between Collins and his father by citing scenes from his novels (see, e.g., the sources for the notes on pp. 306–10). Yet although it is true that Davis' use of fiction as biographical evidence is astoundingly naive, Collins' attitude toward his father, and toward the ideal of paternal authority more generally, was certainly a complex one. Critics have noted the

hostile portraits of fathers in his works, as in the early novel *Hide and Seek* (1854), where the repressive patriarch is, like William Collins, a vigorous Sabbatarian. For a recent portrait of the relationship between Collins and his father that is more nuanced than Davis', see William M. Clarke, *The Secret Life of Wilkie Collins* (London: Allison and Busby, 1988), chaps. 2–5.

5 Wilkie Collins, "Memorandum," in Parrish and Miller, *Wilkie Collins and Charles Reade*, 4.

6 Kenneth Robinson, *Wilkie Collins: A Biography* (New York: Macmillan, 1952), 47–48.

7 Klinkenborg, "Wilkie Collins's *Memoirs of the Life of William Collins*," 24.

8 Alethea Hayter, *Opium and the Romantic Imagination* (Berkeley: University of California Press, 1970), 263. There is some evidence that William tried to interest his son in painting, and one of Collins' efforts, a small landscape painting entitled "The Smuggler's Refuge," was exhibited at the Royal Academy in 1849.

9 Wilkie Collins, dedication to *Basil: A Story of Modern Life*, ed. Dorothy Goldman (Oxford: Oxford University Press, 1990), xxxvi.

10 See Eve Kosofsky Sedgwick, *Between Men: English Literature and Male Homosocial Desire* (New York: Columbia University Press, 1985).

11 Robinson, *Wilkie Collins*, 43.

12 "Our Portrait-Gallery: Mr. Wilkie Collins," *Men and Women*, 5 February 1887, quoted in Clarke, *Secret Life of Wilkie Collins*, 19.

13 I am indebted to Jaya Mehta for this insight.

14 Margaret Homans, *Women Writers and Poetic Identity: Dorothy Wordsworth, Emily Brontë, and Emily Dickinson* (Princeton: Princeton University Press, 1980), 18.

15 Wilkie Collins to R. H. Dana, 12 January 1849, quoted in Parrish and Miller, *Wilkie Collins and Charles Reade*, 10.

16 Ibid. Collins describes the paintings as "two of the largest and finest pictures my father ever produced."

17 The phrase is Collins', from his "Memorandum," in Parrish and Miller, *Wilkie Collins and Charles Reade*, 4.

18 Wilkie Collins to Richard Bentley, 30 August 1849, quoted in Sue Lonoff, *Wilkie Collins and His Victorian Readers: A Study in the Rhetoric of Authorship* (New York: AMS Press, 1982), 68–69.

19 See Lee Sterrenburg, "Mary Shelley's *The Last Man*: Anatomies of Failed Revolutions," in *The Endurance of* Frankenstein: *Essays on Mary Shelley's Monster*, ed. George Levine and U. C. Knoepflmacher (Berkeley: University of California Press, 1979), 326–27, where he discusses the numerous "post-Napoleonic works of literature and painting which shared analogous themes of the end of the race or the end of empire." An early pre-Napoleonic

example of this type of work is Volney's *Ruins of Empire* (1791), which the monster hears Felix and Safie reading in *Frankenstein*; a later example is Bulwer-Lytton's *The Last Days of Pompeii* (1834), probably a source for *Antonina*.

20 Wilkie Collins, *Antonina; or, The Fall of Rome,* vol. 17 of *The Works of Wilkie Collins* (New York: Peter Fenelon Collier, [1900]), 38. All references will be to this edition and are cited by page in the text.

21 Davis, *Life of Wilkie Collins*, 44.

22 There is one quite bizarre scene that underscores the importance of domestic ideology in *Antonina* while simultaneously pushing it into the realm of Gothic horror. When the decadent Vetranio holds his "Banquet of Famine," during which selected aristocrats and their lackies propose to commit mass suicide by drinking themselves to death, he places in a curtained alcove the body of a woman he found on the street, "propped up on a high black throne" with her arms "artifically supported" and "stretched out as if in denunciation over the banqueting-table" (501). This black humor is meant to emphasize, with Vetranio's characteristic cynical satire, the presence of mortality and the Romans' impending doom. When one of the plebeian guests, the hunchbacked and sinister Reburrus, rises to toast the figure Vetranio calls the "mighty mother" of "mystic revelations" (501), he realizes with horror that she is in fact his mother, whom he had spurned when she reproached him for his neglect. Overwhelmed with repentance, Reburrus collapses, repeating hypnotically "MY MOTHER! MY MOTHER!" (504). Thus although the figure of the mother here is indeed "mighty," an icon of violated domesticity that enforces that ideology, she is also a Gothic image that terrorizes men, much as does that emasculating female Goth, Goisvintha, whose role I discuss later in this chapter.

23 Dickens' portrait of Madame Defarge in *A Tale of Two Cities* may have been influenced by Collins' Goisvintha, since he could have read *Antonina* either when it first appeared (he had subscribed to the *Memoirs* on their publication) or later, when he and Collins were more closely associated. Although Dickens' portrait of the revolutionary woman, like Collins', was surely also influenced by Carlyle's revision of Burke in *The French Revolution,* there are many specific similarities between Madame Defarge and Goisvintha. Both women are consumed by the desire to revenge their families (Madame Defarge even comes with her own sidekick, the Vengeance), and both egg on vacillating men (Hermanric, Ernest Defarge) who shrink from killing their female enemies.

24 See Thomas Carlyle, *The French Revolution,* in *Works* (Boston: Centennial Memorial Edition, [1904]), vol. I, chap. 4 ("The Menads"), 243: "descend, O mothers; descend, ye Judiths, to food and revenge!"

25 See Georg Lukács, *The Historical Novel* (1937), trans. Hannah and Stanley

Mitchell, with an introduction by Fredric Jameson (1963; reprint, Lincoln: University of Nebraska Press, 1983), especially 171–250.

26 See Rance, *The Historical Novel and Popular Politics* (New York: Barnes, 1975), chap. 1, "The Historical Novel after Scott," 37–62.

27 In general, her *Desire and Domestic Fiction: A Political History of the Novel* (Oxford: Oxford University Press, 1987) charts the rise of this representational strategy; see in particular the chapter "History in the House of Culture," 161–202.

Chapter 3. Basil

1 Review of *Antonina*, by Wilkie Collins, *Bentley's Miscellany* 28 (April 1850), in *Wilkie Collins: The Critical Heritage*, ed. Norman Page (1974; reprint, London: Routledge, 1985), 42.

2 [H. F. Chorley], review of *Antonina*, by Wilkie Collins, *Athenaeum*, 16 March 1850, in *Critical Heritage*, ed. Page, 41.

3 [D. O. Maddyn], review of *Basil*, by Wilkie Collins, *Athenaeum*, 4 December 1852, in *Critical Heritage*, ed. Page, 48.

4 Review of *Basil*, by Wilkie Collins, *Westminster Review* 60 (October 1853), in *Critical Heritage*, ed. Page, 53, 52.

5 "Nine O'Clock!" *Bentley's Miscellany* 32 (August 1852): 222–34. This story, an early example of how Collins combines his interests in history, mystery, and the supernatural, has an oedipal plot that is not, like *Basil*, about a conservative father and a radical son but rather about contrasting radical visions in two generations of a prosperous French family during the revolutionary period. A cheerily rationalist father who reads Voltaire scoffs at the somber and mystical prophecies of his eldest son, although both later die at exactly the time the son foretells. The second son tries unsuccessfully to escape the bloody fate he is warned about by the ghost of his dead brother, but is sent to the guillotine because of his involvement with the Girondin party, overthrown by the Jacobins. The Gothicism of the tale figures the failure of revolution, as the Girondin son adopts the gloomy fatalism of his brother and rejects the belief in progress signified by his father's interest in the philosophes.

6 Albert Hutter, "Nation and Generation in *A Tale of Two Cities*," *PMLA* 93 (1978): 448.

7 Wilkie Collins, *Basil: A Story of Modern Life*, ed. Dorothy Goldman (Oxford: Oxford University Press, 1990), 2. All references will be to this edition and are cited by page in the text. I have chosen an edition that reproduces the text of the revised edition of 1862 for several reasons. The 1862 edition is the standard edition of the novel, as are the revised second editions of both *The Woman in White* and *The Moonstone*. Moreover, the revisions that

Collins made in the text of *Basil* ten years after its initial publication are mainly minor changes that improve and clarify the language. In the cases where I believe a change has transformed the meaning of the novel, I have indicated this by citing the original edition of 1852 (London: Richard Bentley, 3 vols.) after the page number.

8 See back cover of Wilkie Collins, *Basil: A Story of Modern Life* (New York: Dover, 1980).

9 Maddyn, review of *Basil*, in *Critical Heritage*, ed. Page, 48.

10 For a similar argument about the way a Victorian male writer associates women's writing with indirectness or double meanings, see Suzanne Graver, "Writing in a 'Womanly' Way and the Double Vision of *Bleak House*," *Dickens Quarterly* 4, no. 1 (1987): 3–15.

11 Sigmund Freud, "Medusa's Head" (1922), in *Sexuality and the Psychology of Love*, trans. James Strachey and ed. Philip Reiff (New York: Macmillan, 1963), 212–13.

12 Nathaniel Hawthorne to William D. Ticknor, 19 January 1855, *The Letters, 1853–1856*, vol. 17 of *The Centenary Edition of the Works of Nathaniel Hawthorne*, ed. James Woodson, James A. Rubino, L. Neal Smith, and Norman Holmes Pearson (Columbus: Ohio State University Press, 1987), 304.

13 The paranoid male plot in which one man pursues another is also indebted to Godwin's *Caleb Williams*, *Frankenstein*'s predecessor; some of the chase scenes in the later part of *Basil*, in which Mannion dogs Basil's steps, seem particularly influenced by Godwin. I believe that the type of narrative about class and gender in *Basil* makes *Frankenstein* (to which there are many more allusions than to Godwin's novel) a more important and central source than *Caleb Williams*, but it is worth pointing out that here, as elsewhere, I am interested less in an influence-study that tracks down all the Gothic antecedents of Collins' text than I am in exploring his transformation of a Gothic tradition that has particular theoretical relevance to his work.

14 For a discussion of "Bartleby, the Scrivener" as a figuration of the writer in the marketplace, see Michael T. Gilmore's chapter "'Bartleby, the Scrivener' and the Transformation of the Economy," in his *American Romanticism and the Marketplace* (Chicago: University of Chicago Press, 1985), 132–45. *Bleak House*, *Basil*, and "Bartleby" were all published during 1852–53. The other Dickensian characters that Mannion resembles are Carker in *Dombey and Son* (1844–46) and Uriah Heep in *David Copperfield* (1849–50). Carker, like Mannion, has an affair with his employer's wife (although Dickens made the published version of this story less sexually explicit than Collins did in *Basil*). This diabolical figure of the class subordinate reappears in Uriah Heep, who, like Mannion, is the double of a figure for the artist in the marketplace (in this case, David). I am indebted to Charles

Hatten for discussing with me these parallels in Dickens' fiction to *Basil*, a novel he greatly admired.

Chapter 4. Writing after Dark

1 Review of *The Woman in White*, by Wilkie Collins, *Saturday Review*, 25 August 1860, in *Wilkie Collins: The Critical Heritage*, ed. Norman Page (1974; reprint, London: Routledge, 1985), 84–85.

2 Ibid., 84.

3 Ibid., 83.

4 Ibid., 85.

5 As realism became more firmly established as a critical standard in the second half of the nineteenth century, Dickens, like Collins, was criticized for the implausibility of his characters. See, e.g., George H. Ford, *Dickens and His Readers: Aspects of Novel-Criticism since 1836* (Princeton: Princeton University Press, 1955), 129–55.

6 Wilkie Collins, *The Moonstone*, ed. Anthea Trodd (Oxford: Oxford University Press, 1982), 420.

7 Alexander Pope, "Epistle to a Lady," in *The Poems of Alexander Pope: A One-Volume Edition of the Twickenham Text with Selected Annotations*, ed. John Butt (New Haven: Yale University Press, 1963), 560, ll. 1–2. Referring to this poem to condemn Collins' supposed inability to create character seems to have been standard procedure for his critics. An article in the *Westminster Review* claimed ("to slightly alter Pope's words") that: "Nothing so true, as what you once let fall, / His novels have no character at all; / Matter too soft a lasting mark to bear, / And best distinguished by black, brown, or fair." "Belles Lettres," *Westminster Review* (American ed.), n.s., 86 (July 1866): 127.

8 Review of *The Woman in White*, in *Critical Heritage*, ed. Page, 84.

9 See Walter Phillips, *Dickens, Reade, and Collins: Sensation Novelists* (1919; reprint, New York: Russell and Russell, 1962), particularly chap. 2, "The Background of Sensationalism," 37–108.

10 Review of *Basil*, in *Critical Heritage*, ed. Page, 53.

11 Winifred Hughes, *The Maniac in the Cellar: Sensation Novels of the 1860s* (Princeton: Princeton University Press, 1980), 39.

12 H. D. Mansel, "Sensation Novels," *Quarterly Review* (American ed.), n.s., 113, no. 226 (1863): 252.

13 "Belles Lettres," *Westminster Review* (American ed.), n.s., 86 (July 1866): 126.

14 "Our Female Sensation Novelists," *Living Age* 78 (1863): 352. This essay originally appeared in the *Christian Remembrancer* in 1863.

15 [Margaret Oliphant], "Sensation Novels," *Blackwood's Edinburgh Mag-*

azine 91 (May 1862): 565.

16 The writer of the essay "Our Female Sensation Novelists" divides the reader's body into two oppositional and implicitly feminized sites: "Sensation writing is an appeal to the nerves rather than to the heart" (p. 352). This symbolic map pits the heart, a synecdoche for domesticated sentiment, against the nerves, the neurasthenic impulses that similarly define femininity in the language of Victorian biological determinism, but which are associated with the disruptive side of women's nature—hysteria, madness, and sexuality—rather than with the domestic.

17 Jonathan Loesberg, "The Ideology of Narrative Form in Sensation Fiction," *Representations* 13 (Winter 1986): 115–38.

18 Ibid., 118–19.

19 Critical attention has recently been directed at the subversive nature of sensation fiction; see, e.g., Thomas F. Boyle, *Black Swine in the Sewers of Hampstead: Beneath the Surface of Victorian Sensationalism* (New York: Viking, 1989). For the gender ideology of sensation narratives, see Elaine Showalter, *A Literature of Their Own* (Princeton: Princeton University Press, 1977), 153–81; Hughes, *Maniac in the Cellar,* 106–36; and Elizabeth Helsinger, Robin Lauterbach Sheets, and William Veeder, *Literary Issues,* vol. 3. of *The Woman Question: Society and Literature in Britain and America, 1837–1883* (Chicago: University of Chicago Press, 1983), 122–45.

20 See Hughes, *Maniac in the Cellar,* 55–72, for how the sensation novel replaces the dialectics of melodrama with moral ambiguity. Keith Brown Reierstad examines this kind of ambiguity in Collins' heroines in "Innocent Indecency: The Questionable Heroines of Wilkie Collins' Sensation Novels," *Victorian Institute Journal* 9 (1980–81): 57–69.

21 Respectively, by Phillips, *Dickens, Reade, and Collins,* 129; Sue Lonoff, *Wilkie Collins and His Victorian Readers: A Study in the Rhetoric of Authorship* (New York: AMS Press, 1982), 18; and Keith Reierstad, "The Demon in the House: or, The Domestication of Gothic in the Novels of Wilkie Collins" (Ph.D. diss., University of Pennsylvania, 1976), 131.

22 Lonoff, *Wilkie Collins and His Victorian Readers,* 18.

23 Emile Forgues, "William Wilkie Collins," *Revue des deux mondes,* 15 November 1855, in *Critical Heritage,* ed. Page, 66.

24 Nuel Pharr Davis, *The Life of Wilkie Collins* (Urbana: University of Illinois Press, 1956), 120; for Forgues' comparison, see *Critical Heritage,* ed. Page, 63.

25 Wilkie Collins, "A Shy Scheme," *Household Words* 17 (March 1858): 315; quoted in Davis, *Life of Wilkie Collins,* 70.

26 Julia Swindells, *Victorian Writing and Working Women: The Other Side of Silence* (Minneapolis: University of Minnesota Press, 1985), particularly

45–113. N. N. Feltes locates the publication of *Middlemarch* as a case study of the difficulty with which a woman writer defined herself as a professional in "One Round of a Long Ladder: Gender, Profession, and the Production of *Middlemarch*," chap. 3 in his *Modes of Production of Victorian Novels* (Chicago: University of Chicago Press, 1986), 36–56.

27 See Swindell's discussion, "The Gentleman's Club, Literature," in *Victorian Writing and Working Women*, 91–113.

28 Phillips, *Dickens, Reade, and Collins*, 109.

29 For an illuminating survey of the working friendship between Dickens and Collins, see Sue Lonoff, "Charles Dickens and Wilkie Collins," *Nineteenth-Century Fiction* 35 (September 1980): 150–70, and her *Wilkie Collins and His Victorian Readers*, 42–55.

30 See Margaret Oliphant's discussion of *Great Expectations* as a sensation novel in "Sensation Novels," 574–80.

31 Charles Dickens to Wilkie Collins in *Critical Heritage*, ed. Page, 49.

32 James M. Brown, *Dickens: Novelist in the Marketplace* (London: Macmillan, 1982), 41.

33 Eliza Lynn Linton, quoted in Lonoff, *Wilkie Collins and His Victorian Readers*, 42.

34 Charles Dickens to W. H. Wills, 24 September 1858, *Charles Dickens as Editor: Being Letters Written by Him to William Henry Wills, His Sub-editor*, ed. R. C. Lehmann (London: Smith, Elder, 1912), 247.

35 Lonoff, *Wilkie Collins and His Victorian Readers*, 50–51.

36 See Kirk H. Beetz, "Wilkie Collins and *The Leader*," *Victorian Periodicals Review* 15 (1982): 20–29, for Collins' association with the journal, and also Anne Lohrli, "Wilkie Collins and *Household Words*," *Victorian Periodicals Review* 15 (1982): 118–19. Both articles are useful for discussing Collins' early journalistic experience, and Beetz in particular provides valuable evidence about Collins' politics.

37 Beetz, "Wilkie Collins and *The Leader*," 25.

38 One of the reasons that Collins left the *Leader* illustrates this point. As Beetz describes it, Collins quarreled with Edward Pigott over a satire on religion that the journal had published. In a letter to Pigott, Collins proclaimed, "You have made your confession of political faith (and I agree in it, as you know)—but you have made no confession of religious faith" (quoted in Beetz, ibid., 24). Beetz reads this letter as proof of Collins' Christianity that refutes the common view that he was an atheist, or at least an agnostic. Yet the letter sheds light not only on Collins' religious beliefs but also (more significantly in my view) on his ambivalence about being associated with radical politics. Although he parenthetically declares his sympathy with Pigott's socialist views, Collins balks at the journal's identification with the religious skepticism attributed to radicals.

39 Wilkie Collins, preface to *After Dark*, vol. 19 of *The Works of Wilkie Collins* (New York: Peter Fenelon Collier, [1900]), 5–6. All references will be to this edition and are cited by page in the text.

40 William M. Clarke, *The Secret Life of Wilkie Collins* (London: Allison and Busby, 1988), 78.

41 Leonore Davidoff and Catherine Hall, *Family Fortunes: Men and Women of the English Middle Class, 1780–1850* (Chicago: University of Chicago Press, 1987), especially pt. 2, "Economic Structure and Opportunity," 193–315.

42 Catherine Gallagher, "George Eliot and *Daniel Deronda*: The Prostitute and the Jewish Question," in *Sex, Politics, and Science in the Nineteenth-Century Novel*, ed. Ruth Yeazell, Selected Papers from the English Institute, 1983–84, n.s., no. 10 (Baltimore: Johns Hopkins University Press, 1986), 40.

43 Gallagher, "George Eliot and *Daniel Deronda*," 43. As she says: "The author . . . does not go to market as a respectable producer with an alienable commodity, but with *himself* or *herself* as commodity. The last half of the eighteenth century is the period both when the identity of text and self begins to be strongly asserted and when the legal basis for commodifying texts (as distinct from books) comes into being in copyright law. This combination puts writers in the marketplace in the position of selling themselves, like whores" (43).

44 Gayle Rubin, "The Traffic in Women: Notes on the 'Political Economy' of Sex," in *Toward an Anthropology of Women*, ed. Rayna R. Reiter (New York: Monthly Review Press, 1975), 157–210.

45 Gallagher, "George Eliot and *Daniel Deronda*," 40.

46 The one moment where Leah draws attention to her own voice in the stories simultaneously undercuts its authority. At the end of "A Terribly Strange Bed," there appears a "note by Mrs. Kerby" in which she claims that she cannot resist mentioning the incident that caused her husband to remember the tale. After supplying this information, she says that William thought it "scarcely worth while to mention such a trifle in anything so important as a book": "I cannot venture, after this, to do more than slip these lines in modestly at the end of the story. If the printer should notice my few last words, perhaps he may not mind the trouble of putting them into some out-of-the-way corner" (72).

47 Henry J. W. Milley examines "Sister Rose" as an influence on *A Tale of Two Cities* in "Wilkie Collins and 'A Tale of Two Cities,'" *Modern Language Review* 34, no. 4 (1939): 525–34.

48 William Marshall, *Wilkie Collins* (New York: Twayne, 1970), 42.

49 The frame narrative of Collins' short-story collection *The Queen of Hearts* (1859) emphasizes the writer's dependency on the audience. Three elderly

brothers, each a retired professional (clergyman, doctor, lawyer), have no idea how to entertain their young and fashionable niece, who is foisted on them for some time as an odd condition of her father's will. Their Scheherazade-like plan to tell her stories culled from their past figures the audience of the professional writer (the brothers are very proud of their seriousness) as a kind of demanding female despot, a Queen of Hearts.

Chapter 5. The Woman in White

1 As an index of how swiftly the value placed on Collins' writing escalated, compare the £500 that the firm of Smith, Elder offered him to publish *The Woman in White* in book form—a bid made before its popularity in serial form soared, which Collins presciently rejected as too low—with the £3,000 paid by Sampson Low, Son, and Marston for *No Name*. For Collins' income during the period from 1860 to the end of his life, see William M. Clarke, *The Secret Life of Wilkie Collins* (London: Allison and Busby, 1988), 228–29.

2 The word "devoured" is Percy Fitzgerald's, in *Memories of Charles Dickens* (Bristol: Arrowsmith, 1913), 222. In its review (30 October 1860) the *Times* described *The Woman in White* as a "novel of the rare old sort which must be finished at a sitting." *Wilkie Collins: The Critical Heritage*, ed. Norman Page (1974; reprint, London: Routledge, 1985), 95.

3 Review of *The Woman in White*, *Saturday Review*, 25 August 1860, in *Critical Heritage*, ed. Page, 84.

4 Wilkie Collins, *The Woman in White*, ed. Harvey Peter Sucksmith (Oxford: Oxford University Press, 1980), 1. All references will be to this edition and are cited by page in the text.

5 Walter M. Kendrick, "The Sensationalism of *The Woman in White*," *Nineteenth-Century Fiction* 32 (1977): 29.

6 In his introduction to *The Woman in White* Maurice Richardson goes so far as to call Collins a "radical feminist" (Wilkie Collins, *The Woman in White* [New York: Dutton, 1972], vii). In "Wilkie Collins and British Law" (*Nineteenth-Century Fiction* 5 [1950]: 121–39), Dougald MacEachen discusses Collins' critique in *The Woman in White* and other novels of the laws concerning women. More extended feminist analyses include Nina Auerbach, *Woman and the Demon: The Life of a Victorian Myth* (Cambridge: Harvard University Press, 1982), 135–43; Richard Barickman, Susan MacDonald, and Myra Stark, *Corrupt Relations: Dickens, Thackeray, Trollope, Collins, and the Victorian Sexual System* (New York: Columbia University Press, 1982), 113, 114–20; D. A. Miller, "*Cage aux Folles*: Sensation and Gender in Wilkie Collins's *The Woman in White*," *Representations* 14 (1986): 107–36; Philip O'Neill, *Wilkie Collins: Women, Property and Propriety* (Totowa, N.J.: Barnes, 1988), 98–124; and Jenny Bourne Taylor, *In the Se-*

cret Theatre of Home: Wilkie Collins, Sensation Narrative, and Nineteenth-Century Psychology (London: Routledge, 1988), 98–130.

7 Henry James, "Miss Braddon," *Nation* 1, no. 19 (November 1865). James anticipates a Bloomian vocabulary when he says that Collins' innovations were "fatal to the authority of Mrs. Radcliffe" (593).

8 For more on how debates over the institutionalization and treatment of the mentally ill concerned women and gender roles, see Elaine Showalter, *The Female Malady: Women, Madness, and English Culture, 1830–1980* (New York: Penguin, 1985), 23–98; Barbara Fass Leavy, "Wilkie Collins's Cinderella: The History of Psychology and *The Woman in White*," *Dickens Studies Annual* 10 (1982): 91–141; and Taylor, *In the Secret Theatre of Home*, 37–39.

9 Peter Brooks, *Reading for the Plot: Design and Intention in Narrative* (New York: Knopf, 1984), 169.

10 See Marshall, *Wilkie Collins* (New York: Twayne, 1970), 64–65.

11 U. C. Knoepflmacher, "The Counterworld of Victorian Fiction and *The Woman in White*," in *The Worlds of Victorian Fiction*, ed. Jerome H. Buckley (Cambridge: Harvard University Press, 1975), 362.

12 Ibid., 363.

13 In the *Vindication of the Rights of Woman*, Wollstonecraft asserts that women's limited domestic employments, which render them "gentle, domestic brutes," also encourage a "spaniel-like affection" for men (pp. 98, 68). In *The Woman in White*, Percival Glyde terrifies Laura's pet greyhound —"cowardly and cross-grained as pet-dogs usually are" (118)—a moment parodically proleptic of her own fear of her husband once they are married. Other "pet-dogs" include Mrs. Catherick's lost dog, shot by the keeper of Blackwater Park and whose death anticipates that of Mrs. Catherick's lost daughter, Anne; and Count Fosco's tamed wife, who regards him with the "mute submissive inquiry which we are all familiar with in the eyes of a faithful dog" (195).

14 Ann Cvetkovich discusses how the sensationalism of *The Woman in White* is structured by Hartright's desire for class mobility in "Ghostlier Determinations: The Economy of Sensation and *The Woman in White*," *Novel* 23 (Fall 1989): 24–43.

15 Auerbach, *Woman and the Demon*, 139–40, 138.

16 See Showalter, *Female Malady*, especially chaps. 2 and 3.

17 For hysterics and feminine sexuality, see Showalter, *Female Malady*, 129 ff., and for the debate over chloroform and the sexuality of the woman patient, see Mary Poovey, "'Scenes of an Indelicate Character': The Medical 'Treatment' of Victorian Women," *Representations* 14 (1986): 137–68.

18 Henry Dickens, *The Recollections of Sir Henry Dickens, K.C.* (London, 1934), 54, quoted in Martin Meisel, "Miss Havisham Brought to Book,"

PMLA 81 (1966): 281.

19 *All the Year Round*, 26 November 1859, 95.

20 Peter Caracciolo, "Wilkie Collins's 'Divine Comedy': The Use of Dante in *The Woman in White*," *Nineteenth-Century Fiction* 25 (1971): 402.

21 The parallel between women's situation and a revolutionary context is further emphasized by an important source for the novel, the case of Madame Douhault. In this historical incident, a French noblewoman was incarcerated in a madhouse and deprived of her inheritance during the last years of the corrupt ancien régime. For a synopsis of the case, see Clyde K. Hyder, "Wilkie Collins and *The Woman in White*," *PMLA* 54 (1939): 297–303.

22 Nicholas Rance, *The Historical Novel and Popular Politics* (New York: Barnes, 1975), 78.

23 E. P. Thompson, *The Making of the English Working Class* (London: V. Gollancz, 1963; reprint, New York: Vintage, 1966), especially 350–400; Barbara Taylor, *Eve and the New Jerusalem: Socialism and Feminism in the Nineteenth Century* (New York: Pantheon, 1983).

24 See E. P. Thompson, "The Crime of Anonymity," in Douglas Hay et al., *Albion's Fatal Tree: Crime and Society in Eighteenth-Century England* (New York: Pantheon, 1975), 255–308. Thompson's thesis can usefully be applied to the case of Anne Catherick: "The anonymous threatening letter is a characteristic form of social protest in any society which has crossed a certain threshold of literacy, in which forms of collective organized defence are weak, and in which individuals who can be identified as the organizers of protest are liable to immediate victimization" (255). Marian's comment on the letter shows how this type of protest is read as a class marker: "That is not an illiterate letter . . . and, at the same time, it is surely too incoherent to be the letter of an educated person in the higher ranks of life" (69).

25 Miller, "*Cage aux Folles*," 110.

26 See ibid., 109–11, for the association of nervousness with femininity and reading.

27 See ibid., 112.

28 See Leonore Davidoff and Catherine Hall, *Family Fortunes: Men and Women of the English Middle Class, 1780–1850* (Chicago: University of Chicago Press, 1987), especially chaps. 5 and 6. The phrase "labor that is not labor" is Nancy Armstrong's, in *Desire and Domestic Fiction: A Political History of the Novel* (Oxford: Oxford University Press, 1987), 75.

29 For Barthes' theory of "neither-nor criticism" as a mechanism of bourgeois ideology, see "Neither-Nor Criticism," in his *Mythologies*, trans. Annette Lavers (New York: Hill and Wang, 1972), 81–83.

30 See Miller's "*Cage aux Folles*," for another discussion of homoeroticism in the novel, especially the discussion of lesbianism and male bonding on pp. 128–29, 131–33.

31 See Carroll Smith-Rosenberg, "The Female World of Love and Ritual: Relationships between Women in Nineteenth-Century America," *Signs* 1 (1975): 1–29. The relationship among Marian, Anne, and Laura may be read as a notation for the theme Nina Auerbach has called "communities of women" in her *Communities of Women: An Idea in Fiction* (Cambridge: Harvard University Press, 1978).

32 Eve Kosofsky Sedgwick, *Between Men: English Literature and Male Homosocial Desire* (New York: Columbia University Press, 1985), 174–75.

33 Such descriptions of Shelley may be found in Richard Holmes, *Shelley: The Pursuit* (London: Wiedenfeld and Nicholson, 1974), 360–62. The description of Shelley as "weakly" and having a "most feminine" voice comes from an anecdote of Benjamin Robert Haydon's cited by Holmes; William Hazlitt's portrait of Shelley depicts him as a "shrill-voiced" fanatic.

34 See "Counterworld of Victorian Fiction," especially 368, where Knoepflmacher claims that Fosco's "absolute freedom from scruples" allies him with such figures as Scott's Bois-Gilbert, Dickens' Fagin, and Thackeray's Becky Sharp.

35 Review of *The Woman in White*, *Times*, 30 October 1860, in *Critical Heritage*, ed. Page, 101.

36 See also *Hide and Seek* (1854), which anticipates *The Dead Secret* in its plot about an illegitimate daughter, and *Armadale* (1866), which traces the relationship between a son who bears his father's name and a disenfranchised son who forswears it.

37 Tellingly, the other woman with whom the word "vindication" is associated is Mrs. Catherick, the fallen woman who discloses the history of Glyde's mother. In another echo of Wollstonecraft's *The Wrongs of Woman*, Mrs. Catherick claims she came to Welmingham "a wronged woman" (449), yet as Hartright notes, she offers him "an extraordinary practical vindication of her position in the town" (450).

38 See, e.g., Kendrick, "Sensationalism of *The Woman in White*," 29; Brooks, *Reading for the Plot*, 169; and Miller, "*Cage aux Folles*," 117.

39 See Barickman, MacDonald, and Stark, *Corrupt Relations*, 38: "Hartright lingers agog over it ["this grafting of a stereotypic male face onto a stereotypic female body"] as though it were the most significant item in the strange mystery he is recounting."

40 Auerbach, *Woman and the Demon*, 136–37.

41 Mark M. Hennelly, Jr., notes the significance of this name in "Reading Detection in *The Woman in White*," *Texas Studies in Literature and Language* 22 (1980): 453.

42 For more on the regulation of women's labor, see Davidoff and Hall, *Family Fortunes*, 279–89, 304–15.

43 Whereas it is Marian's unexpectedly intellectual-looking head that synec-

dochically represents her in her meeting with Walter Hartright, this metonymic emphasis shifts to her hands once she is relegated to domestic labor.

44 James M. Brown, *Dickens: Novelist in the Marketplace* (London: Macmillan, 1982), 39–41.

45 The phrase is from Julia Swindells, *Victorian Writing and Working Women: The Other Side of Silence* (Minneapolis: University of Minnesota Press, 1985), 95.

46 Sandra M. Gilbert and Susan Gubar, *The Madwoman in the Attic: The Woman Writer and the Nineteenth-Century Literary Imagination* (New Haven: Yale University Press, 1979), 3.

Chapter 6. Blank Spaces

1 T. S. Eliot, "Wilkie Collins and Dickens" (1927), in *Selected Essays: New Edition* (New York: Harcourt, 1950), 413.

2 Wilkie Collins, *The Moonstone*, ed. Anthea Trodd (Oxford: Oxford University Press, 1982), 214. All subsequent references will be to this edition, which follows Collins' revisions of 1871, and are cited by page in the text.

3 See Ross Murfin, "The Art of Representation: Collins' *The Moonstone* and Dickens' Example," *ELH* 49 (1982): 653–54, for another discussion of the ambiguity of Jennings' detective work.

4 Anthea Trodd uses the word "fathered" in her introduction to *The Moonstone*, xv. In the tradition of Eliot, many studies have located *The Moonstone* as an important influence on English and American mystery and detective fiction. See, e.g., Julian Symons, *Mortal Consequences: A History—From the Detective Story to the Crime Novel* (New York: Harper, 1972); Ian Ousby, *Bloodhounds of Heaven: The Detective in English Fiction from Godwin to Doyle* (Cambridge: Harvard University Press, 1976); and Dennis Porter, *The Pursuit of Crime: Art and Ideology in Detective Fiction* (New Haven: Yale University Press, 1981).

5 As Albert D. Hutter says, "What is stolen from Rachel is both the actual gem and her symbolic virginity"; see "Dreams, Transformations, and Literature: The Implications of Detective Fiction," in *The Poetics of Murder: Detective Fiction and Literary Theory*, ed. Glenn W. Most and William W. Stowe (New York: Harcourt, 1983), 242. Hutter's is the most recent and sophisticated of the psychoanalytic readings of the novel; earlier examples include Charles Rycroft, "The Analysis of a Detective Story," in *Imagination and Reality: Psychoanalytical Essays, 1951–1961* (London: Hogarth, 1968), 114–28, and Lewis A. Lawson, "Wilkie Collins and *The Moonstone*," *American Imago* 20 (1963): 61–79.

6 The phrase is Sue Lonoff's; see *Wilkie Collins and His Victorian Readers: A Study in the Rhetoric of Authorship* (New York: AMS Press, 1982), 210.

7 John R. Reed, "English Imperialism and the Unacknowledged Crime of *The Moonstone*," *Clio* 2 (1973): 287, 281.

8 For Orientalist discourse, I draw on Edward Said's classic study, *Orientalism* (New York: Vintage, 1978). Collins' relation to Orientalism, and to imperialism in general, is complicated. In the aftermath of the Indian Mutiny he coauthored with Dickens for *Household Words* the series *The Perils of Certain English Prisoners*, which, as its title implies, focuses on attacks against the colonists during the rebellion. The tone of this work is consonant with Dickens' virulent response to the Mutiny and his strongly pro-imperialist position; for more on this subject, see William Oddie, "Dickens and the Indian Mutiny," *Dickensian* 68, no. 366 (1972): 3–15; for the British reaction to the Mutiny more generally, see Patrick Brantlinger, *Rule of Darkness: British Literature and Imperialism, 1830–1914* (Ithaca: Cornell University Press, 1988), 199–224. Yet, as Anthea Trodd points out, Collins' own response to the Mutiny, "A Sermon for Sepoys" (*Household Words* 27 [February 1858]: 244–47), is "pointedly unexcited" (introduction to *The Moonstone*, xviii); it is, in fact, pointedly enigmatic, a fable that warns against cruelty but praises the Moslem faith. Given Dickens' violent response to the Mutiny (he wished to "exterminate the Race upon whom the stain of the late cruelties rested"), it might have been difficult for Collins to voice any more explicit reservations about imperialism. One wonders if, after an initial enthusiasm, Dickens disliked *The Moonstone*—whose construction he labeled "wearisome beyond endurance"—because he disapproved of its portrayal of race and imperialism (for Dickens' response to *The Moonstone*, see *Critical Heritage*, ed. Page, 169). Sue Lonoff sees the critical picture of imperialist greed in *The Moonstone* as Collins' response not only to the Mutiny but also to another controversy in which Dickens adopted a strong pro-imperialist stand—the debate during the late 1860s about Governor Edward Eyre's brutal repression of a Jamaican rebellion (*Wilkie Collins and His Victorian Readers*, 178–79). Soon after *The Moonstone*, in fact, Collins wrote and staged with Charles Fechter a play called *Black and White* (1869) set in the West Indies before emancipation. Despite stereotyped portraits of blacks, the play, which supports an antislavery position, ends with the mulatto hero marrying a white heiress.

There may be, moreover, an intriguing, though studiously buried, allusion to anti-imperialist discourse in a scene late in *The Moonstone*. Among the books in Franklin Blake's room that Ezra Jennings dismisses as soporific "Standard Literature" (464) is Henry Mackenzie's *The Man of Feeling* (1771), which contains a critique of the spread of British imperialism in India that is both scathing and unusual (for Collins' day as well as Mackenzie's): "You tell me of immense territories subject to the English: I cannot think of their possessions, without being led to enquire, by what right they possess them"

(Henry Mackenzie, *The Man of Feeling*, ed. Brian Vickers [Oxford: Oxford University Press, 1987], 102; see also 103).

9 Charles Dickens to W. H. Wills, 30 June 1867, *Charles Dickens as Editor: Being Letters Written by Him to William Henry Wills, His Sub-editor*, ed. R. C. Lehmann (London: Smith, Elder, 1912), 360.

10 Leonore Davidoff, "Mastered for Life: Servant and Wife in Victorian and Edwardian England," *Journal of Social History* 7 (1974): 406–28. Rosanna's love for a man who is socially "above" her is interestingly reminiscent of the relationship between Arthur Munby, a middle-class writer, and Hannah Cullwick, a Victorian maidservant, which Davidoff analyzes in her essay "Class and Gender in Victorian England," in *Sex and Class in Women's History*, ed. Judith L. Newton, Mary P. Ryan, and Judith R. Walkowitz (London: Routledge, 1983), 17–71. Although Munby and Cullwick, unlike Blake and Rosanna, were mutually attracted and lived together for many years, the dynamics of power in the relationship—Munby's manipulation of Hannah and the masochistic overtones of her devotion to the man she called "massa"—shed light on the kind of gender and class issues to which Collins is drawing attention in *The Moonstone*. Like Franklin Blake, for example, Munby was the reader and editor of Hannah's journal and other autobiographical sketches she wrote at his instigation; like Rosanna's letter, however, these texts represent more than a woman's obedience to a male imperative and constitute a powerful testimony to Hannah's voice. See *The Diaries of Hannah Cullwick, Victorian Maidservant*, ed. Liz Stanley (New Brunswick, N.J.: Rutgers University Press, 1984). Like the relationship between Cullwick and Munby, Collins' relationship with his mistress, Martha Rudd, whom he met in the 1860s, was also a cross-class one.

11 In her discussion of the Road Murder, Mary Hartman theorizes that Constance's father was the murderer and that his daughter covered up for him with her confession to the crime in 1865. Hartman's account is useful for its analysis of the contemporary reading of the crime as a moral fable about female rebellion and depravity. See her *Victorian Murderesses: A True History of Thirteen Respectable French and English Women Accused of Unspeakable Crimes* (New York: Schocken, 1977), 85–129. To see how Collins drew on details of the case, compare the statement by Constance's father that his daughter's "wish to be independent" was a quality laudable in a boy, but not a virtue for a girl (109) with Mr. Bruff's opinion that Rachel's "absolute self-dependence is a great virtue in a man. In a woman it has the serious drawback of morally separating her from the mass of her sex" (303).

12 I am indebted to Charles Hatten for drawing my attention to this point.

13 Hutter, "Dreams, Transformations, and Literature," 246.

14 The phrase is Lonoff's, in *Wilkie Collins and His Victorian Readers*, 198.

15 Among the relevant discussions of nineteenth-century medical discourses

about femininity, hysteria, and the language of the hysteric are the volume of essays entitled *In Dora's Case: Freud-Hysteria-Feminism*, ed. Charles Bernheimer and Claire Kahane (New York: Columbia University Press, 1985); Nina Auerbach, *Woman and the Demon: The Life of a Victorian Myth* (Cambridge: Harvard University Press, 1982), 7–34; and Mary Jacobus, *Reading Woman: Essays in Feminist Criticism* (New York: Columbia University Press, 1986), 197–274. For a discussion of hysteria in *The Moonstone*, see Jenny Bourne Taylor, *In the Secret Theatre of Home: Wilkie Collins, Sensation Narrative, and Nineteenth-Century Psychology* (London: Routledge, 1988), 200–201.

16 I am indebted to Navin Girishankar for pointing out to me the significance of Rachel's position at the birthday dinner.

17 Hélène Cixous, "Castration or Decapitation?" trans. Annette Kuhn, *Signs* 7 (1981): 49.

18 Ibid.

19 It is significant that Miss Clack, the female narrator and poor relation, is also a ressentiment-ridden version of the artist in the marketplace, since Franklin Blake pays her to write her section of the text (an arrangement she refers to with much, presumably hypocritical, grumbling). Miss Clack is also a member of women's clubs and reform groups—female communities that pose an implicit challenge to the world of men; as Gabriel Betteredge paraphrases her conversation with Godfrey Ablewhite at the birthday dinner, "all the women in heaven would be members of a prodigious committee that never quarrelled, with all the men in attendance on them as ministering angels" (76). Miss Clack is thus associated, as was Anne Catherick in *The Woman in White*, with a kind of feminist millenarianism, a vision that here—even more so than in the earlier novel—is mercilessly satirized and devalued.

One target of this satire is women's writing; Miss Clack's favorite author is the tract writer Miss Jane Ann Stamper, whom no one wants to read. As in *The Woman in White*, however, the novel's devaluation of female community is more important as a function of the story it tells about heterosexuality. Mothers die and potential female communities are disbanded so that women can "grow up" and get married. The spinster Miss Clack is associated with Rachel's mother, who had befriended her and whose place she tries to take after Lady Verinder dies. Yet Miss Clack is rebuffed as a mother surrogate by Rachel, who goes away with Mr. Bruff and later marries Franklin Blake. In this context it is ironic that, since Collins' own mother died while *The Moonstone* was being written, the dedication of the novel is "In Memoriam Matris."

20 D. A. Miller, "From *roman-policier* to *roman-police*: Wilkie Collins's *The Moonstone*," *Novel* 13 (1980): 168.

21 Ibid.

22 Collins' use of piebald hair as a symbol for miscegenation is striking, but not original. In his *An Account of the Regular Gradation in Man, And in Different Animals and Vegetables; And From the Former to the Latter* (London: C. Dilly, 1799), Charles White, a gynecologist who propounded a theory of Anglo-Saxon racial superiority, relates stories of "pyebald, blotched, or party-coloured, black-and-white people" like the following one about the child of an interracial union: "In 1759, a girl was born in Somersetshire, with the hair of her head of two remarkably distinct colours. After she was grown up a little, the hair on the right side appeared of a jet black, resembling the father's; whilst that on the left side was of a carroty red, resembling the mother's; each occupying one half of the head, from a vertical section of the front" (123). I am indebted to Susan Meyer for introducing me to White's book.

23 Taylor, *In the Secret Theatre of Home*, 189. For Taylor's discussion of Ezra Jennings, see 189–92. Although I agree with Taylor that Jennings is a "cross-category figure," I would not say as she does that he thus breaks down "all the systems of difference in the novel" (189). Rather, I would argue that Jennings' role is to underscore the unresolved tensions between the dualities he embodies. Another reading of Ezra Jennings as a figure for the writer is Murfin, "Art of Representation"; a useful reading of Jennings' relation to Victorian medicine is Ira Bruce Nadel, "Science and *The Moonstone*," *Dickens Studies Annual* 11 (1983): 239–59.

24 As this discussion of Jennings indicates, he is a character with a past in Collins' novels. He recalls not only Mannion but also (in his association with a thematics of blankness) his fellow scientist Louis Trudaine in "Sister Rose," whose chemistry can erase writing (Jennings, of course, restores other people's erased words while erasing his own). I believe that this type of hunted outcast with a buried past, a figure most evocatively realized in Ezra Jennings, is of all his fictional creations the one in which Collins had the greatest emotional and artistic investment. Certainly, versions of this character haunt Collins' works, which resurrect him (or sometimes, as in *The Dead Secret*'s Sarah Leeson, her) again and again. Although one could say he appears in some form in almost everything Collins ever wrote, Ezra Jennings' most immediate antecedents are the figure of Mr. Lorn in the short story "The Dead Hand" (which appears in *The Queen of Hearts* and was inspired by Collins' meeting with a strange-looking medical assistant while on a walking trip with Dickens), and Ozias Midwinter in *Armadale*. Midwinter, from the novel written just before *The Moonstone*, strikingly anticipates Jennings in his association with feminine hysteria and racial difference (Midwinter's mother is of black West Indian origin).

25 Compare Mr. Candy's letter to Franklin Blake (511–13) with Severn's letter

to Charles Brown of 27 February 1821. Keats's request to Severn to lift him before his death ("be firm, and thank God it has come") is echoed by Jennings' similar request to Mr. Candy to lift him as he is dying ("It's coming"). In addition to echoes in the accounts of their deaths, there are other connections between Keats and Jennings. Keats had medical training, and Jennings was his mother's maiden name. One source in which Collins could have encountered these details and Severn's letter is *The Life and Letters of John Keats* by Richard Monckton Milnes, Lord Houghton, originally published in 1848 but reissued in 1867, the year before *The Moonstone*'s publication (the edition I refer to in subsequent notes). Collins not only knew Lord Houghton, whose biography was the important early one of Keats, but had even met Joseph Severn while on a trip to Italy with his family during his adolescence; see William M. Clarke, *The Secret Life of Wilkie Collins* (London: Allison and Busby, 1988), 31.

26 Milnes, *The Life and Letters of John Keats* (London: Edward Moxon, 1867), 323.

27 Compare Keats's request (recorded in a letter by Severn dated 14 February 1821 and reproduced in Milnes, *Life and Letters of John Keats*, 320) with Jennings' request of Mr. Candy (512).

28 Mary Jacobus, "The Buried Letter: Feminism and Romanticism in *Villette*," in *Women Writing and Writing about Women*, ed. Mary Jacobus (London: Croom Helm, 1979), 57.

29 It is significant in this regard that the critical attacks on Keats were motivated by his connections to radical circles; as Milnes says, "it was . . . at once assumed by the critics that Keats was not only a bad poet, but a bad citizen. " *Life and Letters of John Keats*, 165.

30 Kenneth Robinson discusses the stage version of the novel in *Wilkie Collins: A Biography* (New York: Macmillan, 1952), 286–87.

Epilogue

1 Wilkie Collins, *The Haunted Hotel: A Mystery of Modern Venice*, vol. 22 of *The Works of Wilkie Collins* (New York: Peter Fenelon Collier, [1900]), 245.

2 Sue Lonoff, *Wilkie Collins and His Victorian Readers: A Study in the Rhetoric of Authorship* (New York: AMS Press, 1982), 169; see also p. 77.

3 The shade that the hero, Oscar Dubourg, turns is described as "blackish-blue" (*Poor Miss Finch: A Domestic Story*, vol. 15 of *Works of Collins*, 191). The allusion to race is made clearer still when the blind girl, Miss Finch, says, "If I married a man with a dark complexion, and if I recovered my sight afterward, I should run away from him" (120). An anecdote is told later in the novel about the child of a colonial officer in India regaining her

sight and screaming with terror at the sight of the "dark Indian nurse" who tends her (354).

4 Algernon Charles Swinburne, "Wilkie Collins," in his *Studies in Prose and Poetry* (London: Chatto and Windus, 1894), 127.

5 Discussions of gender in Collins' late novels include Coral Lansbury, *The Old Brown Dog: Women, Workers, and Vivisection in Edwardian England* (Madison: University of Wisconsin Press, 1985), 133–41, for a reading of *Heart and Science* that links antivivisection to nineteenth-century feminism; Christine Moreau, "'With Theatrical Exaggeration': The Sensationalism of 'Excitable Women' in *Heart and Science*" (paper presented at the Wilkie Collins Centennial Conference, Victoria, B.C., 30 September 1989); the reading of *The Law and the Lady* in Richard Barickman, Susan MacDonald, and Myra Stark, *Corrupt Relations: Dickens, Thackeray, Trollope, Collins, and the Victorian Sexual System* (New York: Columbia University Press, 1982), 144–47; the discussion of *The New Magdalen* and its reception in Elizabeth K. Helsinger, Robin Lauterbach Sheets, and William Veeder, *Literary Issues*, vol. 3 of *The Woman Question: Society and Literature in Britain and America, 1837–83* (Chicago: University of Chicago Press, 1983), 163–70; the reading of *The Fallen Leaves* in Philip O'Neill, *Wilkie Collins: Women, Property and Propriety* (Totowa, N.J.: Barnes, 1988), 32–75; and Jenny Bourne Taylor, *In the Secret Theatre of Home: Wilkie Collins, Sensation Narrative, and Nineteenth-Century Psychology* (London: Routledge, 1988), 207–42.

6 Jenny Bourne Taylor also sees Collins' writing polemical fiction in the latter part of his career as a strategy for seeking a popular (rather than a highbrow) audience. *In the Secret Theatre of Home*, 210.

Index

All the Year Round, 92
Armstrong, Nancy, 36, 56
Ashley, Robert, 3
Auerbach, Nina, 135
Austen, Jane, 13

Balzac, Honoré de, 9, 25
Barickman, Richard, 3
Barthes, Roland, 128
Beetz, Kirk, 93
Bentley, Richard, 49
Bloom, Harold, 9–10
Braddon, Mary Elizabeth, 6, 86, 87
Brontë, Charlotte, 3, 88–89, 90, 161
Brooks, Peter, 115
Brown, James, 91
Bulwer-Lytton, Edward George, 38
Buried writing, 1, 4, 12, 143–44, 156–63
Burke, Edmund, 13, 14, 22, 27, 29, 30, 31, 32, 35, 121
Burkean Gothic, 14–15, 27, 29, 31, 35, 44, 121
Butler, Marilyn, 23

Caracciolo, Peter, 122
Carlyle, Thomas, 50, 54, 87, 93, 121
Chartist movement, 39, 44–45, 49–50, 125
Chorley, H. F., 58
Cixous, Hélène, 153
Coleridge, Samuel Taylor, 39
Collins, Harriet, 42, 43, 96–97, 192n19
Collins, Wilkie: autobiographical sketch by, 39, 41; career in *1850*s, 83, 88–93; as contributor to *Household Words*, 8, 82, 92–93, 101, 106; as contributor to the *Leader*, 93; critics' responses to, 3–6, 7, 8, 58–60, 83–85, 88–89,

Collins, Wilkie (*continued*)
110–11, 143, 164–65; decision to become writer, 40–41; desire for respectability, 162–63; friendship with Dickens, 90–93; income of, 110; influence of female Gothic on, 1–12, 16, 36–37, 39–40, 113, 167–68; later career of, 164–68; masculine artistic identity of, 41–42; maternal tradition and, 9–10, 39–40; mother of, 42, 43, 96–97; as opium user, 162; and professionalization of literature, 7–8, 83–88, 89–93, 168; relationship with father, 38–39, 40–41; religious views of, 183n38; on women writers, 89
—*After Dark*: female sexuality in, 98–99; female writer in, 96–101, 167; frame narrative of, 11, 82–83, 93–101, 115; "Gabriel's Marriage" in, 108; male artist in, 11, 82–83, 94–96, 128; metaphor of procreation for writing in, 100–01; prostitution in, 98–99; "Sister Rose" in, 82, 101–09, 121, 122; "A Terribly Strange Bed" in, 107–08
—*Antonina*: bourgeois manhood in, 52–53; class allegory in, 61; compared with *After Dark*, 99; critics' responses to, 58; domestic ideology in, 54–56, 80; fall of father's authority in, 39–40, 48–49, 59, 60; female rebellion in, 51, 53–54, 60, 62, 67, 121; as historical fiction, 11, 38, 48–57, 82; influence of female Gothic on, 60, 65; oedipal narrative in, 50–51
—*Armadale*: critics' responses to, 6, 143; as fantasy, 165; illegitimacy in, 132; misogynist overtones in, 94
—*Basil*: adultery in, 59, 60–61; compared with *After Dark*, 95, 96, 98; compared with "Sister Rose," 103–04, 107; compared with *The Moonstone*, 159; compared with *The Woman in White*, 118, 122; critics' responses to, 58–60, 85, 88–89; and Dickens, 76, 90–91; domesticity and the female Gothic in, 17, 40, 62–71, 93, 111; family and revolution in, 60–61; female sexuality in, 8, 166; male artist in, 11, 38–39, 41, 63–65, 69–74, 74–81, 82, 85, 92, 98, 128; misogynist overtones in, 94; monstrosity in, 74–81, 104, 118, 159; narrative voice of, 98; reissue of, 110; ressentiment in, 75–79
—*Dead Secret, The*: buried writing in, 1; compared with *The Moonstone*, 193n24; female sexuality in, 3, 8–9; female subversion in, 3; illegitimacy in, 1–2, 3, 94, 111, 132; mother-daughter relations in, 2–3, 9, 10; serialization of, 7
—*Fallen Leaves, The*, 166
—*Haunted Hotel, The*, 164, 167
—*Heart and Science*, 166, 168
—*Hide and Seek*, 8, 110, 111
—*Law and the Lady, The*, 167
—*Man and Wife*, 4, 166, 167
—*Memoirs of the Life of William Collins*: art in, 40, 42–48, 72, 73, 74, 80; Chartist movement in, 39, 44–45, 49–50; compared with *After Dark*, 95–97; as dead end, 38, 39; father's dominion in, 11, 39, 60, 72; mother's absence from, 42, 43, 51, 70; Nature in, 41, 42–43, 45–48, 66, 74, 96; professionalism of father in, 92, 116
—*Moonstone, The*: buried writing in, 1, 12, 143–44, 156–63; critics' responses to, 4–5; as detective

fiction, 11–12, 142–44, 166; Ezra Jennings' role in, 1, 156–63, 167–68; female sexuality in, 144, 145–46, 149–51; hysteria in, 152–54, 158; images of resistance in, 10, 147–51; imperialism in, 144–46; invalidation of female language in, 154–55; monstrosity in, 159; multivoice narrative of, 37, 154–55, 98; outcast in, 1, 84, 142, 144, 156–63; psychosexual reading of, 144, 145–46, 151; readings of the theft of the Moonstone, 143–47; Romanticism and, 150, 159–63; social class in, 146–47; symbolism of the Shivering Sand, 149–51; tension between Gothic and detective fiction in, 143, 151–56
—*New Magdalen, The*, 166
—"Nine O'Clock!" 60, 82
—*No Name*: contract for, 110; critics' responses to, 6, 143; illegitimacy in, 1, 6, 84, 132, 166
—*Poor Miss Finch*, 165
—*Queen of Hearts, The*, 184n49, 193n24
—*Woman in White, The*: adultery in, 132–33; compared with *The Haunted Hotel*, 164; critics' responses to, 5, 83, 84, 87–88, 110–11; female Gothic and feminine experience in, 4, 11, 17, 40, 111–14, 167; female mental patients in, 119–21; female sexuality in, 125–26; feminine carceral in, 37, 167; homoeroticism and failed Romanticism in, 127–31; illegitimacy in, 1, 132; male artist in, 11, 111–12, 116–18, 140–41; male insecurity and Walter Hartright's story, 114–18; multivoice narrative in, 37, 98, 155; popular success of, 110–11; ressentiment in, 126–27; restoration of class and gender legitimacy, 131–41; revolution in, 10, 118–27, 143, 148; serialization of, 121–22; terrorist Brotherhood in, 130–131, 145
Collins, William: aristocratic patronage of, 45, 64; art of, 39, 40, 42–48, 80; Chartist movement and, 44–45; conservative philosophy of, 39, 41, 44–46; eye problem of, 96; friendship with Sir David Wilkie, 41–42, 92; as heroic bourgeois, 51; Nature in art of, 39, 74, 41, 42–43, 45–48, 96, 150; professionalism of, 92, 116; son's memoirs of, 38–39, 40–48

Dana, R. H., 43
Daughters. *See* Mother-daughter relations
Davidoff, Leonore, 99, 128, 137, 147
Davis, Nuel Pharr, 40, 50, 89
De Quincy, Thomas, 161
Dickens, Charles: *Bleak House*, 76, 131; characters in works of, 84; Collins' works compared with, 5, 9, 50, 54, 60, 76, 106; death of, 164; domestic fiction of, 160; as editor, 8, 82, 92, 93, 94, 96; friendship with Collins, 90–93, 110; *Great Expectations*, 90; Indian Mutiny and, 190n8; reactions to Collins' works, 58, 90–93, 145; as sensation novelist, 6, 85, 90; *Tale of Two Cities*, 50, 54, 60, 121–23
Doody, Margaret Anne, 14, 15–16
Doyle, Arthur Conan, 166

Eliot, George, 90, 99, 165
Eliot, T. S., 142
Ellis, Kate, 14

Female Gothic: characteristics of, 2, 4, 10, 14–17; class in, 29–37; feminist criticism of, 14; influence on Collins, 1–12, 16, 36–37, 39–40, 113, 167–68; influence on sensation fiction, 6; male writers and, 4, 6–12, 36–37, 39–40, 56–57, 69–74, 82; Radcliffe and, 14, 17–25; sexuality in, 23–24; Shelley and, 29–37; terror in, 22–25; Wollstonecraft and, 25–29. *See also names of specific authors*
Female sexuality, 3, 8–9, 22–24, 98–99, 125–26, 144–46, 149–51, 166
Forgues, Emile, 88–89
Foucault, Michel, 23, 25, 152, 154
French Revolution, 13–15, 30, 32, 49, 50, 54, 60, 125
Freud, Sigmund, 153

Gallagher, Catherine, 99
Gaskell, Elizabeth, 88–89
Gilbert, Sandra, 3, 10, 16, 30, 31, 140
Godwin, William, 29
Gothic novels. *See* Burkean Gothic; Female Gothic
Gouges, Olympe de, 28
Griffin, Andrew, 32
Gubar, Susan, 3, 10, 16, 30, 31, 140

Hall, Catherine, 99, 128, 137
Hawthorne, Nathaniel, 87, 89
Hay, Douglas, 25
Homans, Margaret, 30, 42
Homoeroticism, 125–26, 128–31
Household Words, 8, 82, 92–93, 101, 106
Hughes, Winifred, 85–86
Hunt, Thornton, 93
Hutter, Albert, 5, 60
Hysteria, 152–54, 158. *See also* Mental illness

Illegitimacy, 1–3, 6, 84, 94, 111, 132

James, Henry, 113, 165
Johnson, Barbara, 33

Kahane, Claire, 14, 18
Keats, John, 161
Klinkenborg, Verlyn, 40, 41
Knoepflmacher, U. C., 115, 130

Leader, 93
Leavy, Barbara Fass, 119
Lewes, George Henry, 93
Linton, Eliza, 92
Literary marketplace, 4–10, 71–101, 110–12
Literary professionalism, 7–8, 83–93, 168
Loesberg, Jonathan, 87
Lonoff, Sue, 4, 88, 92–93, 164, 165
Lukács, Georg, 55–56, 91

MacDonald, Susan, 3
Maddyn, D. O., 58–59, 62
Mansel, H. D., 86
Marketplace. *See* Literary marketplace
Marshall, William, 108, 115
Melville, Herman, 76
Mental illness, 119–21, 152–54, 158
Miller, D. A., 5, 125–26, 129, 154
Modleski, Tania, 21
Moers, Ellen, 14, 30
Mother-daughter relations, 2–3, 9, 10, 17–25, 27, 111
Murfin, Ross, 142

Newgate novel, 59

Oliphant, Margaret, 87

Paine, Thomas, 15
Paulson, Ronald, 30
Peel, Sir Robert, 43
Phillips, Walter, 85, 90
Poovey, Mary, 22, 32
Pope, Alexander, 84
Professionalization of literature, 7–8, 83–93, 168
Prostitution, 98–99, 125

Radcliffe, Ann, 2, 10, 14, 17–25, 26, 72, 113; *The Italian*, 15, 23; *The Mysteries of Udolpho*, 2, 15, 19–25, 67, 113, 136; *The Romance of the Forest*, 23; *A Sicilian Romance*, 17–19, 22, 27
Rance, Nicholas, 56, 124
Reade, Charles, 6, 85, 90
Reed, John, 5, 144
Ressentiment, 29, 35, 54, 75–79, 104, 126–27, 158–59, 192n19
Richardson, Maurice, 3
Robinson, Kenneth, 41
Roland, Madame, 28
Rubenstein, Marc, 32–33
Rubin, Gayle, 99
Russ, Joanna, 4

Sadleir, Michael, 13
Sayers, Dorothy, 3
Scott, Sir Walter, 9, 38
Sedgwick, Eve Kosofsky, 41–42, 129
Sensation fiction, 6–8, 59, 83–88, 89
Sensibility, ideology of, 15, 22–23
Severn, Joseph, 161
Sexuality. *See* Female sexuality
Shelley, Mary, 10, 64, 72; *Frankenstein*, 9, 17, 29–37, 43, 60, 62, 65, 66, 81, 82, 100, 102, 103–04, 130, 158, 159
Shelley, Percy Bysshe, 123, 129
Showalter, Elaine, 16, 119–20
Smith, Charlotte, 16
Stark, Myra, 3
Sterrenburg, Lee, 30, 49
Stevenson, Robert Louis, 165
Swindells, Julia, 89–90

Taylor, Barbara, 124
Taylor, Jenny Bourne, 8, 119, 158, 193n23
Terror, in the female Gothic, 22–25
Thackeray, William Makepeace, 5, 84
Thompson, E. P., 124–25
Tuchman, Gaye, 7, 69

Verne, Jules, 165

Wilkie, Sir David, 42, 92
Wills, W. H., 92
Wollstonecraft, Mary, 10, 15, 16, 18–19, 28, 35; *Maria, or The Wrongs of Woman*, 16, 17, 19, 25–29, 30, 31, 37, 123, 124, 133; *A Vindication of the Rights of Men*, 13; *A Vindication of the Rights of Woman*, 14, 18–19, 20, 22, 25, 27, 32, 35, 36, 67
Wood, Mrs. Henry, 6, 86, 87
Wordsworth, William, 39, 42, 45

Yates, Edmund, 7